SOUL
Connection

A Mother's Love continues into The Afterlife

Diana Thomson

ISBN 978-0-620-61651-5
eISBN 978-0-620-61652-2

Published by Author using Reach Publishers' services,
P O Box 1384, Wandsbeck, South Africa, 3631

Printed and bound by Mega Digital Printers

Edited by Vanessa Finaughty for Reach Publishers
Cover concept by Debby Thomson, designed by Reach Publishers
Website: www.reachpublishers.co.za
E-mail - reach@webstorm.co.za

Dedication

To my son, Michael, who was cut down in the prime of his
life by a gang of heartless thugs.
Michael, you brought chest-bursting pride, love and fun
into my life.
Only you know what a crushing, heartbreaking blow your
death was to me.
Thank you for coming back to me in spirit and guiding me
in writing this book. I hope I have done you justice.

I love and miss you.

I'll lend for a little time, this son of mine he said,
for you to love while he lives, and mourn for when he's dead

It may be six or seven years, 22 or three, but will you 'till I
call him back, take care of him for Me.

He will bring his charms to gladden you, and should
his stay be brief, you'll have lovely memories as
solace for your grief.

I cannot promise he will stay, since all from earth
return, but there are lessons taught down there I
want my son to learn.

I've looked the wide world over, in search for
teachers true, and from the throngs that crossed life's
lanes, I've selected you.

Now will you give him all your love, nor think the
labour vain, nor hate me when I come and call to take
him back again.

I fancied that I heard you say: Dear Lord, Thy will be done.
For all the joys this man shall bring,
the risk of grief we'll run.

We'll shelter him with tenderness, love him while
we may, and for the happiness we've known, forever
grateful stay.

But should the angels call for him much sooner
than we've planned, We'll brave the bitter grief that
comes and try to understand.

Contents

Foreword

To lose a child is anguish beyond belief... but to have one brutally murdered is incalculable.

That is what Di Thomson went through. Her son, Mike, was killed by a gang of thugs as he fought to the death to protect his wife and young children. His courage in those awful final minutes, when he stood alone and barehanded against scum armed with a gun and knives, is valour beyond words.

So, too, is the courage of his mother. Di not only had to come to terms with her son's horrific murder, she and her family had to deal with the vagaries and, at times, sheer incompetence of the South African judicial system.

This is the story of a mother's indomitable love, a mother's bravery, a mother's refusal to be defeated and a mother's granite will to see something good come out of absolute evil. It is a true triumph of the human spirit.

It is also a fascinating chronicle of communicating with departed loved ones. For those who think spiritualism is either 'woo woo' or some arcane occult, this is a refreshingly honest and simply told account of how supernatural connection and comfort can come in many different ways.

Sadly, this is also a snapshot of South Africa today, where crime is a way of life that touches and scars us all. The torment and distress of those left in its bloody wake is something that should both haunt and shame the leaders of this beautiful country of such promise.

In short, this is a remarkable book by a remarkable woman.

Graham Spence

Introduction

In a split second, a phone call from our son, Allan, changed my life forever.

He phoned with the news that our second son, Mike, and his wife, Lorna, had been held up in their home and Mike was dead.

My grief was beyond measure. However, our love for Mike would not allow us to let evil prevail when they had cut down a really remarkable man. We would make good come from his death… somehow.

My healing process has been slow, but, through Mike, I have been taken on a journey I could only previously have dreamt about. He has taught me that there is life after death. He has taught me that love and guidance can still be received and given through the veil. He has helped me through the grief by guiding me to mediums when I needed one and by unfailingly coming through to me… leaving me feeling as if I have just had a long distance phone call with him.

The story of how hundreds of young people have had their lives changed through the Mike Thomson Change a Life Trust needed to be told. The remarkable achievement of Ursula Du Plooy, one of Mike's colleagues at Computershare and his boss, Stan Lorge, who have spearheaded the anti-crime trust, is another story that needed to be told.

I have encountered some negative reactions to my open belief in seeing a medium as a tool for healing. I am convinced that, without it, I would not be where I am today. I have found my times with Mike such a comfort that I have felt compelled to write about it. I am convinced that our loved ones actually *do* want us to communicate with them after passing just as much we want to know if they are okay – so convinced that I have written this book with the hope that my experience will encourage other people suffering such heartbreaking loss to put aside their fears and misgivings and find a good medium.

I often get the reply, "I am too frightened that they won't come through and then I will be hurt all over again."

No, in my experience, this will not happen with a reputable medium. You only have to ask your loved one who has passed over the night before to be there for you and they will!

In any event, what do you have to lose?

My dear friend, Sandy Croswell, was one of the first people to read my draft copy, and this is her comment:

"Woven into the pages of this remarkable book is a courageous journey undertaken by a devoted mother after the brutal and senseless murder of one of her beloved sons, Michael Roy.

Many readers will be comforted by the realisation they are not alone in emotionally crippling circumstances, while others will be filled with hope and profound inspiration.

Above all, this book portrays the unconditional love and overwhelming determination of Diana to overcome a devastating family tragedy."

Acknowledgements

The most important person I need to thank is my late son, Michael. Not only did he guide me to my first medium and, indeed, all the others, including the 'bad' ones, but he has been my inspiration all along in writing this book. He has been 'looking over my shoulder' and giving me approval all the way. I needed to see the 'bad' mediums in order to appreciate the very good ones.

The next person I need to thank is my medium, Laureen, who has been pivotal in my journey of growth, healing and learning to live with my grief. She has brought me more comfort than she can ever know by enabling me to make contact with my beloved son. She continues to be a source of love, understanding and support. Her accuracy, together with her compassion in her readings, endeared her to me from day one!

I am so grateful to my husband, Brian, who has been so patient with me spending so many hours at my desk. He accepted that I needed to do this on my own. Thank you for your love and understanding when I know there were times you felt shut out. You know the reason. Thank you for the regular answers and help with grammar and vocabulary when asked.

Thank you to Graham Spence, who is not only a very busy best seller writer and journalist, but is also my cousin. When I embarked on this project, I asked him if he would help me, as I have never written a book before. He immediately agreed and has taken the time to read it chapter by chapter as I went along and gave me such valuable help and advice. He also wrote the foreword, for which I am deeply indebted.

Debby, my oldest daughter, took over the first editing. She

also managed the entire computer layout, which I could not do. How Debby managed to fit this into her very busy schedule escapes me! Not only that, she was able to correct me on a few timeline recollections that, in my state of grief, I had confused. I am so grateful to her. Thank you so much.

My younger daughter, Carol, has also been a sounding board, a thesaurus of note and the maker of many cups of coffee! Thank you.

To Allan, our first born: thank you for your reaction when I first mentioned this book. Your approval was so important to me. I hope the result meets with your approval.

To Janine Daniel, a book publicist and daughter of a friend... thank you for reading the first draft and pointing out repetitions and other errors. I also appreciate your advice and suggestions.

To my friend and beautician Gilly Leontsinis who was a sounding board during every treatment of all the "Experiences" and who suggested the initial title of "A Watch, a Rose and a Mother's love" which we did not use in the end but it did describe the book exactly.

Finally, to my friends and family, who helped me, believed me, supported me through my grief and encouraged me to document all the various messages and validations that we experienced after Mike was taken from us. My sister, Verna, and cousin, Robyn, my dear friends, Sandy Croswell, Jeremy Anne Hopkins, Pam Heeley, Ronny and Pete Black and Linda Timmers, who were always ready to lend an ear and take an interest.

There were many others and they know who they are. Thank you from the bottom of my heart.

Chapter One

The night of 27 September 2007 was a dark and stormy night. Mike Thomson, aged thirty-nine, was looking forward to his fortieth birthday in two weeks' time. He was enjoying the evening with his wife, Lorna, his daughter, Megan, aged eleven, and his son, Nick, aged nine. They were all warm and snug in the main bedroom watching TV and feeling safe from the raging storm outside. The youngest, Annie Rose, aged seven, was already asleep in her bed down the passage.

Their bedroom opened out onto the swimming pool enclosure, which was surrounded by walls and an electric fence, which, until that night, was always considered supposedly secure.

While lying on the bed with his family, Mike happened to cast his eyes outside towards the courtyard and noticed that his pool was overflowing, presumably as a result of the amount of rain that had fallen that evening. He went outside to do a back wash and get rid of some of the water in the pool.

While running the backwash on the pool, Mike moved across to the corner of the courtyard to throw out the contents of the leaf basket from the filter. As he approached the small garden and shrubbery in the corner of the courtyard, to his horror, he noticed the intruders hiding within.

"Hey, what do you want?" he shouted.

Without warning, the sharp crack of a handgun added to the crescendo of the thunder. It was all that Lorna heard. In that small moment and with that one sound, the lives of the Thomson family were changed forever....

Brian and I were happy in our small garden flat in Paulshof, where we were living temporarily before moving to Hartbeespoort Dam, north of Johannesburg.

It belonged to our oldest son, Allan, who was planning to sell it sometime, but it suited him to have us stay there until we were ready to build our new dream home. After years of running a big rambling family home, it was a novelty to be in such a small and easy to maintain townhouse. Life was good; we were planning our new home for our impending retirement and looking forward to the prospect of the families coming out to Hartbeespoort Dam for weekends. Brian, my husband, was busy designing the house for our retirement; smaller than the family home, but bigger than the Paulshof flat. It was to be a 'lock up and go', easy to maintain and small enough that we would not need full time help, but big enough to be able to have family and guests stay over.

The development on the Hartbeespoort Dam was a French province design and we anticipated a very pretty house with stone taken from our new property, wrought iron railing and shutters. Brian has a talent for house design and was enthusiastically planning this last home for us. Allan (our first born) and Mike (our second born) spoke about buying a boat together and housing it in a boat house at the dam. They talked of having a yacht and teaching the children to sail. They both had three children, a girl and two boys, and a boy and two girls respectively. Both lived in Johannesburg, were very close and spent a large amount of time together. Our grandsons weren't so keen on the idea of a yacht, however, as they wanted a big motor boat for skiing! It was fun planning our future.

Our third born, Debby, had, many years ago, moved to Hoedspruit in Mpumalanga and was, and still is, self-employed there. She is qualified in nature conservation and has turned her many talents to a variety of activities. Currently, she is managing projects for the Kruger to Canyon Biosphere, which she co-founded almost twenty years ago. It has been recognised by UNESCO. In her not so spare time, she is a fixer, mainly for the BBC and their wildlife documentaries, as well as for other international production companies.

In addition, she has just launched a project that she has spent many years working on. It is a product called Ranger in a Box, which is a double CD set, equivalent to having a qualified ranger in your car while touring in the many game reserves in Southern Africa.

Carol, our youngest daughter, was also living in Johannesburg, running her own business of managing children's parties and hiring out party equipment. She, too, lived alone, but in Douglasdale in the northern suburbs of Johannesburg.

I have never had any ambitions of being a corporate businesswoman. I just wanted to be a mother and to be the best mother I could be. However, when my last child left home, to avoid the empty nest syndrome, I started landscaping people's gardens. This grew into a very time consuming and successful little business. However, after sixteen years, it was enough. I was very happy with my family, running my home and loving being a granny with all my grandchildren around me.

I was winding down my gardening activities. When I moved out of our big house, I closed down my landscaping business, paid off my staff and started teaching gardening to many of the gardeners I had come across during the course of my work. They were mostly gardens that I had landscaped and then taught the gardener how to look after it. I saw the gap, took it and loved what I was doing, but, after a few years, I felt it was time to retire and enjoy our twilight years.

Brian was also negotiating the sale of his business. He had been in the incinerator/cremator business, designing and manufacturing for the past forty-three years. Business had been good, but, at this time, it was a very stressful and corrupt business to be in. Not wanting to be part of paying bribes and tired of battling the less-than-informed Powers That Be, he was ready to retire and get out. Although no concrete offers had come in yet, several people had shown an interest in purchasing his business and negotiations in this regard were underway. There was so much to look forward to in the years ahead.

The universe, however, had a different plan for the Thomson family:

It was 10:30pm on the night of Thursday, 27 September 2007, a night like any other. We were both in bed, Brian gently snoring next to me, and I had switched off my bedside light after some reading and settled down to sleep.

Outside, the welcoming roars of thunder were silencing the constant sirens of the emergency vehicles, which had their headquarters over the road. The drumming of the raindrops on the roof tops had a gentle soporific effect. I was happily drifting off to sleep.

Suddenly, the phone rang. I leapt out of bed; at that time of night, it could only be something wrong. With my heart pounding and my mouth dry from anxiety, I answered the phone. It was Allan, our oldest son. Will I ever forget that voice? It was full of anguish and despair.

"Hello Mom."

I knew there was trouble by the tone of his voice.

"Son, what's wrong?"

"Mom, Mike and Lorna have been attacked by an armed gang at home and cleaned out."

"Oh no! Are they all right?"

"No, Mom, it couldn't be worse…. Mike is dead!"

"That can't be, no, no, not our Mike! How? Are Lorna and the children okay?"

"I don't know, Mom, but I am coming now to fetch you and Dad to go there."

Mike is dead. Mike is dead. Mike is dead. The words rolled endlessly through my paralysed mind. *Did I really hear what my oldest son had just told me…? Is this really happening to us?*

I woke Brian and told him. His stunned silence just said it all. We held each other without saying a word. There was total disbelief. *This can't be happening to us; this sort of thing only happens to other people.*

We threw on some clothes. I was shaking; I was freezing that nervous freeze that has nothing to do with the weather and couldn't think what to do next. We stumbled out of the door into the darkness and went down to the gate to wait for Allan and Sarah. The night had become so cold, yet, somehow, so terribly hostile and lonely.

Within minutes, they were there, but we seemed to wait forever. I can't remember how we got to Mike's house in

Craighall Park. I kept thinking that this must be a dream and I would soon wake up and find all was well again. I was so, so wrong! It was a nightmare and we were living it!

We arrived to find police cars all over the place and uniformed men everywhere. They would not let us in, but made us go to the house next door. The neighbours, Perry and Ronelle Hutton, had Mike's little family with them and they were taking care of them. The children were huddled on the floor at Lorna's feet and she was sitting on a bed or couch, sobbing. She kept saying, "I can't live without Mike. He is my life. How can it be that I am now a widow? What am I going to do? What am I going to do?"

There are no words to describe the shock, horror and disbelief that we were all experiencing that night.

I wanted to see Mike; however, they would not let us enter his yard. His body was in the pool and we had to wait for the police photographer to come over from Germiston, about thirty-five to forty kilometres away, before they would allow anyone else enter the crime scene.

I know the police were just doing their job and they had procedures that had to be followed, but, for me, it was just too much to handle that Mike had to stay lying in the pool until the photographer came. How is a mother supposed to emotionally comprehend that? The photographer was at least three quarters of an hour away! How could they leave my son in the water all that time? How can people be so insensitive and inhuman?

But then, I was only his mother! What did it matter to them? He was dead anyway.

Most of that time is a blur, but I do remember a nice young man, Jade, who was a volunteer with the Parkview victim support unit. He was so kind and an unobtrusive, comforting presence. When the photographer arrived, Jade went next door and took off Mike's wedding ring and his watch. He returned and gave them to Lorna.

He turned to us and said, "They have taken Mike out of the

pool and you can go across now."

Jade and his colleagues had a profound influence on future good that was created out of this tragedy.

We left Lorna and the children with Sarah, Allan's wife, as well as Perry and Ronellle, and Brian, Allan and I went, with very heavy hearts, across to see what they had done to our boy.

There is nothing that can prepare a parent for seeing their beloved child lying lifeless on the ground. Mike had the world at his feet and was in the prime of his life. He was taken just two weeks before his fortieth birthday. Why? What did he do to deserve this?

"No, this can't be happening to us? Not to our family?"

At this stage, I was not crying. I was too numb to feel anything. I think I was in denial and shock. Perhaps there was a mistake? I was still shivering, but still not from cold. I knelt on the hard, cold paving next to him. At last, they had removed Mike from the water and laid him on the ground next to the pool: he was very wet and oh so very, very cold. I will never forget the coldness of his body next to mine. Gently, as though I might have hurt him, I lifted his shirt and saw a bullet wound in his side, as well as numerous stab wounds all over his upper body. They were no longer bloody from being in the water. They were clean and very visible.

"One, two, three, three, four, five, six, seven… the bastards, how could they do this? Eight, nine, ten, eleven… you poor darling, did it hurt? Twelve, thirteen, fourteen. Can you believe that they needed to stab him fourteen times? It must have been a screwdriver, because the entrance wounds were the size of screwdriver head. I wonder how deep they are?"

Allan then noticed another bullet wound at the back of his head. That must have been the 'coup de grace'.

"Oh Mike, my darling boy, what have they done? Not you, not you," I cried out to him. I held his face in my hands and told him I loved him, and said I would look after his family and oh how I was going to miss him.

A parent's role is to protect your child. Both Brian and I felt so helpless that, in spite of the tools we had given him to protect himself during his life, we were unable to do anything to help him this time. Not even the best fighter in the world can stop a bullet!

I should not be saying a final goodbye to my beloved son. It is not the way things should be. We have always been so very proud of him. These evil people have taken our special boy. We had reason to be proud of all of our children, but Michael had always been an exceptional young man. Everybody loved him.

Why? Why? What did he do to deserve this? He never harmed a living thing. Not even an ant was killed by Mike. What did any of us do to deserve this? I only ever wanted to be a mother and create a wonderful family. Why us? Why us?

Why should Lorna be left without a husband and my three little grandchildren grow up without a dad?

It was some time before I realised that, in reality, the question should not be why us, but rather, why *not* us? We are no different to any other victims of crime.

How dare these evil people come and destroy the life that had been so successful in every way? From childhood achievements to excelling in high school and then, as an adult, giving so much of himself to society. What a waste! What a travesty!

With broken hearts, we left our boy lying on the ground to be removed and taken to the mortuary. At the risk of repetition, I cannot describe the desperation we felt at being unable to help our son and brother. However, his family needed our love, help and support, so we went back to Lorna and her brood to arrange to take them home to Allan's house and away from the nightmare that had only just begun.

While we were waiting for the police to finish at the house, Lorna told us her traumatic story....

It was 8pm. Supper was over, and the children bathed and in their pyjamas. Their youngest, Annie Rose, had already been put to bed for the night and the rest of the family was sitting in Mike and Lorna's bedroom watching TV together, as they did every night. It was storming outside, the rain pouring down and the night black and menacing. Even though it was a very heavy storm, it is always comforting to hear the rain falling outside while you are warm and safe inside. Everyone was feeling content and cosy in the safety of the main bedroom. Megan and Nick were totally engrossed in the movie on TV.

Their bedroom opened out onto the pool area, which was completely walled in. There was an electric fence on the one side and a high retaining wall on the other. There was a huge impenetrable thorny Bougainvillea and gate on the third side. On the fourth wall of the house, there was a flower bed above the retaining wall and his lovely garden going on from there. Mike had heard his dogs barking earlier, but had not taken any notice of them, as there was a genet that lived in the garden and the dogs often barked at it when it started its night time activities. He was quite justified in thinking he was safe in his pool enclosure. There were locked wrought iron gates on two sides.

At about 8:30, the rain stopped and Mike looked outside and noticed that his pool was overflowing.

He went outside to attend to his pool. As he was bending to pick up the leaf catcher, he saw four armed men hiding in the bushes. He shouted at them, "Hey, what do want?"

They replied with a gunshot to his side.

Lorna, who was inside, heard his shout, followed by a shot. Silence followed. She did not know if Mike had been hit or not. He had, in fact, been shot in the side and the bullet had penetrated his lung. The next thing, Lorna realised with terror that two armed men were rushing into their bedroom. Two armed men remained outside with Mike, and he must have seen the two other intruders heading into the bedroom to his wife and children.

Being a black belt karate instructor, he was not about to let a bullet in his side stop him from doing all in his power to save his family.

Mike and Allan were partners in a Kushido Karate school in Bryanston. However, Mike had had two back operations as a result of rugby injuries and was struggling to continue with his training. He was a big man, both in build and courage, and was prepared to fight to the death to protect and save his family. I hoped the adrenalin prevented him from feeling any pain from the gunshot wounds, the multiple stabbings or from his back.

From what we have been told from a confession made by George Nyembe, one of the accused, and what we were able to surmise, Allan found some unspent bullets lying on the ground (the police did not find them). Allan thought that could only have happened if the gun had fallen to the ground. We believe that Mike attacked the first man who shot him. The identity of this man, was understood to be Razor Zulu, the gang leader but later refuted by him.

We subsequently found out that this man's modus operandi is to rape the women and sometimes torture them with a hot iron. With one man down and apparently disarmed, Mike then turned his attention to the second attacker, George Nyembe. We thought that they might have fallen into the pool in a scuffle, but a subsequent confession by George said that Mike had pushed him into the pool, gone in after him and was drowning him. The attacker, George, seeing that he was now in trouble, took out a long screwdriver and stabbed Mike fourteen times. Mike must have been getting weaker and weaker with the loss of blood and the screwdriver penetrating very deep. He could no longer defend himself. These stab wounds alone would have killed him, but then Razor must have gathered himself together and picked up the gun and finally shot Mike in the back of his head.

It was over outside. Mike was dead.

Lorna heard none of the happenings outside as she was being forced at gunpoint around the house. She had to open the safe and show the other two where their belongings were. They found Mike's gun in the safe and took it. Having finished their work outside, the two went inside to continue the night's work, one very wet and one dry. They also put guns to the children's heads and started demanding money and cell phones, etcetera. They would not let Lorna go to Annie, their youngest daughter. In hindsight, that saved her from the trauma the others had to endure, but was of no comfort to Lorna at the time. She did not know how many men there were and what the others might be doing.

The men demanded money, of which there was precious little in the house.

"Where is your jewellery?"

"There is none; it has already been stolen before."

"Show us the cameras and give us your cell phones."

"Where is your laptop?"

They helped themselves to TVs, cell phones, a laptop, linen, cameras and whatever else they wanted. They also stole Nick's club soccer kit, which he only realised when he needed them two weeks later! After all, they had all the time in the world! They loaded whatever they could into Mike's car. They roughed up the family a bit, but, thankfully, nothing serious other than emotional trauma. They then proceeded to tie them up with belts and neckties. Lorna said that, by this time, the other two had come into the house. She kept referring to them as 'the mean one' and 'the wet one'.

While they were tying them up, one of the robbers noticed that there were speakers in the corners of the rooms. Mike loved music and he had music piped into every room. They mistook them for CCTV cameras. Nick, who was only nine years old at the time, was the only one not yet tied up, so they took him at gunpoint and said roughly, "Show us where the cameras are!"

The terrified boy had no idea what they were talking about. "You've already got our camera!" he nervously told them.

After constant denial, they eventually believed him; they gave up and tied him up with Lorna and Megan. Megan was only eleven at the time.

All the while, Lorna was pleading with them and asking, "Where is my husband? Where's my husband?"

"Don't' worry. He's sleeping," they said.

Little did she know what they really meant.

Finally, they said, "We are going now."

They loaded up Mike's car with as much as they could and told her, "Stay like this for one hour. Do not move. We are leaving one of our men behind. If there is an anti-hijack unit in your car, we will call him and he will shoot you all!"

They then left. The fact that Razor Zulu had not attacked Lorna and the girls shows that Mike did achieve what he had tried to do – by wounding or tiring out this vicious rapist, Mike had protected his family.

Lorna thought that, recently, Mike had disconnected the

anti-hijacking unit, as it had been troublesome. She prayed that he had not fixed it. She had no doubt that they would carry out their threat if they found it working. Before they left, they cut the phone wires.

I cannot begin to imagine the anguish, terror and despair as she waited with the two children for the hour to pass. She could not wait the complete hour, as she was so worried about Mike. They managed to help each other get untied. She went and woke up their youngest daughter, Annie Rose, and, terrified of what they were going to find, they went to look for Mike. They called and called and heard nothing… absolutely nothing. They searched the entire area, but to no avail. Lorna then climbed onto the top of a table that was standing next to the pool in the courtyard to shout to her neighbours next door to please come and help them.

Lorna stood at the neighbour's wall and screamed, "*Helllppp! Helllppp!* Please, please help us!"-

An unfriendly elderly couple who used to complain about the sound of the children having fun in the pool lived next door. Their bedroom window faced that side and Lorna was sure they must hear her, but no. Just silence.

On receiving no response, she turned around to climb back off the table and it was only then, from this view, that she saw Mike lying at the bottom of the pool. She knew the worst had happened. Her beloved husband was dead.

The Thomson family needed help. They could not use their cell phones, as they had been taken. They ran back inside to the landline, only to find it dead. Frantic, they went to the wall at the other side of the house and shouted again for Perry Hutton, their friendly neighbour. There was an inter-leading gate between their properties, which they entered, screaming for Perry. Thank God, he heard and instantly came to their aid. He called the police and then he called Allan. They tried their best to console our hysterical, heartbroken and frightened

Lorna and her children.

It was at that point that we arrived. After hearing the tragic story of Mike's courageous fight to the death, everything went hazy. I remember seeing men in uniform and bullet-proof vests, milling all over the house, not doing anything in particular. There were so many police cars with their blue lights flashing. I remember an ambulance in the street and seeing them load my boy onto a stretcher and into the vehicle. I wanted to run up to them and tell them to take care of him, that he would be okay... but my heart knew he was gone for good. The body bag said it all.

At some stage, Lorna gave me Mike's watch, which I put on my wrist immediately. I was so touched by her action. She could have kept it, but she still had time to think of me. She had his wedding ring, which she has since worn on chain around her neck.

I later believed that Mike, in spirit, prompted her to give it to me for a very special reason, and a reason that I have felt the need to share with you in this book, with the hope and intention of helping others find comfort and communication in the loss of loved ones.

Having called Mike's sisters during the long and arduous wait for the police photographer, we now had to face the task of letting the rest of the family know what had happened. It was well past midnight, but we felt that the more immediate family would want to know immediately. One of the first people I called was my cousin, Robyn, and her new husband, Derek Milton.

Robyn is my closest cousin; we grew up like sisters. She and Derek were newly married, both having lost their first spouses to fatal illnesses. In fact, the last time I saw Mike alive was at their wedding party a week or so before. We had such fun that evening. I can so clearly see Mike and Lorna arriving a little late and walking into the marquee. He looked so handsome in his bright blue- and white-striped shirt. I looked at him with such pride, knowing that happy couple belonged to Brian and I. (Sadly, that shirt now hangs in my spare cupboard, never to be worn again unless, one day, Mike's son, Nick, would like it.)

I knew Robyn would help. I called her. The phone rang for ages and, eventually, a sleepy Robs answered, already on the alert, as only bad news comes at that time of night.

"Dinny, what's wrong?"

Sobbing, I said, "Robs, Mike has been murdered."

"Oh my God, no!" She was instantly awake. "How? Why? When?"

"We will tell you later. Please can you help?"

"Of course; what must I do?"

"Please can you go over to Carol's flat and fetch her and take her to Allan's house? We are on our way there now."

"We will leave at once."

Sarah had already phoned our other daughter, Debby, in Hoedspruit to let her know, while we were all waiting for the police photographers. Debby, who lives alone, was beside herself and said she was coming up immediately.

"Please, darling, don't travel alone until it is light. I really don't want you driving alone in the middle of the night when you are so distraught."

The following was the beginning of our experience of love and support from friends. The first people Debby called were Helen and Derek Smith, good friends of hers and the family who have lived in the area for many years.

Knowing, firstly, that her friend, Helen, was planning a JHB trip for business in the next few days, and knowing that neither Helen nor her husband answer their phone late at night, Debby sent through an SMS asking if there was any chance Helen would be on her way up to JHB the following day and if Debby could get a lift up with her. At the time, Helen was in bed asleep and Derek had come downstairs to the kitchen to get a drink of water. As hardworking business people, they have always had a policy of ignoring their phones after hours to avoid the 24-hour work scenario. To this day, Derek cannot explain what made him look at the phone, and, after reading this book, you may be able to surmise the same reasoning that we have to date – something told him he needed to see the SMS that had just come through. Sensing something was wrong, he immediately took the phone up to Helen and suggested she call Debby immediately as something must be wrong. On hearing the situation from Debby, she and Derek made a decision there and then that Helen would drive Debby throughout the night, to get to the family as soon as possible, and so, at 11pm that night, Debby and Helen left for a six-hour drive to get to Johannesburg to be with the family in the days to follow.

Back at Craighall, I remember us all piling into Allan's car, along with Mike's three dogs, Charlie, the Labrador, Vaalie, Mike's hero-worshipping Maltese cross rescue from the Vaal Triangle, and Torie (Victoria), a pavement special. This made a total of eight people and the three dogs. Vaalie, who had witnessed the whole event, was found hiding and shaking under the bougainvillea in the pool enclosure. He sensed his master and hero was dead. He would miss Mike as much as we would!

Our departure from 89 Buckingham Ave, Craighall that night at 1am on 28 October 2007 closed the chapter on a very happy marriage, a lovely and loving family, culminating in the brutal death of a devoted husband.

All of the Thomson lives were irrevocably changed that fateful night.

Allan drove our broken, weeping family home to his house, where we tried to get the children to bed. At that late hour, Allan could not find an emergency chemist to get something for Lorna and me to calm us down. We clearly needed help, as Rescue Remedy was not enough for such trauma; we tried it, but we might have been drinking water for all it did to help us. Allan headed up the road to the nearest hospital, which happened to be close by to where he lives, and explained to the person on duty what had happened and please could he have a sedative for tonight for his mother and sister-in-law. Their response was, in a nutshell, rude and brutal. No, they said, we must come in person to the emergency room and get a doctor to prescribe something.

"I don't want a schedule drug," he replied. "Just give me something over the counter that will help them for now. They are in no state to come out at all."

"Sorry," said the unhelpful man. "How do I know you aren't a drug addict trying your luck?"

With his patience fast running out, Allan could do nothing more than reply, "Do you think I can make this sort of thing up? Where is your compassion, man? Please let me talk to the doctor."

Once again, he was met with a cold and unhelpful 'no'.

It was at that point that the night's events came to a head and, quite simply, Allan lost it. In his anger at the insensitivity of his brother's murder, and now followed by the insensitivity at a place of assistance, he punched their very large glass door at the entrance to the hospital. It broke in an instant and came tumbling down around him. "What the #*%#@ has happened to human kindness?" he yelled.

Back at Allan's home, Sarah, Allan's wife, was showing her true mettle as well – she was a star. In a flash, her home became a non-profit hotel and was invaded by all and sundry and their dogs! I think, with all the family dogs, there were nine! Helen stayed a couple of days finding space on a couch, as did Carol. Helen also became the never-ending tea maker – a small service that is worth so much at a time such as this.

After some hot coffee and tea and a short discussion about who would call who, we set about letting people know.

I called my sister, Verna, first. She had only just returned to Malawi from an extended visit to South Africa. She had spent time with her daughter, Barbie, in Cape Town and about a week with me. She did not hesitate, and said she would be on the first plane back. Verna Henderson and I are very close, although she is eight years older than I. I needed her.

My sister Verna.

I then tried to get my brother, Malcolm Spence. He was away in Mozambique and could not be reached. I am not sure who in his family persevered and finally gave him the news, but I will

Robyn (my cousin), Malcolm (my brother) and Pam (lifelong friend).

never forget his call. He was heartbroken and just sobbed and sobbed on the phone. He said he would be with me as soon as he could get back. Malcolm was not well himself. He had been fighting cancer for some years and was doing a 'bucket list' of travelling the country visiting old friends and family on his huge BMW motorbike.

It was not long before the phones started ringing off the hook. I took every call that was for me. I found it helped to talk and hear my friends' and families' voices. I needed to be occupied all the time.

We were all in a disbelieving automatic mode.

Chapter Two

It is strange how certain things stick in one's memory and others become hazy. I remember Sarah called her dad in Cape Town to tell him about Mike and she did not know how to word it. She said, "Dad, there has been a terrible accident."

Both Allan and I said simultaneously, "There was not an accident; he was murdered!"

"But that is such a harsh word."

In unison, we both said, "What they did was harsh and it was no accident!"

Allan, our oldest son, married Sarah Hannekom in 2002. It was his second marriage. His first marriage was sadly not always a happy one, but it did result in a very beautiful daughter, Shannon. Shannon has always been called Shanny, as that is what the grandchildren called my mother. Allan was very blessed to have Shanny live with him almost from the start of their marriage. Up until then, he and Zelda (his first wife) shared 50% custody. Happily, it was a very amicable divorce and all of us are still friendly. Shannon and her mum have a good relationship.

Sarah was one of my clients. I met her just after she had got divorced and she had bought a new home, which needed a garden designed and landscaped. Over a period of a few years, Sarah and I developed a very good relationship and, a while after Allan was divorced, I introduced them! She has been and still is a very good stepmother to Shannon and a wonderful daughter-in-law to both Brian and me. Sarah had no children from her first marriage, but she and Allan have now been blessed with two dear little boys, Dylan and Brian, just twenty-two months apart. It was like history repeating itself, as their age difference was much the same as my sons, Allan and Michael.

Allan called Mike's boss, Stan Lorge of Computershare, and told him that Mike would not be returning to work.

About a week prior to his death, I had called Mike for a chat. I asked how work was and his response was, "Mom, this is the most amazing company. I have never worked for a company like this. I just love my work and I look forward to going to work every day!"

I was soon to find out why.

Stan's immediate response and everything subsequent has

been nothing short of remarkable and a true testament to him as a man and the company that he runs.

That morning, we were visited by the investigating officer of the Parkview Police Station, who came to get a statement from Lorna and the children. They were very sympathetic and patient. Two ladies came from the Parkview Victim's Support Unit. They were also so kind. They brought a little gift bag with goodies for the children. I don't recall what was in them, but I know they were special. They offered to shop for the family and do anything required to help us. They are an amazing group of people who do this wonderful service out of compassion and for no fee. Debby, Mike's sister, was so impressed with them that, when she returned to her home town, Hoedspruit, Limpopo, she started up Hoedspruit Victim's Support Unit there and, to this day, it is up and running and performing a wonderful service to the community. It was one of the first positive things to emerge from this awful tragedy.

At about 10am, Stan Lorge, Mike's boss, arrived from Computershare with his assistant, Mbali. His genuine grief and warmth was incredible. He offered so much assistance. Counselling for the whole family would be paid for by the company. They assured Lorna that they would continue to pay his salary for several months, as well as his medical aid. He said just how shattered and upset everyone at the office was, as they loved and respected Mike so much. We discussed contacting a private investigator. Richard Moss, Mike's best friend from school and university, arrived with his wife, Louise. He mentioned he knew of one and said he would contact this man, who had a very good reputation.

I remember sitting on Allan's patio with Stan, Richard, Brian, Allan, Debby and Mbali, and being part of the discussions, yet not comprehending that this was really happening. How could we be talking about my boy's death? I have never felt so helpless and bewildered and, for the first time in my life, out of control of what was happening around me. This was just beyond anything I had ever had to cope with and I was only too grateful to have someone else making decisions, giving advice and just being so practical.

Allan had already called his own work, the Johannesburg Stock Exchange, and told them about the tragedy. In no time, the network was spreading the news. It was not long before flowers started to arrive for Lorna, for us, and for Allan and Sarah. Visitors and people were starting to pour in one after the other, and many at the same time. Although we had first class support in Debby's friend, Helen, who kept a constant supply of tea going for everyone as they came and went, catering for whoever was there over meal times was fast becoming a challenge. During initial calls of support, when asked what anyone could do to help, the answer was always a standard and fairly numb, "There is nothing at the moment, thank you." However, it did not take long before we answered with a revised, "Please send food, cakes and drinks." We were, on average catering, to anything between twenty and forty visitors at a meal, apart from our own substantial family, and this in itself was becoming a challenge. A roster of mums from Rivonia Primary School days was organised by one of the stalwart mothers of our time there. She organised a daily delivery of something until the day of the funeral. We so appreciated and needed the support of everyone visiting; however, making sure we could cater for them all was a necessity and a challenge. It was not long before a panel van arrived, full of drinks of all sorts, beers, hard tack, wine, cold drinks – enough for a huge wedding. This was sent by the JSE. This was to see us through the next week of constant visitors and support. At lunch time, another delivery van arrived with a hot lunch to feed at least twenty people. This, too, was to continue daily for a week until the funeral. This came from Rand Merchant Bank, where Allan had worked at least four years previously. We were totally overwhelmed and speechless at this outpouring of love, support and generosity.

Mbali made an appointment for the whole family to see a counsellor, whose office was quite far away. We all went together late in the afternoon. The appointment was 4:30. After battling the evening traffic, we got there in time and were kept waiting for at least fifteen minutes. The children were getting very restless and agitated, and we were all feeling somewhat let down at this delay. Eventually, a lady appeared and asked why we were there.

This, we did not need. Surely she *must* have been told – did she care that little? There was no 'sorry for your loss' or 'I am so sorry to hear what you have been through' to Lorna and the children. She then said that she did not 'do' children. We made a group decision that, if she did not 'do' children, she would not be 'doing' any of us. Somewhat traumatised and disappointed, we left. Computershare were very apologetic and grateful for the feedback. They would not be using her again in the future! They were still prepared to pay for any other counsellors we found ourselves.

To identify the days of the next week is not possible. It was a succession of friends and family arriving, answering the phone, meetings with people and family being met at the airport. Each one a new greeting with tears and wracking sobs. Trying to sleep at night was impossible until my dear friend, Bea, arrived with a script for sleeping pills from our mutual doctor friend, Ruth. Every evening, Brian and I left for our little home emotionally exhausted, leaving the rest of the family to stay with Allan and Sarah, where there were people and dogs sleeping on settees, mattresses and even sharing beds. Although I wanted to stay with my family, I also found it somewhat of a respite to cocoon ourselves for a few hours for some rest and reflection. To get some pill-induced sleep was so welcome. Before I was given the pills, I would lie in bed and could not get Allan's voice out of my head saying, "Mom, it couldn't be worse; Mike's dead."

It repeated over and over until I would end up crying myself to sleep in the early hours of the morning. Five years on, that desperate voice of Allan's still haunts me.

What I do know is that my sister, Verna, arrived on the Saturday. Someone went to fetch her from OR Tambo Airport. She came straight to us at Allan's house. It was one time I wished that she did not have to be there, but it was such a relief to have her with us. Her love was such a support and presence. She would be with me in our flat for quite a while. The next day, Malcolm, my brother, arrived.

Malcolm came with his wife, Naomi. I was so relieved that he, too, had come to be with us.

Malcolm held a very special place in Mike's heart, as, in his youth, Malcolm had been a Springbok athlete. He ran the 400m race at the 1960 Rome Olympic Games and won the bronze medal with a torn Achilles tendon. Malcolm had always displayed enormous courage and stoic perseverance, which had stood him in very good stead for his later battle with cancer. He never complained and, on inquiring about his health, his reply was always, "I'm fine." Mike also used to run the 400m and often phoned Malcolm for advice on timing and training. His uncle was his role model in athletics.

Debby called Neil,

Lorna's dad in Scotland, who was shattered and devastated. He, too, just broke down and sobbed over the phone. Lorna told him not to come out, but I felt that she needed to have him here and, also, he needed to be here for himself. When he asked what he should do, I replied, "Please come, Neil; Lorna needs you."

He caught the first plane out he could. He loved Mike so much. He used to say to his friends and relatives in Bathgate, in his broad Scots accent, "Our wee Lorna, she has found herself a real man."

Mike, too, was very fond of Neil and loved having him to stay and taking him to our holiday home in the bush. Neil seemed to attract such good game sightings. On his last visit to South Africa, he woke up one morning to find a pride of eight lions outside his bedroom window. They remained there on a kill for about two days. Mike managed to get some amazing photographs! We had been going there for about twenty-five years and had never had such luck!

Funeral arrangements could not be made, as we had not yet had the autopsy report, nor had Mike's body been taken to the funeral parlour – he was still at the state morgue, where the official autopsy is conducted. That, too, was very stressful. I tried not to picture the scene, but, in my lowest moments, it was impossible not to imagine him on the autopsy table. I had seen too many CSI programmes on TV. It was quite some time before I could watch one again.

Lorna's last two employers, Rosie Deans and Janie Quirk, who used to be sisters-in-law and are still very close, have both always regarded Lorna as family. Lorna lost her mother when she was ten, so I was really grateful when Janie flew out from England and Rosie came up from Plettenberg Bay in the Eastern Cape immediately to support her. Lorna needed them so much and they were there for her. There was a time when the three were sitting on the patio, Lorna was crying and asking them how she was going to cope without Mike. She had no sooner said that when an African mask that has been on the wall for ages suddenly fell off. They put it back firmly and, a little while later, it fell off again.

I was stunned. Was that the start of Mike's messages to us? Was that too much to hope for or too farfetched?

Lorna trained as a nursery nurse and nursery school teacher. She came out here as a nanny to Rosie's, and later Janie's, children. When their babies reached nursery school age, she was able to run a nursery school at a friend's house and she became extremely popular with mothers of the northern suburbs of Johannesburg.

Rosie and Janie took Lorna and her children to Sandton City to shop for clothes for the funeral and to go to Build a Bear.

This is a shop where children choose a soft toy, which is just the skin, and they 'build' it. They stuff it, they put a heart in the right place and it gets stitched closed. The toy is then given a name, an identity document, a passport and a set of clothing, which is beautifully made. There are many accessories for the chosen 'one'. I believe that a mortgage on the house may be necessary to pay for a full wardrobe! I think our children got two sets of clothing each for their animal. They spent the afternoon building their stuffed animal. Megan built a giraffe, which has always been her favourite animal, Nick built a monkey and Annie Rose built a black puppy. I seem to recall that Nick chose bush clothes and a karate gi for his monkey. Nicky Tom called his monkey 'Mike the Monkey' and this stuffed animal never left his side. As time wore on, we could always tell just how Nick was coping. If he was beginning to relax, the monkey would be put down, but, if he was feeling down, the monkey was back in his arms.

I always felt so grateful to those two women in Lorna's life. I was not capable of doing anything like that for my grandchildren. It was taking all my strength just to keep myself together, let alone be of support to anyone else.

Sarah and Allan noticed that their children were feeling the stress of the whole situation without really comprehending much about it all. All the attention was directed at Lorna and her children, thus leaving Allan's children feeling somewhat sidelined. It was not deliberate, but just the way things were. They asked the boys if they would also like to go and make a bear at the Build a Bear shop. Dylan said, "Yes please, Dad."

Brian Jnr said, "*No* dowa." (Don't want to.)

Anyway, they did go. Shanny made a bunny rabbit, Dylan made a monkey that he called Mike, and Brian eventually made a lion, which was called Dowa, because he 'dowa' make one! Dylan hero worshipped his big cousin, Nick, hence the copying of the monkey. Nick, however, was having none of it. Dylan's monkey was allowed to be called Mick, but not Mike.

I think it was Wednesday when we were called to say that Mike's body was now at the funeral parlour. Brian and I wanted to go and say our last goodbye. Lorna came into the room.

"Lorn, we are going in to see Mike this morning. Do you want to come with us?"

"No, thank you; I will go this afternoon and take the children with me," she replied.

Somewhat taken aback, I asked, "Surely you do not want them to remember seeing him like that?" I did not want to be prescriptive, but I was not happy about it.

Her reply came as a surprise, but I completely understood. "I want them to come with me, as I want them to see and understand that he really is dead and that he has not just left them and they could somehow feel responsible for their dad not being there." Lorna, better than most, understood how children so often internalise tragedy and feel responsible. She did not want this to be the case with her children.

Unusual, but it made sense.

That morning, Brian and I made the trip into town. We were shown into a chapel, where Mike was lying in an open coffin. When I looked down at my beloved son, I was filled with rage that had obviously been suppressed the past few days. What enraged me was most probably irrational, but they had covered his head with a white cap that had lace on the edge. His head had obviously been cut open and that had to cover the cuts, but lace on my big, rugby-playing, karate black belt instructor man? No, no, no! A bandage would have been a far more sensitive covering. Then, on top of that insult, there was a single blue Dutch iris on his chest. That, to me, just symbolised death and funeral, and I wanted nothing to do with it. It was bad enough; I did not need those extras!

I took the iris and threw it as far as I could and as hard as I could across the room, accompanied by a heartbroken cry.

"No, not my Mike, not that strong man reduced to this. I won't have it!"

Whilst I was by no means at peace, he, at least, did look at peace. I could see that his spirit had left his body. What had been my fun-loving, full of character, affectionate, teasing, lovable Mike had gone. That white, expressionless face was not my beloved son, Mike. It was only the vehicle that had housed his wonderful, indomitable spirit.

Brian and I once more held each other without saying a word.

I gave Mike my last kiss on his cold lips and my tears fell on his chalk-white cheeks, and Brian and I left the room.

I remember nothing of the journey home.

Chapter Three

The funeral was arranged for Friday, 5 October at the Bryanston Catholic Church and, afterwards, a celebration of his life at the Bryanston Country Club.

Lorna told Allan and Debby how she wanted the funeral arranged. Together, they organised the service at the Bryanston Catholic Church where they had got married. Mike was neither a Catholic nor a church-goer, but I know he would have been happy with whatever Lorna wanted. Lorna is a devout Catholic and she needed to have a special service for her much-loved husband. Among the eulogies was a beautiful letter written by one of Mike's students, Dee Knight, who trained at the dojo with her daughters, Michele and Cathy. Dee, sadly, was overseas at the time. She sent a very moving letter, which she requested to be read out at the funeral.

Sarah went into town to get a piece of Thomson Tartan from Rob Roy, the supplier of Scottish paraphernalia, to drape over Mike's coffin, and, while she was there, she was offered a piper, which she accepted. That was to be a wonderful touch. I asked two of my close friends to get flowers from Mike's garden. Like his mum, he was a keen gardener. They picked roses and orchids, and we a made simple bouquet. They were to go early to the church and put them on his coffin before people started arriving. That was all we planned to have on his coffin: a Thomson tartan drape, the Thomson family crest and the flowers from his garden. It was simple, but powerful.

A family friend, Nikki Bush very kindly came and gave us some ideas of how to go about organising the celebration of Mike's life. She had just organised her grandmother's funeral, so it was very fresh in her mind. We were finding it very hard to be creative at such an emotional time. Mike deserved more than just a funeral. She was able to give us guidance on how to go about organising the best send-off that we could possibly give Mike.

I arranged for a DJ whom I had met a couple of weeks earlier at Dylan's nursery school fun day to come. He was quite reluctant to come at such short notice, but, when he heard the story, he rescheduled everything so that he could be there. He not only played CDs, he also sang and played the keyboard. He was requested to play gentle music in the background – but with one exception: to play the music from *Star Wars* loudly in the beginning when people arrived. Mike was not just a *Star Wars* fan, he was a *Star Wars* nut and he must have watched the movies dozens of times! That was going to be a very fitting tribute to him. We also requested that he play Neil Diamond,

Queen and *Mama Mia* and music from *Les Miserable*. These were some of Mike's favourites. I know he appreciated it.

I arranged for someone from each stage in his life to just say a few words. Richard was asked to be the master of ceremonies, and Debby made a lovely slideshow of her brother's life, which was to be flashed onto a large blank wall non-stop during the afternoon. Pete Upfold was another university friend of Mike's, and he and his wife, Rose, had become very close friends of Mike and Lorna. Pete put together another slideshow of Mike, his mates and years at Wits University, and some later pictures of their wonderful visits to Ntsiri, our game reserve and holiday home where we were shareholders. Many of the photos beautifully showed the fun and mischief that these boys got up to.

Ernie Saks was Mike's headmaster at primary school and had always been very fond of Mike. In fact, he had awarded Mike the Chairman's Cup of merit in his final year at primary school. We all loved Ernie and, before his retirement, he was considered one of the best headmasters in the education department. I knew he would do Mike proud.

Two very proud parents on the day Mike received the Chairman's Cup of Merit at Rivonia Primary School.

I then asked Colleen Travis Lee, who was head girl together with Mike when he was head boy at Bryanston High, to say a few words about their time together. They worked and got on so well together. Charles Lourens from Computershare was asked to say few words as, sadly, Stan could not be there; he was going overseas on business straight after the funeral service. We would have loved Stan to do us the honour, but it was not to be. Allan agreed to talk about his brother on behalf of the family in general. Richard was to end the celebration of Mike's life with a letter from Brian and me and from his sisters, as we knew we would be too emotional and unable to speak ourselves.

Carol, Mike's youngest sister, undertook to arrange helium balloons, which were to be released by the children there, each with a message to Mike tied to them. Although initially envisioned as an activity for the many children at the funeral to participate, so many of the adults felt they strongly needed to send Mike a message that they, too, attached their heartfelt words to each of the balloons released.

All the arrangements were made; we now had to get through the next few days.

During that week, there were so very many acts of kindness and love; too many to mention without becoming tedious. However, one that stands out in my memory is of his high school sweetheart, Vivian Shultz (nee Mitchley). They met each other in Standard 7 and they were inseparable until their Matric year.

I remember so well the last day of school when they were in Standard 9. Both Mike and Vivian had been tipped to be head prefects. Vivian's mom, Sandy, and I were very anxious at home time and were sitting in the car together outside the school waiting for the assembly to close and hear the news. It was a very tense time and it seemed to take forever. Suddenly, the school children started pouring out and coming up to the car before our children had got to us. They were congratulating both of us! What was the news? Yes, Mike was made head prefect and Vivian was made deputy head prefect! We were two very proud mamas!

Sadly, that year, they parted company and went their separate ways, but still remained good friends. Viv eventually married an accountant. It pained me at the time to have to concede that he was, in fact, a very nice young man and we wished them well.

They had been living in Cape Town for quite a few years and, on hearing

Vivian and Mike.

of Mike's death, Vivian was on the first plane she could get to Johannesburg. She stayed with Nikki Bush, who, coincidently, was one of Allan's old girlfriends. Vivian spent a whole day cooking different meals for Brian and me. I will never forget her coming to see us at the flat and bringing this huge cooler box of delicious meals she had so lovingly prepared. I did not cook for months.

What a friend!

It was so comforting to have my two siblings with me, both of whom had experienced their own personal losses. My brother, Malcolm, lost his oldest son, Bruce, when Bruce was only twenty-eight, to a fatal asthma attack. If anyone understood what Brian and I were going through, he and his wife, Naomi, did. My sister had also lost her life partner, Sandy, ten years previously and was still grieving for him. It is very special when families come together in a crisis.

Neil, Lorna's dad, arrived from the UK looking exhausted and so, so sad. I was so pleased to find a kindred soul who cried as much I did. We could not talk about Mike without the two of us dissolving. Richard and Louise very kindly offered to accommodate some of the visitors. Both Neil and Rosie (Lorna's surrogate mother who came up from Plett) stayed with them.

Verna stayed with us in our compact home. She was a star. She took over so many of my daily chores and was just so sympathetic and kind. My inability to stop crying was a very big concern for her. She was just unable to console me in our private hours on our own. She had a very good friend, Yolanda, who came to visit. Yolanda did a certain amount of counselling and I think Verna was hoping that Yolanda would be able to sort me out. Sadly, it was to no avail. She said to Verna when she thought I was out of earshot, "Di is not dealing with it. She is just not dealing with it. She needs help!"

I unreasonably reacted rather unkindly, as she only meant well. "Please tell me, how do you deal with your son being taken from you in such a brutal fashion and how do you deal with your grandchildren being left without a father? Unless you have been there and walked in my shoes, you cannot possibly understand! What I need is time and lots of it before I can try to 'deal' with this. In the meantime, the only thing I can do is cry!"

Poor Verna stood by helplessly. She had tried her best and I am ashamed to say that, at that time, I did appear to be ungrateful.

Mike's death barely made the newspapers. There was a photo of him on the bottom of the second page of *The Star* – a major Johannesburg daily – a few days after his murder. At the time, we were requested by the police to please keep this out of the papers, as they find that the perpetrators tend to go ground immediately when a public spectacle is made and it is then harder for them to be found. Once again, in our numb and sheep-like state, we did exactly as we were told and initially turned down the many calls and enquiries that were being received from journalists. Thus, only a small story made the papers.

About a week or two later, a well-known South African musician was also murdered, and his story was splashed all over every form of media possible and, surprise, surprise, it was only a matter of days before the media reported that the perpetrators had been identified and apprehended and, not long after that, charged in court and sentenced.

Was the advice given to us loaded with ulterior motive or was it just bad advice?

Not being a hundred percent confident that the 'lack of media coverage' would assist in finding and apprehending the perpetrators, we still continued with the hiring of our own private detective to look further into Mike's murder. Richard managed to contact his private investigator friend, Ollie, and arranged a meeting with Allan, Stan and Ollie at Allan's house. Ollie agreed to do what he could to track down these gangsters, starting with tracing the whereabouts of Mike's cell phone and laptop. Brian and I were at the meeting, as was Debby, and we were so grateful for the offered help in apprehending these thugs who kill and torture innocent people with impunity and, in particular, our son. It was at this meeting that the concept of the Mike Thomson Change a Life Trust was conceived. The aim of the trust was to do something about crime prevention.

It is at this point that I need to introduce Vanessa Lynch. Vanessa Lynch is a dynamic young lawyer who was, coincidently, at school with Mike. Her father had been murdered at their family home some time before. In her despair at the lack of police work, crime scene protection and collection of possible evidence, she decided to do something to improve matters. She formed the DNA Project, which was to develop DNA use in South Africa and to get laws changed in order to create a DNA database in this country. Not really knowing just how far she had got with this project, we also called her to find out if she was able to help us in looking for DNA in Mike's house and maybe helping on that side. Sadly, she was not that advanced with her project and was battling to get sustainable funding. It was there and then agreed that she would be the first recipient of funds raised by the Mike Thomson Change a Life Trust.

We all had a really difficult few days building up to Friday – the day of the funeral.

Debby and Allan were sorting out Mike's affairs. Lorna had to go over to her home and let the police in again to look for fingerprints. I believe that they were successful, but they left the house covered in black powder!

All the week's events were certainly taking their toll on everyone. A new counsellor had not yet being found, but the need became extremely urgent when, on Saturday, the day following Mike's funeral, Nicky Tom, Mike's son, was found curled up in a foetal position, once again dressed in the same clothes he went to the funeral in, hugging his monkey, Mike, and refusing to speak, eat or drink. Nicky Tom was pretty much in a comatose condition. In desperation, Debby rushed up to a local children's counselling centre in Bryanston Drive, not far from Allan's home, thinking that any help at this stage was better than no help and Nicky Tom was not responding to any of us in any way whatsoever. Debby stood in their reception and begged them to please make a gap on their busy Saturday morning to squeeze Nick in. On hearing the story, they did so immediately, and Debby and Lorna returned a little later with Nick. Whatever they did and said to him in there will never be fully known; however, after carrying a frozen and immobilised Nick into the room, a young boy was able to walk out on his own half an hour later. The change in him was remarkable and we believe was good grounding for how he has managed to deal with his trauma in the years to follow. What a difference from the first lady who did not 'do' children.

Lorna and I also went there for some counselling. I do not know how Lorna found them, but I only had a couple of sessions and then stopped. I did not want to abuse Computershare's generosity. I am afraid that I was not ready for it. I sat there with this very nice young lady who I felt had no idea at all where I was or how to deal with me. My grief was just too profound and no amount of talking was going to help.

After the mask on the wall incident, there were a number of other 'coincidences', which I now truly believe were messages from Mike. The following accounts are true, although, to some, they may be hard to believe. In the first instance, there were two people to corroborate the story.

Debby and Lorna were travelling together in the car, talking about Mike and all the gaps in their lives that were now left to fill. Lorna was not a great cook, so Mike, who loved his food, became the cook in the family. Debs turned to Lorna and said that she would have to start cooking and jokingly said Lorna would have to now get some lessons. The radio had constantly been playing quietly in the background and, at this time, Debby and Lorna were both quiet, contemplating all that was being said, when they both clearly heard over the radio…

"Don't worry, Mrs. Thomson, there is always KFC."

Both Debby and Lorna's jaws nearly hit the floor.

"Did you just hear what was on the radio?" Debby asked Lorna.

"I think so," said Lorna. "Did you just hear 'don't worry, Mrs. Thomson, there is always KFC?'"

"Yes," said Debby. "That is exactly what I heard."

What are the chances that an advert like that – using the correct surname – would come over the radio at *exactly* the right moment in a conversation on *exactly* that very subject?

Coincidence? I wonder. Debby called the radio station to ask about the advertisement and they had no knowledge of it being broadcast at all. I heard it once and never again.

When Lorna and the children were forced at gunpoint around the house and being manhandled, she lost a small diamond cross pendent that Mike had given her. A day or two after the murder, some of the family and Lorna went back to the house to see what was stolen and to start looking for papers. She searched for the cross, as did everyone else at the house. It was nowhere to be found. That night before going to sleep, she asked Mike to show her where it was, as she was heartbroken about it. Those material things become even more precious when the giver has been taken from you. The next morning, back at the house, she walked into the lounge and there was the pendant lying in full view on the carpet. Michael had helped her.

As Lorna and the children moved straight into Allan's house after the attack, their possessions were in an awful muddle, as things had been brought over at different times and by different people. Lorna needed some papers that she had to sign and hand in to Nick's teacher at school for the family fun day, which was coming up. She began to panic, as she could not find them and, at that time in her life, the least little thing that went wrong became a major issue out of all proportion. Again, she appealed to him to help her. "Please, Mike, darling, show me where these papers are. I just cannot let Nick go back to school and be the only one who has not got sponsors and the sponsor money."

A short while later, Lorna went into the bedroom and there they were, scattered on the floor. They had not been there before. Michael had helped her yet again.

One of the visits that really helped fill the time of waiting was from Pat and Eileen Donaldson. Mike had worked for them both at Tanda Tula in the Timbavati game reserve as a game ranger for two years in his 'gap' year between finishing working for his mechanical engineering bursary and finding another job. It was Mike's choice to get bush experience rather than do the usual thing of backpacking overseas, as many of his

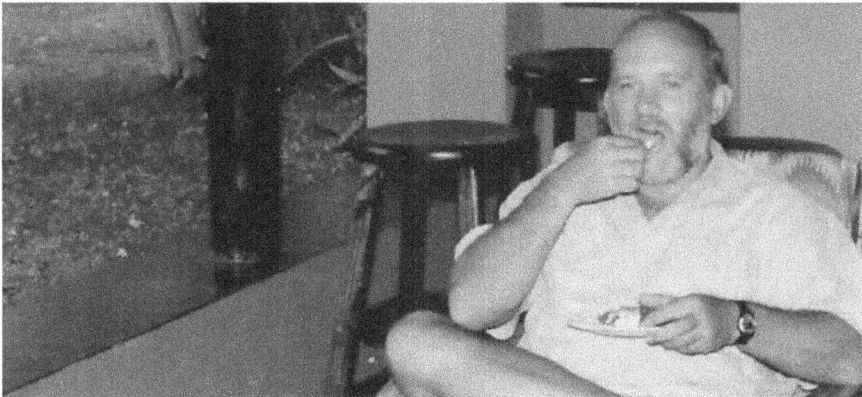

Pat Donaldson.

friends and two of his siblings had done. Pat and Eileen were instrumental in a very successful match making venture when they knew that Lorna was coming to the lodge with Janie and her new husband, Patrick. Lorna had been there before and they knew Lorna and Mike would be a perfect match – and so right they were! We had known Pat and Eileen for many years and it was heart warming to have them come all the way up from the Lowveld to attend his funeral and to see us. Pat told us that Mike had been the finest ranger he had ever had the privilege of working with.

Pat was the manager at Tanda Tula from its inception. My mother and father went there every year and really loved it. Dad loved the bush, but he had to see lions before he was happy. Poor Pat used to send out the scouts every morning to try to find them for Dad. There were occasions when he got so desperate that he would ask a visiting pilot to take him up to do an aerial search! Somehow, by having Pat with us, it brought my mum and dad closer as well. It was from our many visits to Tanda Tula that we invested in our bush home, Ntsiri.

To hear lovely things about our son helped to prepare us for the heartache of the next day.

Chapter Four

I woke up in the morning with a feeling that this was all surreal. I was going through the motions of cleaning my teeth, having breakfast, taking a shower, washing my hair and all the routine stuff without really being aware of what I was doing. I did not want to take any sort of tranquiliser, as I wanted to be aware of everything that was going to happen. I could not decide what clothes to put on, should I get ready now, or should I get ready later? What should I wear? Not black; that was too sombre. Not my new yellow top, as that was too bright and cheery. Verna helped me to finally settle on a not-so-new lilac slack suit, which was neither too bright nor too dreary. It was so hard to make any decision, which is very unlike me. What did it matter, really, yet I felt I needed to honour my son with the right clothes.

I have no idea what I did in the morning to while away the time. It was impossible to settle down or concentrate on anything. However, Brian and I sat at my computer for a while and tried to compose our very difficult letter to Mike. How do you put into words the excruciating pain that you are feeling in the middle of your solar plexus and the lump of lead that is in your heart? How do you put into words the loss to you and to your family? How do you convey the love you have for your children and that the pain would be the same no matter who it was who was taken from us? How do we do it?

We decided to make it as simple as possible, as, in reality, there are not enough words to describe Mike and to convey what his death was doing to us all.

Peter Upfold very kindly came to collect Verna, Brian and myself so that we did not have to drive ourselves. He arrived in good time for us to be at the church by 2pm. We got there at 1:45. I was gob smacked to see how many cars were already in the parking lot; it was nearly full, with no parking visible anywhere! Peter drove us slowly up to the front door of the church and dropped us off there. As I got out of the car, I could hear the bagpipes playing a beautiful but hauntingly sad lament. The piper was slowly marching up and down in front of the church. I do not know what it was called and, at the time, was in no state to find out, but it has been indelibly printed on my memory.

We got out of the car and walked into the church. To now finally see the coffin at the front of the altar with my darling son, Michael, inside was something I had never for one moment thought I would have to experience. It was something for which I was not prepared in any way. Particularly as we had only been in that church for happy occasions such as their wedding and later to attend the christenings of the three children. I was not supposed to go to my son's funeral there. I looked around and comfortingly noticed all my family there. Lorna, looking so small and vulnerable, sat in the front pew with her children next to her. The children were allowed to choose their own clothes. Nick and Meggie were very smart in their new outfits and little Annie, who had escaped into her own little world, was dressed in a fairy dress. I was amazed to see people whom I had not seen for maybe fifteen to twenty years coming in.

On time, the priest came in and the service began. I was overcome with emotion when I saw the whole karate dojo there sitting in a block, all dressed in their gis and barefoot as if they were in class.

Between Lorna, Debby and Allan, a really beautiful and moving service had been organised. Peter Kenyan, another friend of Mike's, gave such a warm and sincere eulogy, followed by another tribute from one of the seniors, Amelia, from the karate dojo. She spoke on behalf of the all the students. Amelia, five years later, gave birth to a baby boy, who she called Michael. What an honour!

Michelle, another student, paid tribute to her hero and read out the beautiful letter from her mom, Dee. Michelle spoke of how much Mike had meant to her, her sister, Cathy, as well as her mom, Dee. My heart was not just broken, it was also swollen with pride on hearing just how loved our boy was. That was our Mike they were talking about!

"I'm speaking on behalf of the Knights family, also known as the motley crew,

Dee Knight.

especially on behalf of my mom, Dee, who is somewhere in Turkey and, unfortunately, couldn't be with us today. When my mom, Cathy and I started karate, Mike and Allan thought we'd last three months at most. Five years down the line, I think we've proven them wrong, but a large portion of our continued persistence is due to Mike.

"Mom loved him from the second class. He was like a lion, immensely strong, but as gentle as a kitten. He always inspired you to give your very best. When Mom fell and scraped her elbow, Mike gave her much sympathy and then said 'now get back on that mat'. And there was always the promise of a sweaty hug after pulling us through a tough class.

"Many times throughout her training, Mom had to put on her 'Mike face' to keep her going and I think we've all used our Mike faces every now and then. From my side, there is much I owe Mike. He taught me so many things I could never learn any other way. He was a great teacher in teaching me how to control a class of unruly children.

"But I'll always love him not only as a great teacher, but also as a phenomenal person. He is one of those who leave a mark on the world, and in everyone's hearts.

"Some final words, directly from my mother: 'He is the wind, he is the sky, he is the stars, and he is the rain. Mike, wherever you are, I hope there's lots of glitter.'"

– *Michelle Knights; Cathy Knights; Dee Knights; 4 October 2007*

Dee wrote that there had been times when she was going to quit, as it was getting tough, and it was Mike's encouragement and teaching that kept her going. (She posthumously rewarded him by being awarded her black belt.)

The very special order of service was handed out at the door and I think they ran out, as there were so many more people than we expected. I looked across the aisle and saw people reading it and tears flowing unashamedly. Was this really happening? There was Barbie, Verna's daughter from Cape Town, and, behind her, Malcolm's children. Next to us was Peter Todd, Brian's nephew from England. So many people had made a huge effort to be there.

The priest, Father Michael Fitzpatrick, spoke with such passion, as well as anger. He had married this man and, through the evil ways of others, he was now burying this man. It was such a moving tribute to Mike.

When the service was over and he had closed with the prayers of commendation, he called on the pall bearers to come forth. They were obviously Brian and Allan, behind them Neil, Mike's father-in-law, Richard Moss and Dale Goldschmidt, his groomsmen at his wedding, and Peter Upfold, a university friend and our driver to the church. Of his own accord, our brave little Nicholas, all of nine years old, went up and joined the men in walking out with his daddy. If that was not heart wrenching enough, as the coffin was taken past the karate group, they all stood up together and bowed to him and said in unison, "Sayonara Sensei Mike."

My courage and composure left me. I broke down and could not control my weeping.

I somehow got myself out of the church and, before I could get to the car, I was surrounded by people wanting to offer condolences. I had lost Brian and Verna in the masses. They were also being surrounded by friends. I could not get away; that has to be the worst nightmare for any bereaved person at a funeral. In front of me was a sea of heads, but no faces; they were clouded by my tears.

We estimated that there were about eight to nine hundred people there, and they all seemed to be in the queue waiting to speak to me! I looked at all these people and right in front of me was my very dear friend, Gloria McPherson, who had been a neighbour since our children were small. I said to her, "Please get me away from here to the car; I can't do this anymore."

I felt my knees starting to buckle and I did not want to collapse there.

Peter, our caring driver, brought the car in and we tried to get out so we could make our way to the Bryanston country club, where a celebration of Mike's life had been arranged. We found ourselves caught in a traffic jam! It took more than half an hour to get there and it was only about ten minutes away with no traffic. By the time we arrived at the club, the room was packed with people. There were friends, family and colleagues and people who were at primary school with Mike, their parents, his teachers from primary and high school, and work colleagues. The staff from Craighall Primary came, as well as the staff from Thabile Nursery School, which I had started some thirty-five years ago and where Mike and Lorna had sent their two younger children. There were just too many people to remember them all. It was overwhelming, to say the least.

We arrived just as the DJ was ending the *Star Wars* theme. I was sad to have missed that. It seemed an interminable time that we mingled and chatted to people who had come to pay their respects and have snacks and drinks. Richard eventually called everyone to please come and sit down on the chairs provided and to get the celebration of Michael Roy Thomson's life underway. He introduced himself and spoke a bit about their friendship, and then called on Allan to speak. My heart went out to my remaining brave son. I do not recall all he said, but one thing has stayed with me. He spoke without notes. "On behalf of Mom and Dad, Lorna and the rest of the Thomson family, I want to welcome everyone here this afternoon and thank you for coming to pay tribute to Mike, my brother. All my life, I have had a brother and I cannot remember any time when Mike was not there for me. I cannot remember any time I did not have a brother. Now, I do not have a brother and I don't know how I am going to adjust to life without Mike." The details of his eulogy escapes my memory, but I do remember being so proud of him. He was battling to stay composed and not break down.

The next person to speak was Ernie Saks, Mike's headmaster from Rivonia Primary School. He also had wonderful memories of Mike and the wonderful camaraderie there was between the parents of that time. What a happy time it was for all of us, including the pupils.

Colleen Travis Lee then had a few words to say about their time as co-head prefects. Again, I do not have the details of her contribution, but I do remember her saying that he was mature beyond his years and that he was such a support to her, and they had a wonderful working relationship. She ended by saying that she always considered him her 'head man', not her head boy.

Before the proceedings began, Debby was showing a slideshow of his life. It was non-stop, starting with babyhood through nursery school, primary school, high school, university and Ntsiri. It included his time at Tanda Tula, where he had been a game ranger, his wedding and his babies, taking his children to the bush, and, finally, all his pictures of him with the children. I realised just how important taking photos of *all* the stages of your children's life is. That is all we have now; photos and memories.

Peter Upfold did his own slideshow of his time with Mike; it was mixed with sadness, amusement and love, which were welcomed.

Mike and Colleen.

Those young men were full of fun and mischief when they were at university. With Pete's photos to back up the escapades, he managed to bring some humour to the occasion, which Mike would have liked.

Charles Lourens from Computershare then spoke about Mike. Charles had known him for the shortest time; nevertheless, Mike had managed to make his mark on the company. Finally, Richard read out the letter from his sisters and the one that Brian and I had written in the morning.

Michael Roy, from his loving parents

How we wish that either of us had the courage and strength to read this ourselves, not only to let you know, but also to be able to tell the world the depth of our despair, heartache and unimaginable anger. We know that you will understand that Dad and I would not be able manage one line.

When Dad and I set out on this then-exciting path of marriage and then parenthood, we were young and romantic and, in many of our discussions for our future, we always said 'would it not be wonderful to have two boys and then two girls'. We then set about the task of building a family – the Brian and Di Thomson family. Not in a million years did we ever dream we would be so successful; *two boys and two girls*. Each of you exactly what we wanted and exactly when we wanted. All our children know how they are loved and how they loved each other. The depth of their pain and grief is as deep and searing as Lorna's, her children's and ours.

Mike's history is here today represented by all of you who have come to pay your last respects to him. All of you played your part in making his life what it was. Mike must be totally overawed when he looks down on us all today to see the love and respect shown to him and to all of us.

All of us Thomsons would like to thank you all for your presence here to share in our grief and help us through this awful period. We know so many of you have already walked this path. Anyone who has not been there will be unable to believe how helpful it is to have the house full of friends and family and love...

This is for Mike.

Dad and I are so proud of the wonderful, loving son and man you had become. Our lives will never be the same again, but rest assured we will take good care of your beloved Lorna and your very precious children. I promise you that, when this is over and we are stronger, your family and friends will not allow you to have lost your life in vain. Some good will have to come of it. You are our hero and oh, my, how we will miss you.

Rest in peace, our darling boy.

Dear Mike – from Cally

Dear Mike,

You had the most amazing patience with everyone and everything around you…

In karate, it never seemed to faze you when you were asked to demonstrate something for the umpteenth time. You simply explained it and showed how it was done without making a fuss about how we should know, as you had already demonstrated how to do it!

Your deep love of animals showed in the way every stray or abandoned animal found its way to you and absolutely worshipped you.

Your patience with your children was infinite – explaining and answering all their questions. At the farm, you were quite happy for the kids to wake you up at the crack of dawn to take them on an early morning drive only to land up sitting or watching them catch butterflies, then to have your afternoon sleep interrupted as they fought over climbing into the hammock with you or insisting on you taking them up to the Scotia with you. Your pride in your children was plain for all to see.

A large part of what made our home such fun was the endless stream of your friends who treated our house as their own.

Mike, the void you are leaving behind can never be filled; you will be sorely missed!

Dear Mike – from Debby

How does one even start to explain what it means to have had a big brother like you, Mike, and just how much your loss will mean in my life?

Following you around as a little girl, always wanting to play with you and your friends, and, when most boys were running away from their little sisters, you so often found some way for me to join in.

In high school, you gave me the hardest and biggest shoes to fill that any sibling could ever be faced with. Often not known by my own name, but rather 'Little Thomson' or, if I was lucky, just simply 'Mike's sister'.

From your first days at Bryanston, you excelled at everything, from academics to sport and even, your little known secret, at dramatics too. Your short-lived theatrical career starting off as the honourable, and very apt, Prince Charming in Rivonia Primary's *Cinderella*, through to the lead role in the high school musical – *South Pacific* – a role that I recall included a very short-lived singing career as well.

Your speed on the athletics track was unbeatable and with a reputation to follow. I recall, in Standard 7, being told I had to run the 400m, which was a race normally open to seniors from Standard 8 to 10 only; however, it was presumed that, as I was 'Little Thomson', it must go without saying that I would be as good as you always were, and obviously if I was only half as good, then that would still be more than enough than they felt they expected in others. I can still remember my extreme disappointment at coming third as a junior in a seniors' race, which, in hindsight, may have been quite impressive; however, it was not good enough for me, as I had not been able to live up to what everyone else had grown accustomed to expecting from a *Thomson*.

The pride I felt at so many occasions, that you were my

brother, and after Allan had started a dramatic rise in the Thomson name at school – you just made it fly. I went through school bearing the Thomson name with pride. There was no greater compliment anyone could pay me than to refer to me as Mike's little sister.

As an adult, I truly treasured the times and moments we've shared from our initial days of working in the bush together – the parties at the Orpen Gate Research Station and Timbavati and Klaserie HQs; from the 'double dating' weekend visits when both Lorna and I would make the long drive to Hoedspruit every odd weekend, she to visit you and I to visit Bruce; to the lengthy emails and phone calls over the years to discuss family visits/issues and other family details, and, of course, how can I forget all the nights meeting for dinner at the deli in Hoedspruit, while on your way to Ntsiri, with yourself, Lorn, the kids, usually four or five others, and often all climbing out of the same car – your car – one of the few men I know who chose to drive a larger family car, because that's who you are – your family is your life.

Although I hold everything clearly in my heart and in my head – your laugh as if I heard it yesterday, your smile from a few minutes passed, and your presence that I still feel filling this room as only you can, I am terrified that, with time, they will fade.

I vow to you this day, Mike, that I will ensure, together with Allan, that this senseless, despicable deed will not be left as yet another statistic. If this *had* to happen, we will ensure that it has happened for a reason – as a catalyst for a major and critical upheaval and change to this unforgivable and unacceptable situation that has taken over our country.

Your loss had left a huge void so much greater than anyone could ever imagine. Please just know that we will be there for your little family that you love beyond words, for Lorn and the kids; there will be no task too great to do for them, because we know it is what you would have done for them too.

I could never have asked for a better big brother over all the changing years of our lives.

I look forward to the days when I can once again mention your name and speak of you with the same pride and admiration that I always have, instead of this heartbreak, pain, anger and lack of comprehension.

Mike, I loved you and I always will. You will still remain a shining star in all that I do, all that I am and all that I will ever be.

Goodbye, my big brother; I look forward to sharing times with you again in the next phase.

All my love,

Debby

A fitting end to a very emotional, but amazing, tribute to a very special young man was when all the children and many of the adults present wrote notes to him and tied them to a helium balloon. There were far more than his own children there, as he had been such a wonderful karate teacher to the juniors and host to so many children in his home. When all the messages were tied to the balloons, they released them all at the same time.

I know Mike got his messages and he would have loved that!

Chapter Five

Two brothers with their first born Shannon and Megan.

After the funeral, the family and some close friends went back to Allan's house, emotionally drained. Everyone was sitting in the lounge chatting and having a drink. We were talking about Mike and how well the afternoon had gone. We were remembering the fun times we had all had with him and his family and how we were going to miss him. After some time, I noticed that a strange whirring sound had started.

"What is that noise?"

"Must be the wind," said Verna.

"No," I said. "Look outside; there is no wind. Could it be a child's battery toy that has been left on?"

Sarah got up to have a look, but could not find a toy. "It sounds like it is coming from the fireplace," she said.

Richard then got up to look and said, "Yes, it is coming from the fireplace. It sounds like a fan."

"Can't be," said Allan. "We don't have a fan."

Allan and Sarah had been living in the house for about five years and were not aware of a fan in the fireplace.

Richard confirmed it was, indeed, a fan and found the electric cord. He followed the cord behind the furniture to behind the TV and saw it was plugged in. Richard switched it off. There was much discussion about how it could possibly have been turned on when no one knew it was there. I thought about it and wondered if I should voice my thoughts. They would probably think I was losing it, but I decided to anyway.

"I believe that was Mike telling us he is with us here now and he was with us today."

My comment was met with silence. No one said 'you are talking rubbish', but no one had the courage to agree with me. There were too many sceptics in the room, but I was sure it was Mike.

However, I was not alone, because, later, Debby said she also thought it was him, as she had been noticing a few unusual occurrences that week.

Debby had also received a phone call in the middle of the funeral service on her phone, which she had forgotten to switch off. Her ring tone is the call of a woodlands kingfisher, which, with Mike having been a keen birder, was almost a fitting sound; however, after receiving a number of dirty looks from the rest of the family, she had switched if off immediately. After the funeral, she had switched the phone back on in order to phone the person back and apologise for having to reject their call, only to find that there was no record of the call at all – no missed call, no rejected call, no recent calls logged – nothing registered at all.

As we have come to learn that electronic equipment is one of the easiest and most popular methods of communication from the other side, we now suspect that this was once again Mike calling through to let us know he was definitely there.

During the weeks to follow, there were several messages from Mike. On more than one occasion, my cell phone would ring, and, just as had happened to Debby, when I answered it, not only was there was no one there, but, similarly, there was no 'missed call' or 'unknown number' that showed up. As with Debby's phone during the funeral, on these occasions, there was nothing. I knew in my heart of hearts that it was Mike.

Debby stayed on in Johannesburg to assist the family for a few months after the event and was still staying with Sarah. Allan was away on business for a night and, knowing that I was not having a good day, they, together with the little boys, Dylan and Brian, brought some supper to us. During the course of the evening, Dylan, who was five years old at the time, went into our little office and knocked some papers that I had been working on onto the floor. Sarah picked them up and put them back on my desk. After they had gone, I went into the office and there on my desk on top of the papers was Mike's ID book. This had been safely stored in a stack of Biddy drawers (a set of plastic office drawers to store documents) standing on the corner of the desk. I could not understand how it had got there. I called Sarah to ask if she had put it there or picked it up from the floor.

"No, Di, definitely not. It was not there when I picked up the papers."

I immediately knew how it had got there. It was Mike.

It was a couple of days after the funeral and we were at home. I was unable to settle on any sort of household chore. I was mechanically topping up the flowers that filled my flat and rearranging those that were dying. It was really all I was capable of doing. I was thinking of these messages from Mike and I was convinced that Mike was trying to contact me, and the only way I knew how was to find a medium.

I turned to Verna and said, "I must find a medium. I must

know if Mike is okay and I need to know more about what happened. I need to know where he is and what he is trying to tell me."

"No, I don't think you should," she said. "That is not a good idea and it is stuff you must not meddle with. It is not healthy. Dad and Sandy would not have approved and I don't think it is right."

"How can it not be healthy? He's my son, for heaven's sake!"

"You must leave him be and allow him to move on."

I paused and took a deep breath. "I can't explain, Vern, but I have to see one. I have this overpowering need to do so and I know one will find me if I don't find one first."

I could see there was no point in arguing and she could do nothing to make me change my mind.

Three more incidents made me all the more determined to find someone to help me. One was when I went to sit down in the lounge and a glass candle stick on the table next to the couch suddenly fell with a loud thwack! It did not just fall over; it fell with a force that made it sound as though it was pushed.

The second one was just before we went to the game farm in December. Brian and I were having lunch at our dining table in the flat. We were talking about Mike and I was saying that I was missing his little contacts, as I had not been aware of any for a few weeks. A second or two later, the toaster just popped up. We did not push or see the on/off lever go down and we had not been making any toast. We both felt the toaster and it was hot, and we just looked at each other. We both knew he was making contact.

The third one was, in my mind, the strongest message of all. I went into the office and there on my computer keyboard was Mike's death certificate. I had received this awful document in a big brown envelope. I hated seeing that certificate, which said in big black letters that Michael Roy Thomson had died on 27 September 2007 from unnatural causes with such a passion that I put that, too, in the Biddy drawer, in the envelope under other papers to keep it out of my sight. How on earth did it get there? If that was not a message from Mike saying 'Mom, I need to contact you', I don't know what was.

The longing to know how he was, the longing to find out if he suffered and where he was now become all consuming. I had to find a medium and I had to find one *now*.

I mentioned this to my friend, Pam Heeley, who I have known since I was five years old. She had lost her husband some years previously. She said her son, also named Mike, frequently went to see a medium when he needed to communicate with his dad. He felt that the medium, Jacqui Freemantle, was very good. I called her immediately and got an appointment for the next Monday.

Mike was killed just three weeks before his fortieth birthday, which would have been on 16 October. On 13 October, it was not only his oldest daughter, Meggie's, birthday, but, also, the Craighall Primary School was holding a family fun day. Mike had been on the governing body and was very involved in the organisation of this day. They honoured him by calling it the 'Mike Thomson family fun day' and had banners made with that wording along the fences of the school. His spirit at the school on that day was palpable.

We, as a family, felt that we needed to attend this day for him and his family. It must have been very hard for Megs to feel anything like a celebration for her twelfth birthday. We just wanted to be together. It was very difficult for us. There were so many times when I would see a tall man with a child on his shoulders or walking along with a bush hat on and I would think, *There's Mike.*

But, of course, it was not. This function was the first of many occasions when my son was honoured for his contribution to society.

During the morning, a lady went to Lorna, who was running her own stall, and said she had noticed a small truck from which someone was selling rose bushes. She wished to buy one and donate it to the school in memory of Mike. Would Lorna like to choose one?

Lorna replied, "I don't know anything about plants, but my mother-in-law is a landscaper and she would know."

Debby and I walked across to his little stall and we choose a white rose for peace. It was called White Sunsation. I said to Debs that I wanted to change the name to 'White Sensation', as he was a sensational man in every way and also because he was a sensei in karate.

As we were going across to Lorna to tell her what we had done, I felt my cell phone in my pocket vibrate. I quickly took it out and answered it... but no one was there. I looked for a missed call or a number showing. There was nothing. The thought then occurred to me that my phone was, in fact, on ring tone, not vibrate. I knew it was Mike thanking us. I just did.

I could hardly wait for Monday to come. I had my appointment booked with the medium and I was looking forward to making contact with Mike. Verna was very anxious about me going, but I was adamant I had to. Jacqui had given me an address where she had a room in the gym at the Randburg sports club. I found the place and, with my heart in my mouth and full of trepidation, went into the building. What if he did not come through; what if I was wrong? What if she was not as genuine as Pam said she was?

I was early and sat waiting in the reception area. The noise from the gym and the huffing and puffing of the people exercising did nothing for my nerves. I thought this cannot possibly be a suitable atmosphere for someone to communicate with the other side. By the time my turn came, I was a nervous and emotional wreck and battling to control my tears.

I was ushered into a small austere little room, where Jacqui sat behind her desk, which had a photo of her son on it. I was quite blown away by my misconception of what a medium may be. Jacqui was young, blonde and quite beautiful! She had very large, blue, blue eyes and a lovely friendly demeanour. She was not at all 'woo woo', as my sister would say.

I sat down in front of her and she explained how she works. She did not want any information from me unless I was validating what she told me. She said straight away that she had a young man with her who had died a violent death. She said he was not ready to go and was crying.

This upset me so much.

She then said that he was asking me to buy a white rose and plant it in my garden. This surprised me, as he knew that I had a very small garden and no room to plant another rose.

I then asked her how she was receiving this message; was she seeing him, hearing him or interpreting a vision?

She said she could see him and he was holding out a white rose to me. I straight away realised that her interpretation was not correct, but the message of the white rose was real. Mike was referring to the rose that we had selected in his honour that weekend. That was validation enough for me.

The message of the rose was a pivotal and important step in my journey, as it was a major confirmation that I was, indeed, communicating with my son and there was truth and validation in what I was experiencing.

Jacqui continued to give me messages from Mike. She said

that he had felt no pain during the entire incident and that he was in a white-hot rage. That was a comfort. She said he fought two men and that there were another two who went into the house. She said that he had broken the ribs of one of the men he fought. He told her they would be caught and that one of them would die before they were sentenced. The broken ribs were impossible to verify. However, one of the gangsters, Razor Zulu, who went inside to Lorna and the children, is known for raping and sometimes torturing the women with an iron. Lorna and Meggie were not raped. Did Mike, in spirit or with the energy expended in fighting him, manage to stop him? I believe in my heart of hearts that he did.

He said he would not reincarnate soon, as he wanted so much to be around and help his children grow up. Michael was an exceptional father who was totally dedicated to being the best dad he could be. I believe that he wanted to be around us and especially his family for a while longer to be true. (For any reader who is unsure of reincarnation, I suggest reading Dr Brian Weiss – he has a number of books on the subject that may give a different perspective to conventional thinking.)

My hour with her just flew and I had to wrench myself away. She told me that Mike had very strong vibrations and that, as I was open to spirit interaction, I must look out for messages and signs, as they will be there. Most people do not recognise them and so do not receive them. She said that spirits actually want to communicate with their loved ones and that, in recent times, had found it much easier because of the energy waves that man has harnessed through advanced electronics.

In effect, what she was saying was that the first few months after he left us, he did his best to comfort me by sending so many messages in many various ways. It was due to seeing her that I was able to recognise them.

I needed to know more about life after death, so I started reading books, mainly by well-known mediums from all over the world, such as John Edward, John Holland, Dr Brian Weiss, Lisa Williams and Gordon Smith.

A passage from John Holland's *Spirit Whisperer* really grabbed my attention. In a section on messages from loved ones, called *Electricity*, he says: "Lights flickering, television sets going on and off by themselves, radios and stereos acting up for no reason, electric clocks gaining or losing time or just stopping at the time of person's death, cell phones ringing and registering the number of the person who has passed or not registering anything at all. These are just a few examples of how spirits use electricity to grab our attention."

After reading this confirmation, I needed no more convincing that Mike was truly contacting us. In only slightly differing ways, we had experienced every one of the methods that he described and more.

On the Saturday after Verna left to go home, Brian and I were watching the semi-finals for the World Cup rugby match. Mike loved watching rugby and we were both very aware of his absence that day. It was not South Africa playing, but it was a brilliant game. At the end, Brian said, "Mike would have loved

that game." Then he switched off the TV and put the remote on the coffee table. The TV came on again. Brian picked up the remote, turned it off again and put it down.

It came on again. This happened three times.

I said to Brian, "That is Mike saying he did watch it with us and he did enjoy it."

"Of course," said Brian. "Goodnight, Mike." He turned off the TV and put down the remote.

It stayed off. This, for us, was yet another confirmation of interaction and communication with Mike. Brian has related this story to friends so many times and, each time, he is still emotional about it.

Chapter Six

Mike with his first born Megan at Boulders near Simonstown in the Cape.

Once again, that overwhelming need to see Jacqui was starting to take over my thoughts. Part of me said it was too soon, as she did not come cheap, but the other half said I could not put a price on the comfort that contact with Mike brings to me. How could it be too soon? A voice inside my head was urging me to go.

I called Jacqui and booked an appointment. This time, I

went with eager anticipation and without the trepidation of my previous visit. Jacqui told me that I had come just in time, as she was moving to White River. She confirmed again that Mike was, indeed, there and he said, "Thank you for coming, Mom. I was asking you to come back." He said that he was very worried about Lorna, as she was at breaking point and he was worried she was going to have a breakdown. He knew that she was not accepting help and he understood my sadness over it. He asked that I just keep trying. He said he had been trying to reach her, but she was blocking him. Lorna, being a Catholic, was afraid of her church not approving.

He also told me he was very concerned that Debby and Allan, who were going through all his papers, had not found a document that contained details with a new and additional policy that would mean extra money for Lorna. Through Jacqui, he said it had a black and gold logo in the top right corner, and she tried to describe it with her hands.

Jacqui said quite a few things this time that I could not validate and came away feeling a little let down.

I told Allan and Debby about her message concerning the document. They both were very confused and said, "Not a chance, Mom. We have been through absolutely everything and there are no documents that have not been found."

However, they both then returned to Mike's house in the following days and re-went through all the paperwork in his filing cabinet, this time to just look for anything that had a gold and black logo as Jacqui had described to me.

However, even with a new search, they were still unable to produce anything and I had no choice but to file this information away in my mind together with the other messages Jacqui had given me that I had not been able to confirm.

I accepted that and thought it was part of the stuff of which I could not make any sense or was nonsense.

About two weeks later, I got a call from Allan.

"Mom, you are not going to believe this. When the robbers took Mike's computer screen, keyboard and mouse, etcetera, they did not take the computer box, probably because it looked old and they had already taken his laptop anyway. Debs and I went into it to help Megs set up her new iPod and thought we might as well do it on the computer that Lorna would eventually take with them when they moved out to wherever they may stay next, and so we went into Mike's home computer for the first time since that night."

Lorna had bought Megs a new iPod for her birthday on 13 October – a mere two weeks after Mike had been killed – as that is what Mike had wanted to get for her and it obviously made sense to both Allan and Debby to set up Megs' new iPod on the computer that they would eventually take with them.

"It is the first time we have opened his computer," Allan continued, "and there we found a folder with some of Mike's additional personal documentation and you won't believe what we found."

Low and behold, there on Mike's home computer was the document with a black and gold logo, which contained information on an additional policy that Mike had taken out fairly recently and it was for extra money for Lorna. Jacqui was so right!

We were gob smacked! I now regret that I did not record the other stuff that she told me that I thought was of no value. Maybe, in time, that would also have been revealed to be right.

Lorna was very unhappy and stressed at the idea of living in Jo'burg. She and the children decided to go back to Scotland for December and have Christmas with her dad and her aunts in Bathgate. She was considering returning to live in the UK. We were desolate at the prospect, but understood her need to return to her own family.

It was a very sad little family that we said goodbye to at OR Tambo Airport and two very sad grandparents left behind.

Brian and I had always shared a love of the bush and, when our children were still at school, we bought a share in a nature reserve called Ntsiri in the Umbabat game reserve bordering the Kruger National Park. We built a lovely but simple and comfortable home ourselves. Mike's girlfriend at the time was Vivian, who was in his class at Bryanston High School. Her dad, Peter, was a builder and good friend of ours. He took his team of builders and lived down there for twenty-three days and, during that time, built the house. To save money, he did no finishing or inside fittings. Over the years, in the school holidays, we as a family worked on the house until it was completed. It was a wonderful bonding experience for all of us and, in particular, it was there where Mike had developed his love and expertise of the bush.

Mike was accumulating a vast knowledge of the bushveld, including the flora and fauna. I loved having someone who shared my love in trying to identify the wild flowers as they popped up in the different seasons. It was this passion that led him to be become a game ranger for two years doing a 'gap' period between finishing his degree, working off his bursary and starting his career.

We heard that Pat Donaldson of Tanda Tula in the Timbavati nature reserve adjoining the Kruger Park was looking for a new game ranger and he decided to apply, as he had just finished working off his bursary. He had been there many times as a young boy with us, and he and Allan had previously helped out there in the school holidays. He knew that one of the traditions there was to finish up an early morning game drive at a picnic spot for a delicious cooked breakfast in the bush. In his application, he said he had the following talents: he could fry thirty eggs in a large pan on the fire at one time, he could open a bottle of beer without a bottle opener (before the days of twist-off caps) and he would be able to service and repair the bush vehicle!

This fine accolade of bush-required skills got him the job without hesitation!

Pat Donaldson demonstrating the skill of bush breakfast cooking at Tanda Tula.

One of my fondest memories of our times together in the bush was the two of us both enjoying a glass of Jameson's whisky in the evening around the fire. We were the only two in the family whose favourite whisky was Jameson's. Mike always had one for me at his home and I did the same for him at my home. However, the best was being in the bush with the family sitting around the crackling fire, a full moon illuminating the surrounding bush and, in the background, hearing the night sounds. The potjie pot (a three-legged cast iron pot traditionally used for cooking over a fire) bubbling away with the vegetables or pap to accompany the meat. (Pap is another traditional South African food. It is a stiff maize porridge that is eaten with gravy or a type of local salsa.) Mike would be bustling about with his head lamp on, cooking our meat on the braai (barbeque), and the rest of the family discussing the events of the day or playing cards or backgammon with the children. The bubbling and sizzling coming from the fire were often accompanied by the 'oh Lord deliver us' of the African night jar or the whooping of a hyena on their nightly rounds. Of course, we were always excited to hear the roar of lions in the dark. If we did, we would often drop everything, cover the fire, and jump into our bush vehicle and go and look for them.

Early in December 2007, Brian, Carol and I decided to go down to our bush home, as it had been some time since we had been there. It would be our first visit since Mike died.

"When we are sitting around the fire, I will have a Jameson for me and then I will have one for Mike. If I want a second, I will have one and, if I think Mike wants a second, then I will have a second one for Mike," I told the family, as I knew this was going to be a very emotional trip. A little light hearted chat together with this shared whisky helped to relieve the sadness.

It was, as predicted, a very sad and emotional visit to the farm. After the first evening when I had enjoyed my Jameson, I went to bed and cried myself to sleep. I did not have to be strong for anyone or put on a brave face; I let go and sobbed from deep down where the pain in my solar plexus would not go away. I was wearing Mike's watch and, at 5am, the alarm went off for the first time. It woke me and I did not know how to turn it off. I put my hand on the face of the watch and it stopped. I assumed that Mike had set it for 5am to go swimming or something, but was confused, as I had not heard it before and I had been wearing the watch since it came off his body. I certainly did not set it myself, as I did not know how to operate his watch. At first, I did not link it to Mike, but, when it went off a few days later after another tearful night, I began to suspect it was another form of communication. Again, I only had to touch the face to stop it. I was only aware of it going off twice during that time.

After Lorna and the family left for the UK, Christmas was looming, with no one really having any enthusiasm for it. The last Christmas had been a big family affair with Lorna's dad, Neil, her brother, Michael, and nieces coming out from the UK, as well as friends and other family members being invited. It was a lovely day and we treasure the memory. Brian and I and the girls decided to join Allan and Sarah and the family for a short while at Shelley Beach for Christmas.

Shelley Beach is a holiday resort on the KwaZulu-Natal South Coast. Verna, Malcolm and I inherited a townhouse in a delightful complex of only seven duplex townhouses right on the beach. Malcolm did not want his share, so Verna and I bought him out immediately. Many of our families had enjoyed lovely holidays there with each other and their respective children.

After Sandy, Verna's husband, had died while on a family trip at Shelly Beach, she found it very difficult to be there on her own. She wanted to sell and I wanted to buy Carol her own home, so we were both looking at selling. Thank goodness Allan wanted to buy it in partnership with another family member. It remained in the family, but the responsibility of maintenance was passed down to younger members.

It was during this time that I began to initiate communication with Mike by requesting him to make use of the alarm on his watch that I was still wearing. Each and every time, Mike responded. Initial communications happened on sporadic days – following my request to Mike, but always at 5am. Brian was unsure about this, as he felt that the watch must be set for 5am and that perhaps I sometimes did not hear it, as he had heard it on some occasions and I had not. This put some doubts in my mind and I hoped that I would be able to prove to myself in time that it was Mike.

As predicted, Christmas was a difficult time for us all. We went through all the motions of Christmas for the little ones, but none of us had the heart for it. We returned home after New Year to face the prospect of learning to live without Mike and helping his little family to pick up the pieces and carry on.

One evening soon after we got back, one of my clients, Hillary Dunnet, called me to see how I was getting on. She told me that she had lost her daughter a year ago. We made small talk about work and coping with grief when she said to me, "I get messages from my daughter when I am in the shower. The light flickers."

To find another person with similar experiences was so welcome. "Hillary, I am so pleased to hear that, as we also get messages." We also found that we were reading the same books.

"Have you ever considered seeing a medium?" asked Hillary.

"As a matter of fact, yes, I have already seen one, but she has moved to White River. Do you know of a good one?"

"Yes, I do; her name is Laureen and she works out of Alberton. I will SMS her number to you. I get so much comfort from seeing her. I always come away feeling that I have had a long distance phone call from my daughter."

"Thank you so much. I will contact her soon."

What did I say to Verna when she was with me? "If I could not find one, one would find me!" I was fast learning that there are no coincidences in life.

That night, before I went to sleep, I asked Mike if he would like me to see Laureen and, if so, to please make the alarm go off again the next morning. Well, true to my hopes, it went off and I took it as sign of approval that I call Laureen that day.

I made an appointment for 28 January 2008. I got hopelessly lost trying to find her, as my GPS was not updated enough to deal with the new road closures and road works. I finally got there half an hour late and in an awful state.

As I walked down the passage, she came out of her consulting room to greet me. She said, "There is a gorgeous young man in a red shirt walking down the passage behind you. Oh, I am being told that he is your son."

I knew then I had come to the right place. He was there for me and he did have a red shirt! Again, she was not what I expected. Laureen was young, somewhat funky with short, almost spiky, hair and again not a bit 'woo woo'. She had a simple consulting room with two chairs, a small table next to her with a glass of water on it and a clock. Why did I have this preconceived idea that a medium would be weird and different, perhaps sitting in front of a crystal ball or going into some sort of trance? It was nothing of the sort.

She confirmed that she had a young man with her who had recently crossed over. She said it was a violent death and that he said he could do nothing to stop it.

Laureen asked me if I could explain why she was feeling wet and why she had a terrible pain at the back of her head. She kept hitting the back of her head; she said that was the final thing that took his life. I was immediately convinced that she knew what she was doing. I confirmed and explained about the pool and the shot to the back of his head.

She was quiet for a while and looked at me quizzically, then said, "Now, I don't understand what I am about to say to you, but perhaps you can explain. What is this thing between the two of you and alcohol? You don't look like a 'soak' to me, but I have such a strong taste of alcohol in my mouth. Mike is laughing and he is saying 'thanks for the drinks, Mom.'"

Of course, I knew immediately what she was talking about. Good old Jameson's whisky! She told me that he talked about a brother and how glad he was that they had patched up a difference of opinion over a karate matter. I was so relieved to hear that. Laureen said that she was seeing two letters, D and C, and that he said it was his sisters. He wanted to honour them by covering the letters in flowers. He said he loved them both.

She then said he was with Dad Dad and Mike quickly corrected her and she said, "Sorry, no, he is saying Da Da."

That was music to my ears. The grandchildren called my father Dan Dan. I knew my parents would be there for him.

My father, Ralph Spence, had passed on New Year's Eve eleven years before Mike did. My mother, Bernice, joined him just seven months later. I had not had any spiritual contact with them and was so comforted to know that they were there to receive my boy.

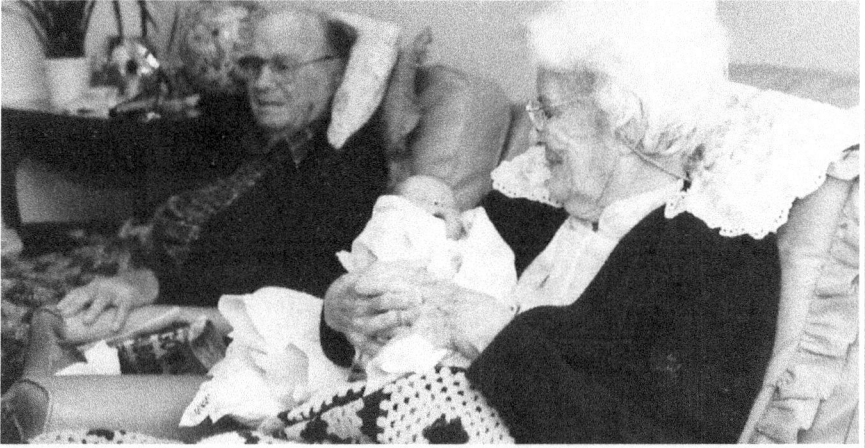

The watch alarm went off on intermittent days, always at 5am, for quite some time. There were some days that I woke up before 5 and waited for it. There were times when it did go off and there were definitely days when it did not go off. There was no pattern except that he seemed to always answer my questions by triggering the alarm the next morning, or in response to a bad day that I had experienced. Most of the time, I did not need to do anything more than touch the face and the alarm would stop. However, one morning, it would not stop. I eventually had to get a pen to push in a little button on the side that was flush with the casing.

Did that mean that the messages through his alarm were coming to an end? Please no.

Chapter Seven

Our house at Ntsiri was on the bank of a mostly dry river bed. Directly on the opposite bank was a very old, very large *Schotia Bracypetala* (weeping Boer been). I am sure it must have been over a hundred years old.

Since the first time we went there, when Mike was still a young boy, he loved to climb that tree and sit high up and have a commanding view of the surroundings. Very often, he could see elephant or buffalo making their way in his direction and he would sit and wait there for them. Frequently, he had elephant right underneath him, resting in the shade and feeding off the tree.

As he grew older, he started taking his children up the tree too. First, it was Meggie, who was still in nappies, and Lorna would have to pass her up to Mike and he would go up higher and sit quietly with her.

As each baby came, they would all be taken up into the tree to wait for passing game or just to enjoy the view and peace the tree brought them. There were odd occasions when the remains of a leopard kill were left hooked between two branches and Mike would take up a child or children to inspect the carcass.

Our last visit to Ntsiri with the family was Easter 2007. For some reason, in all the years of this favourite pastime of his, we had never photographed Mike in his tree. There he was, as usual, up there with the children and their Aunty Carol.

"Brian, please get your camera and take a picture of this? It is such a special picture and I want to preserve it for posterity."

Did I have a premonition that this was to be our last visit with Mike? I did not recognise it as such at the time, but, in hindsight, I think it might have been.

That very photo became an important centrepiece in our memories of Mike. Debby made a beautiful collage of Mike in his tree with all sorts of family pictures around it. We all have a copy up on a wall in our homes. The decision was made that under the *Schotia* tree was a very suitable place to scatter Mike's ashes. I could not contemplate the thought of having him buried in a small container somewhere. He had to be free and in a place that he loved.

Ironically, he was cremated in Nelspruit in a cremator built by his dad. Mike was working for his father at the time and he had, in fact, commissioned that unit himself. Martin, the owner of the crematorium, kindly drove up to Johannesburg and collected Mike. We knew it would be done with integrity and respect. We knew that the ashes that we received would really be those of Mike. To add to the irony, it was not much later that Martin himself was cremated in the same incinerator. He was killed in a freak accident while canoeing off the coast of Mozambique. He went over a big wave and the paddle hit him on the head and knocked him out. He drowned. I believe that Mike would have been there to greet him and help him cross over.

5 February was the weekend we decided to take Mike back to Ntsiri. Lorna was not keen to go back there just yet, but, as usual, she faced the ordeal with the courage that she had already demonstrated. She wanted to keep some of his ashes, which we readily agreed to.

Lorna and the children, Allan and Sarah and their three, Brian and I, together with Carol, all travelled down for the occasion. Debby, who lives in the area, came and joined us for the weekend. Dale and Nicky Goldsmidt, good friends of Mike and Lorna's who also lived in the area, came across for the day. Debby first had the stressful task of driving to Nelspruit, where she collected her brother's ashes from Martin for us. It was not an easy task for her.

I really do not remember very much about that weekend. It was

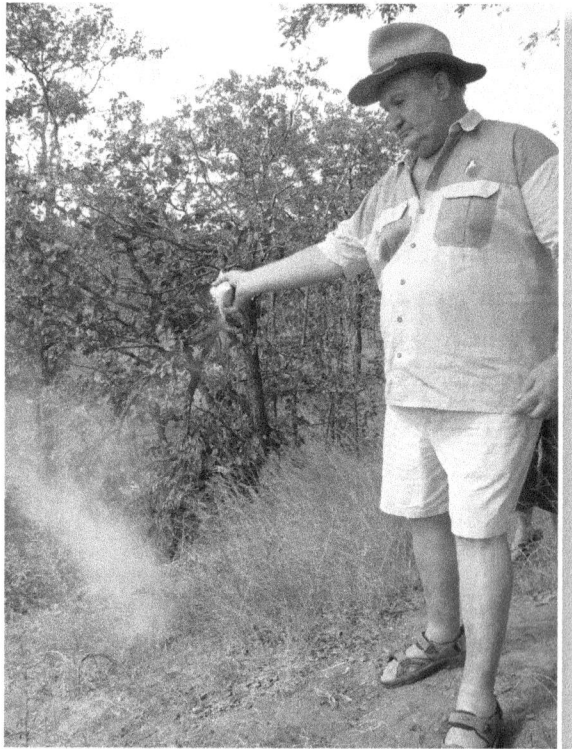

Brian scattering Mikes ashes under the *Scotia* - one of the hardest things Brain has ever had to do.

just too painful. I wrote a little speech, which I read out when we were all under the tree.

Writing this brings tears again. It is supposed to be therapeutic; who said so?

Brian then took the wooden casket and scattered his son's ashes: dust to dust. Probably the hardest thing he has ever done.

That night, as I was going to sleep, I asked Mike to say hello to me in the morning. Sunday morning at 5am, the alarm went off. This time, I just touched the watch again and the alarm was immediately silenced. I then tried something new. It was very hot and still. There was no breeze in the room. I asked him to let me feel something. There was a very gentle breeze across my back. I said thank you; what about my face? It moved to my face. I so treasure that small contact, yet it was so frustrating because I want so much more and I have not experienced that again.

On our next visit, we attached a plaque honouring Mike to the tree.

My letter to Mike the day we scattered his ashes

5 Feb.

Darling Mike,

I, as your mother, the one person who had the closest umbilical bond with you until you met your darling Lorna and created your own special family, wish to say what is in my heart today.

Mike, we both know that all of us here today are just some of the people who were special in your life. You were, and always will be, loved and respected beyond description. I know you are here today with us and will be watching over all of us forever.

You told me only the other day through Laureen that love has no barriers and no boundaries. We will always remember that and knowing that will help each of us through our dark and sad days when we are missing you.

Whilst we are struggling to carry on our lives without your physical presence, we are learning to live with your spiritual love and support. I, your mother who gave birth to you, loved you and nurtured you as you were growing up, have this to say. I am desolate at your passing, but have come to understand that you were lent to us for a time only. Dad and I were privileged and blessed to be given the opportunity to be your mother and father for nearly forty years. We will always treasure the time we had together as a complete family.

I hope you approve of the place where we are leaving the remains of your earthly body. We all know how you loved this tree and you loved this place. It is your other home and will be a spiritual place for all of us. Today, we set you free. You can be wherever you want to be. Our bond of love can never be severed. Be at peace, my darling son. Till we meet again. Enjoy the elephants and lions that pass this place.

Your loving mum

On our return to Johannesburg, we were invited to the unveiling of a portrait of Mike, which had been done by a friend of Dee Knight from the dojo. The karate students had organised a very simple little ceremony on one of the mornings of a grading. I was not sure what I felt about the portrait, as Mike's hair was made black and he did not have black hair. However, as time has passed, it has grown on me. Dee read out a very moving letter from her daughter, Cathy.

Letter from Dee's daughter in England read at the unveiling of his portrait at the dojo

Mike taught me how to hug again. He reminded me that hugging was not a sign of weakness. That it was a way to give strength to another. Secretly, I used to look forward to his warm hugs, but, being stoic me, I never told him this... it would have given him another reason to laugh at me (it was bad enough with my pink gi). His strong arms could hold any weight and his spirit was always big enough to lend to my own smaller one. He reminded me that it was okay to love with the heart – that no pain in this world could ever shatter the spirit completely. His philosophy seemed to laugh louder, give more and live more. He taught me that, to live, you needed to experience life – you needed to laugh when it was funny, grin when it was happy, scowl when it was bad and cry when it hurt.

Like the lion he was, he put his family first, defending them with his every action. Like a lion, he could bellow a loud roar and protect those he loved. Like a lion, he carried his 'mane' for all to see – displaying his pride and courage without fear.

His booming voice will echo forever in the walls of the dojo. His footprints are ingrained in the wooden floors. And his spirit lives on in all of us.

As I have mentioned previously, a couple of weeks after Mike's murder, there was yet another murder; this time of a high profile musician called Lucky Dube, who had been shot in a botched hijacking. Within two days, his killers were arrested and brought to court. His death made big media headlines and I heard it discussed on the Redi Direko show on Radio 702. I felt incensed that Mike's murder had only been reported on the second page of the *Star* in a very small article and photo and that we had been encouraged to keep the story out of the papers. This prompted me to write to her and voice my desperate opinion! This is what I wrote:

25 October 2007

Dear Redi

I have also emailed and faxed this letter to John (who is also a presenter on 702). Can you imagine how the family of a young man feels when his brutal murder goes barely unreported? We hear daily of policemen killed in the line of duty. They all just become a number and the man in the street becomes immune. However, a celebrity is killed and, within two days, his killers are found. Are his children and family any more traumatised than mine are? Is the loss of Lucky a greater loss than that of Michael Thomson, who was a pillar of his community? Michael was my son. All of our lives in the Thomson family have been shattered and there are three little people without the loving, exceptional father they had.

I will try to explain simply why I need your radio station's help or suggestions. For you, the media, his death is now old news, but, for my family, it will remain forever. Three weeks ago, my son, Michael Thomson, who was thirty-nine years of age, was brutally murdered in his home, two weeks short of his fortieth birthday. He died a hero fighting off three to four men armed with guns and knives, trying to protect his wife and three little children. It happened in Craighall Park at 8:15 in the evening. His murder has just become an addition to the statistics, as there have been so many in the past couple of years in the suburb. Unless we all do something, it will remain just that, a statistic.

The reason Mike's brutal murder did not make headlines was twofold.

1. *We were asked to keep it low profile to assist the police in their investigations. They did not want the murderers to go underground. For us, and me in particular, the time for silence is over!*

2. *He was not a high profile figure, but my, did he dedicate his life to this country! There was never any question that he would not remain here and make this country work for all its citizens. I could tell you so much more about him, but there is not enough time. The fact that there were more than eight hundred people at his funeral: all of them filled with grief and anger, asking what can we do to save our country?*

On Friday, there was another high profile murder, and Mara Louw (a well-known South African singer) called in. I tried to call, but to no avail. She spoke so eloquently. She spoke for us all who are now desperate about what is happening to this country and about the corrupt people who are at the helm of almost every department in the government. She spoke for us all and I want to thank her. We are all so worried about each other and we are frightened of the future for our children and grandchildren. This is now far, far worse than ever it was in the past. We used to feel safe in our homes, but now no one does. There were always corrupt politicians, but now it is so blatant and so condoned. We need to stand together and let the world know what is happening to our rainbow nation and to the dreams that we all had for a united future. This is not a black on white issue or vice versa. It is about getting rid of the people who are not only allowing this to happen, but who are perpetuating and benefiting from the crime and only paying lip service to the nation.

I know and appreciate your anti-crime efforts, but it is no longer enough! Every time there is a murder or a violent hijacking, you need to broadcast and make a request for informants to come forward. You need to tell the public what actually happened and how many people are left traumatised and suffering.

We would also like to suggest that all the media come together to somehow create a register of all victims in, say, the past five years and get a newspaper to publish it for free... I think the results and information would be staggering.

I found it so hard to get excited about Saturday's fantastic World Cup win, as we would have shared watching it with Mike and his brother, Allan, and their families. It seems so hypocritical to see our president out there enjoying the hype and success when we all know what is really happening back home here. The euphoria will soon be over and there will be more families torn apart like mine and their voices will be silenced.

Mike touched so many lives that his death has been the last straw and so many of the young people with children are now leaving the country. That makes me so sad and so scared for those who cannot go.

Please, I beg of you, Redi, read my letter and acknowledge it... I have listened to 702 for years and have always thought you were the answer to so many people's prayers by giving them a voice.

We are ready and willing to do whatever it takes to help change things. We do not expect a miracle, but we can no longer keep silent about this brutal violence.

Mike died for two cell phones, two TVs, a laptop, some clothing and linen, and a gun that was in his safe.

That brings me to another issue where the law has backfired. In insisting that guns be locked up in the safe, they are impossible to access in a crisis and have resulted in people being forced to open their safes and often land up being killed in the process. In the past, most burglaries occurred while the owners were away. Today, they make sure that the owners are there to force them to open safes. That is why there are so many people killed in their homes.

That may be an issue for discussion one day.

I hope that you will not disappoint me.
Sincerely,
Diana Thomson

Neither my letter to John or to Redi was answered. I got a computer-generated letter from Redi that it had been received and she would get around to reading it. She obviously did not manage to do so. I appreciate that she must get thousands of letters and they have to be vetted by her producer, but can you imagine how helpless and saddened I felt that my son's murder was not worth the time to read about? I did not even get an acknowledgement from John.

Chapter Eight

I had not had the alarm go off for over a week and I was missing it. Before going to sleep one night, I spoke to Mike in my head. I told him that I was missing the alarm and that I was longing for him to just say hello. The next morning, I received my greeting.

I wanted to see Laureen again. This was to be my second visit. I managed to get an appointment for 25 February. There were a number of things I needed to know.

Laureen started by confirming again that he had died violently (she does not always remember everyone from visit to visit, as she sees so many different people with so many different stories).

She, too, confirmed what Jacqui had originally told me. Mike did not feel any pain, as his adrenalin was pumping. He says the first sensation he felt was floating.

Laureen then surprised me.

"Was Mike connected to the martial arts?"

I don't know why, but my pulse started racing. "Yes, he was, very much so."

Allan had started karate at Stellenbosch when he was at university. When he finally came home to Johannesburg, he could not find a dojo that followed the same style. He decided to start his own dojo at the local scout hall so that he would be able to continue training. However, during this time, Mike had joined a dojo of a differing style in Johannesburg. Mike decided to move over to Allan's style and they became partners in the Riverside dojo. With the two brothers each bringing their own individual strengths, skills and personalities, the dojo grew until they were forced to find bigger and better premises. They found the perfect accommodation upstairs in the Riverside shopping centre, where it is today. At the time of Mike's death, he was a third dan and Allan a fifth dan.

Laureen continued, "He tells me that he fought with every fibre of his being and he used everything he had ever been taught. He says he did inflict damage to his attacker, but he was unable to stop them. He said that he would do it again to save his family."

Was that the broken ribs to the gunman or George Nyembe when Mike was trying to drown him? Again, a confirmation of what another medium had said.

She then said, "There were five there that night; one was waiting in the car. One is not a South African and may be difficult to find. They will catch the others, but one will die before he is punished." This was another endorsement of Jacqui's reading.

Laureen then told me that we had been to scatter his ashes and said she had a very high 'feeling' and could not quite understand the message.

"I'm feeling high up. Is it birds; is it flying; is it an airplane?"

"May I suggest something?" I tentatively asked.

"Please."

"Could it be a tree?"

"Yes, yes, that's it. He is in a tree. That's weird; what was he doing in a tree? I can also feel water, but I cannot see it. Why is that?"

"Could it be a dry river bed?"

"Exactly! That is what it is."

I explained to her the story of the tree and where it was. What she said made perfect sense.

Mike said she must thank us; he was very touched and very happy at our choice. He reminded us that he would not be staying there, as it was merely symbolic, but he would be with us all wherever we may be. That was some comfort and time would prove that statement to be of even more comfort to me in particular. He also said that he was very proud of how strong his children and Lorna had been.

On Thursday 28, as I was going to sleep, I asked him if he had enjoyed our session with Laureen as much as I had. Friday morning, he answered me and once again I only had to touch the watch face as usual to stop the alarm. I was feeling very sad, as I was very worried about Lorna. She had moved into Richard and Louise's house in Rivonia, as she was too afraid to stay anywhere on her own with the children. They had very kindly let her have the granny flat above the garage and they were all living in one bedroom and one living room. Lorna was still going across to her house every day to run her nursery school and taking the children to Craighall to their school. They were not eating properly, as she was afraid to cook in the living room, as the thatch roof was low and she was afraid of fire. Lorna was working herself to a standstill just to fill her day and not have time to dwell on things. I wanted to help, but she was being very stubborn and would not let me do anything. We were all finding it a struggle to get through each day.

On Sunday night, I had such a vivid dream that I was being moved into an awful house and I was standing in a room crying. Mike came to me and put his arms around me and hugged me tight. I could feel that hug as though it was real. I did not want it to end, but, of course, it did. It was the first time I had dreamt of him since he died and I have read that loved ones can appear to you in a dream, and it is usually more vivid than a normal dream; which this was. Was it him? I think so.

I asked him that night, but, sadly, the next morning there was no alarm. I was so sure it was him; I now did not know what to think. That night when I was in bed, I spoke to him.

"Please, Mike, if it was you in the dream, give me another sort of message to tell me?"

It had been some time that I had not been woken by the alarm and I decided to give it one more try. I realised that I must learn to live without it one day, but I was not ready to do that yet.

The next morning, I got my confirmation. Again, I did not have to press the button to stop the alarm. I just touched the face of the watch and said, "Thank you, Mike."

Mike and Lorna were very involved with the children's soccer at the Old Parks Club in Bordeaux, Randburg. They used to take Megan and Nick to soccer in the evenings and on Saturdays. They both played in the club teams. Meggie played for the girls' team, but sometimes, when they were short of boys, she would play for the boys' team as well. At one of the soccer practices, a lady unknown to Lorna went up to the coach and asked if Lorna was the lady who had lost her husband.

"Yes, she is. She is Lorna Thomson," the coach informed her.

"Well, there is a lovely man standing beside her in a dark red shirt and a bush hat."

There he was again in his red shirt and his favourite hat.

Lorna had such mixed emotions after she had been told. She was comforted by the fact that he was with her, but she was heartbroken that she could not see him herself. How I identified with her.

I read in the newspaper that South African actor and comedian Desmond Dube had just lost a very good musician friend and neighbour, Bashimane 'Shimi' Mofokeng, right outside his house in a hijacking. He was incensed at this senseless killing, as this was only a few months after Lucky Dube had been killed in a hijacking. Desmond felt very strongly that enough was enough. He wanted to organise a Million Man March Against Crime and was appealing to all South Africans to rally and support him.

I read this article out to Brian. We felt strongly that we should support him, as we had been directly affected by crime.

"I know we are not marchers, protestors and street gatherers, but I cannot with a clear conscience ignore this appeal," I said to Brian. In the same breath, I asked what he felt about it. He agreed with me. I called Mike's siblings and they also felt that they wanted to be part of it.

That night, I asked Mike what he thought. I said if he approved, please send a message by alarm. If I did not get it, I shall assume he believed I should let it be.

After a long gap of no alarm in the morning, at 5am, I got my approval! Once again, I knew it was Mike.

That was all I needed, so I set to work.

Chapter Nine

The following morning, I called Desmond and offered my services. He was very sympathetic and grateful. He asked me to come in and see him at his offices in Oakdene in the south of Johannesburg.

I duly went across town to see him and was immediately impressed by his passion and enthusiasm for the task ahead. He and his wife, Tumi, who was a petite 'blonde' black lady, had taken three months off work to organise this. Desmond immediately came across as a confident and sincere person. He and his staff were to go without a salary while the march was being organised. They were all totally dedicated and his office was a hive of activity and enthusiasm. I was so inspired by this man. As I lived in the north of Johannesburg, to go across to the south daily was going to be too difficult for me. I said I would work from home and keep in touch with him and his office. I gave a lot of thought to how I could actually help him. I decided that my best option was to find buses and try to fill them. We needed buses, as the march was to be in Pretoria and we lived approximately fifty-five kilometres from the Union Buildings, which are the administrative seat of government. Desmond was hoping to hand over a memorandum to the then-President Thabo Mbeki. My suggestion to get buses was not without ulterior motive. I thought if we could go in a group it would save parking problems for everyone and, if we had commitments, people would be less likely to pull out for some arbitrary reason. It would not be easy to change one's mind at the last minute if one had a seat reserved! It also made it so much easier to keep tabs on everyone and keep them up to date with the arrangements.

Desmond requested that I ask Lorna to write a story about their experience. She was reluctant to do so. Therefore, I wrote a letter on her behalf, which they sent to the press, and it was published in some newspapers.

At about the time of Mike's murder, there were several other murders, armed robberies and rapes in the same area. Wrio Denny, who was also an owner at Ntsiri, had been murdered in his home in Craighall earlier in 2007. Mike accompanied Brian and me to his funeral. It is just as well none of us knew that we would be attending Mike's before long.

I called Wrio's ex-wife, Olivia, who had become a friend of mine, and asked her if she and her family would be prepared to get supporters and join in the march. She was more than willing. In addition, her brother was the owner of a bus company, and she approached him to hire his buses at a good price. This he readily agreed to do.

There had been another horrific murder of a friend of theirs; Tessa Goldsworthy had been to collect her grandchildren from school and, as she was driving into her driveway, she was hijacked and killed in front of the children. Her family was eager to garner support.

Another tragic event happened soon after Mike was killed. A young schoolgirl, Emily Williams, had been killed in the crossfire when a gang of armed robbers were running away from the house where Emily's mum, Toni, had stopped to pick up a lift club member. Their security company had been called and their men were shooting at the fleeing robbers. The robbers returned the fire and hit young Emily in the head. Her devastated parents were already making a big noise about crime and had organised their own mini-march a few weeks earlier. I did not know this family, but, once I had contacted them, we realised just what a close community we really are. Toni, Emily's heartbroken mother, had been at school with Allan and she knew Mike well. In addition, Roger, her dad, had business dealings with Computershare. They were very willing to participate and fill their own bus. This tragedy in their lives had prompted them to make plans to emigrate.

Shortly before Mike's murder, there was yet another high profile killing at the Broadacres Super Spar near Fourways (a suburb to the north of Johannesburg). That Spar is owned by the Tarr family. They are lovely people and a very close knit family. There were four sons, two of whom were identical twins. Very early one morning, as the Tarrs were opening the shop, they were attacked by an armed gang. Ian, one of the twins, was fatally shot. I did not know them at the time, but I called in to the shop one day and asked to see Pat, the mother. As soon as I started speaking to her, I knew we were kindred souls. We were both mothers with the same pain and anger. She was also prepared to be a part of our march and to assist wherever she could.

The first thing to do was to find a sponsor or sponsors for the buses.

Computershare offered to pay for two, as did Pat Tarr. I thought that four for a start would be enough. If we needed more, I would cross that bridge when we came to it. I started emailing everyone I knew to get support. It was very heart-warming to find out how many people were willing to give up their day to come and have their voices heard and give us support. My emailing became a network of people happy to be a part of this. I received so many letters of encouragement and acceptance. Many of them were from total strangers.

We decided that each family would have a bus and one of Olivia's friends offered to make us banners to attach to the sides of the buses. This would help to get our message across.

The Dennys and the Goldsworthys were not able to fill a bus each, so they shared one. We had a banner for Wrio on the one side and Tessa on the other side. Mike's bus was full, as was Emily's, both displaying appropriate banners on either side. The banners had a photo of the victim and 'in loving memory of Mike or Emily, etcetera'. In the end, we managed to fill three buses, so Pat only had to pay for one, with Computershare paying for the other two!

The media started to get interested and, as a result, I was invited to appear on TV on the 3 Talk with Nolene show on SABC 3. With me on the show were Desmond, Letta, Shimi's widow, another young woman who was held up in her apartment, but not hurt, and another TV and radio talk show hostess, Criselda Kananda. The topic was the value of the march and what may come out of it.

That TV show was another eye opener for me. It helped me

to understand and appreciate that there were many black South Africans who are just as fed up with the crime and corruption as white South Africans are and want to do something about it. If only our country could be run by the likes of Noleen, Desmond, Criselda and Letta, perhaps we would not be fighting this onslaught of violent crime and misuse of government and municipal funds. I was very nervous at first, but, as soon as we went on air, I felt calmness come over me and I knew that Mike was with me and giving me courage.

Following the TV show, I was asked to join Kayseree Moodley on Querishne Naidoo's show on Sunday at 5:30am on Talk Radio 702. Both these women were not only lovely to look at, but really warm and sincere people. That, too, was an opportunity to promote the march and its purpose and to field questions from the public. They expected a listenership of approximately 80, 000 at that time of the day. Brian and I left home in the dark at 4:30am. While we were driving there, Mike called on the alarm to let me know he was with me.

We fielded quite a few questions and, thankfully, all were encouraging. Both Kayseree and I did our best to promote Desmond's objective for the march. What he hoped for was to try to get the mindset of people changed and, in particular, the mindset of the black youth.

Desmond said, "When the ANC first came into power, it was okay if a young unemployed son brought an obviously stolen microwave oven home for his mother. She would accept it with the attitude that it had previously belonged to a white person and it is now the right of the blacks to have it."

Desmond then added, "No, that was stolen from someone who had worked hard to acquire their possessions. What must now happen is that, when your child comes home with obviously stolen property or if you see that there are stolen cars next door, do not turn a blind eye as has been done in the past. Either make your son return it or report it!"

He said he hoped that he could get it across to people that crime is wrong and, for the country to succeed, we *all* have to change. Desmond wanted role models to be people whom the youth could admire because of their morals and principals, not the gangsters who have flashy cars and designer clothes. He hoped that other movements to counteract crime would be born from this.

At the same time as all this positive energy was being mobilised, Desmond received some very negative reaction. In particular, a radio host from an early morning show, tore this endeavour to shreds and said it was a waste of time and nothing good would come of it.

I then called in and said, "Good morning, John. I want to take issue with you over your trashing of this march against crime. It may not be your cup of tea, but then you have not been personally involved with violent crime. You have not had one of your children murdered. What right do you have to tell people not to march because you consider it a waste of time? You actually have the ability to influence this one way or the other, as you are heard by millions of people. It may not be what you would do, but shame on you for denigrating someone else's efforts to do something positive."

John's reply was, "If all those millions of people got together to do something positive, how much better that would be."

I replied, "Yes, I agree, in a perfect world it would, but you know and I know that that cannot and will not happen. This at least gives the people who do not have the ability to get up and 'do something positive', as you say, an opportunity to unite with others who want to see the high crime rate brought to the authorities' attention."

John was very vociferous and trashed it totally.

I then said, "I think it very sad that you have chosen to bring down a sincere and positive man in an endeavour to unite people in their anger and frustrations. Also, what you are doing is trying to silence someone who is speaking on behalf of hundreds of thousands of victims and their families."

We could find no common ground.

"John, you have not experienced firsthand tragedy; you cannot represent people who have, with your views."

He angrily replied to me, "Don't tell me I have not experienced tragedy firsthand. I have been called out in the night to help when the daughter of a friend was raped. Don't tell me I don't know."

I decided to give up, as it was useless arguing with him. All I can say, even now, is: "John, in spite of what you think, you have *not* walked that path, and, until you have, you do *not* know. It was not *your* daughter."

This was followed by a lot of calls to the radio, some agreeing with his viewpoint and others violently opposed to it.

Desmond and his team valiantly pressed on with their plans. He kept saying, "Evil prevails when good men sit and do nothing." That was to be their slogan for the march.

One of the people who heard my spat with John on the radio was someone by the name of Gaby Burgmer, who is the owner of the Heia Safari Ranch just outside Johannesburg. Her father had recently been murdered by his housekeeper, who had put a hit out on him, as she had heard that she was a beneficiary in his will.

Not only was Gaby very keen to join the march with all of her staff, she very kindly invited the whole Thomson family out to her ranch for breakfast and a game drive.

This invitation came as a very pleasant surprise and diversion, as we were still all feeling so shattered from our horrific loss. It was, indeed, helpful for the whole family to have something different to do on that Sunday morning. We all went out there for breakfast and were warmly welcomed by Gaby, who had organised a very pleasant morning for us.

This safari ranch, to a bush-loving South African, is not a

safari ranch in the true sense of the words. The hotel part is very pleasant and has a bush atmosphere, but there are semi-tame animals such as zebra, wildebeest (gnu), warthog and impala roaming around the camp and in between the guests. The property is not large, but a very pleasant game drive gives foreigners a small taste of the bush not far from town, and I imagine that, if they are short of time, they would love it.

We went on the promised game drive, but, to be honest, our sadness and reminder of Mike, who was usually the driver up front in a bush vehicle, did not do justice to her generosity and empathy.

The children at the Heia Safari Ranch with their animals from Build a Bear.

I had not had an alarm call for some time and was beginning to think they were coming to an end. Again, I was wrong!

All the plans were in place. The march was scheduled for Tuesday 10 June.

On the Friday before, a rumour went out that the march was cancelled. It was announced on the news broadcast of many radio stations. I heard it, called the offices and was devastated to find that it was someone making mischief and not true. My heart went out to Desmond. He spent the day trying to put out the fires and telling the media it was not cancelled! I sent out emails to all the supporters on our buses to tell them to *please come*! We did what we could to resurrect the momentum, but huge damage had been done. People who had offered sponsorship for all sorts of things pulled out and left him high and dry. They did not want to be part of a sinking ship.

Who was responsible for this? Had it been started by criminals who had a vested interest in maintaining the status quo regarding crime; i.e. crime does pay? Had it been started by some politician who did not want the ANC to show up as being indifferent to violent crime in South Africa? Had it been started by those who considered the march a waste of time and wanted it to fail to prove a point? We will never know, but the fact is this backlash was started and it succeeded in doing severe damage to the whole project. Desmond and his team did not deserve this malicious rumour mongering.

Desmond asked me if I would please be one of the main speakers and tell my story from the stage on the day. I had not done any public speaking since my school days and the debating society! The thought filled me with terror!

However, I decided that, for Mike, I had to do it!

This is one of the letters I received in support of the march. I did not know Mirko until the day of the march.

Letter from Mirko

Hello Diana,

Thank you for taking my call earlier on today. My heart and prayers go out to your family for your loss. Before I begin, I just want to say *thank you* for doing this all and being proactive in our society. I know this is in honour of your son and must be difficult with the pain you feel, but your actions will benefit our society in many ways in the future. *Thank you.*

I have emailed all the people I can and sent them the notice below and I hope I can get the synergy going.

We have so much to offer as people, yet we are restricted by 'pigs' in our society. I was very straight in my email and raw about the issue, but we need to get the ball moving and, if one has to be honest and direct to get the message, then so be it (if I offend any law-abiding citizen, my apologies).

Well, I would really like to play any part possible and help in any way possible.

Please forward me any information possible to promote this campaign.

God bless you, Diana and family.

Mirko

This is the notice I sent out today

Hi everyone,

Yes, it's me again trying to get people to be more active in the fight against crime....

Whose life is worth R2? R2 is what a bullet costs to destroy a life.

The next time someone spends R2 buying an ice cream or whatever, think of the loss of life a bullet caused to someone in

our society. Yes, our society, not their (criminals) society, by some criminal. We all live together and we need to act together.

I received an article this morning from a friend and was so astounded that finally someone has put something in motion (God bless Mr. Dube) and I want to help in any way possible.

Like I have mentioned before in my 'presidential elect' emails, as some of you called them (as if I was going for the presidency), we as a people need to do something. **It's time, people, it's time**.

I spoke to the lady on the attachment this morning (Diana) and she lost her son to crime, and she is cut so deep. Wouldn't any of us be destroyed by this loss?

Yes, we hear it all the time, but I could sense the pain she was feeling. I don't want to feel that ever in my life. Come on now. **Let's be proactive** and get our marching shoes on for 10 June 2008. If you want to be part of it all and want more information, visit: http://www.millionmanmarch.co.za

Corporate businesses, please, let's all do something together; let's sponsor buses or whatever to get the masses there. Let's get the synergy moving now.

Anyway, once again, if anyone has any ideas, please forward them to me. God bless all of those involved in this project.

Mirko

If you want me to stop nagging… *I won't.*

Let not fear and ignorance prevent progress.

Chapter Ten

The Mike Thomson Change a Life Trust

Extract from the Mike Thomson Change a Life launch brochure

"In 2002, Computershare (international) set up a global charity programme. In February 2007, Computershare staff from around the world took part in a cycle event in order to raise funds for Change a Life. With cycling becoming the fastest growing executive sport in South Africa, a regional cycling event in aid of charity seemed a natural next step.

"Simultaneously, Computershare South Africa was becoming more active in anti-crime initiatives and, after the brutal murder of its Johannesburg-based senior manager, Mike Thomson, in September 2007, it seemed natural that Computershare Change a Life initiative in South Africa should focus on combating crime."

In 2008, a cycle challenge was planned for participants to ride from Victoria Falls in Zimbabwe, down the one side of the Zambezi River to Katima Molimo, and back on the other side of the river. It was to take four days and end at Victoria Falls in a gala dinner. Each participant would be obliged to raise R20, 000.00 in sponsorship as an entry requirement and Computershare Australia would match the funds rand for rand. The funds raised would be allocated to the Mike Thomson Change a Life Trust and to the worthy children in the Wilderness Programme.

This whole programme was headed by a Computershare staff member, Ursula Du Plooy, and her team. Ursula was just beginning to demonstrate her brilliance at organisation and facilitation.

One morning in March 2008, there was a call from the security guard at the gate of our complex to say we had a visitor. We were curious, as we were not expecting anyone. However, the guard was instructed to let him in, as he was from Computershare. He was delivering a perfect invitation to the launch of the trust. It was a beautifully scrolled invitation attached to the stainless steel frame of a mini torso. Dressing the torso was a perfect miniature cycling shirt in purple and white (their corporate colour scheme) and their logo, 'Computershare Change a Life cycle challenge', was on the front and back. This was our introduction to Ursula's ingenuity and attention to detail.

The invitation was for a breakfast to be held on 28 May at the JSE (Johannesburg Stock Exchange) to launch the Mike Thomson Change a Life Trust and the proposed cycle challenge.

All the family was at this launch. We were treated to a delicious finger breakfast. Everyone was given a name tag and a portable electronic hand-held auction device. We were intrigued, as we had never encountered anything like this before.

After breakfast, we were ushered into an auditorium for the proceedings to begin. Stan Lorge, Computershare's CEO, opened the gathering with a very moving speech. He spoke of Mike and how much his loss meant to them all. I found it very hard to keep my composure; it just did not sink in that all this was happening in my son's name.

Ursula then went onto the stage and gave the details of the cycle challenge and the route, and told the audience that there were still a few places left. They could only take seventy, as that was what the accommodation provided by Wilderness Safaris could manage.

When she had finished, she called on Gerald De Kock, who is a well-known sports commentator in South Africa and no mean cyclist himself. He started the auction and was excellent!

Well known sports commentator Gerard de Kock has become a solid institution himself in the annual Cycle Challenges.

Brian and I had discussed the bidding before we went in and decided that we would bid on whatever was being auctioned up to about R2, 000.00. Imagine our chagrin when the first cycle to be auctioned opened at R5, 000.00! My finger lifted to press the button and stayed lifted throughout the auction! We were just not in that corporate league!

There were about five top of the range bikes donated by

various cycle shops and we were heartened to hear Allan alongside us bidding against his boss and, between the two of them, they pushed the price up to R20, 000.00! Allan got the bike. The other bikes were also sold for what I thought were very large sums of money. A young cyclist, Martin Dreyer, who was a cycle and a canoe marathon champion, offered to ride tandem and sell the back saddle to anyone who wanted to join the challenge, but was not fit enough to do it alone. That back seat sold for R50, 000.00!

In no time, all the places were taken and Ursula set about organising the cycle challenge, which was to be the experience of a lifetime for all who participated in whatever capacity they had chosen. Ursula herself had started training and she was going to ride as well. Stan was not riding, but going in an advisory capacity and along for the trip. Ursula has told me on many occasions that Mike has not only changed the lives of many children, he has changed her life through the trust and cycling.

This was, for the Thomson family, a very touching and emotional experience. How would I ever be able to thank Stan for making my promise to Mike come true? This was far bigger and more far reaching than we could ever have done on our own. We would have loved to have been able to join them, but, at that time, it was just not possible, as well as 'no spare accommodation'.

With what promised to be a very successful well-planned event, we were starting to feel a very strong sense of amazement at the continued impact Mike would have on the lives of others around him. This helped us to move forward and continue with our plans and work in trying to make the hugely damaged Million Man March another such success.

Chapter Eleven

Mike holding his new son - Nicholas Thomas Thomson.

10 June 2008 – The Million Man March

It was still dark when we left for the New Life Church in Bryanston in the northern suburbs of Johannesburg, where we had been given permission to leave our cars and be picked up by the buses. I was very apprehensive before we left, as it had turned out to be a bitterly cold morning and I just wondered if some people not directly involved would be put off.

I need not have worried. All my family in Johannesburg and their children were there, and all my friends who were in JHB were there. Friends of friends, clients, Brian's clients, Allan's colleagues, his friends, Carol's friends and Sarah's friends all came to give their support. Craighall Primary parents came and some staff members were there. Computershare sent a contingent from the office and, of course, Lorna and her children showed their usual courage by taking part. I was unsure, until the day arrived, whether she would be there or not. She could not decide, but, in the end, she came.

It was a very moving sight as we drove into the parking lot. There were the three buses in a row with the banners on the side ready for us to all make a stand. What energy there was that morning!

MMM Mike bus.

The buses left on time and drove in convoy to Pretoria. It was bitterly cold. Thank goodness everyone arrived, prepared and well wrapped up in scarves, beanies, jackets and gloves. On our bus, we had TV media from Holland and Germany. Lorna and the children were interviewed by both. *Carte Blanch* went on the Williams bus and, sadly, I think that was apparently all the media support we were getting. However, SABC 3, one of our local broadcasting channels, was covering the event at the union buildings for the whole day.

We left home early, because we were warned that parking was going to be a problem. It turned out to be no problem at all; we just drove into the grounds and had carte blanche choice of parking! This was the first disconcerting sign.

We were to meet with the other organisers at the Sheraton Hotel, which was bustling with people, helpers and politicians from opposition parties, and some media, both international and local, but apparently more of the former! The hotel was across the road from the Union Buildings where it was happening. From the patio, it had a commanding view of the area where the proceedings were to take place. The march was due to end at 10am at the buildings where the speeches and memorandum were to be delivered. We had got there much earlier than anticipated and were told that we were not expected to march, as they required us to be at a candle lighting ceremony. We now had time to kill. The family went into the dining room and had a very pleasant breakfast together.

Every few minutes, one of us would get up to see if the grounds were filling up. Slowly, people were arriving, groups of school children from St Mary's girls' school. A bunch of Democratic Alliance politicians, including their leader, Helen Zille, started chanting and toy toying (a traditional method of protest, dancing and singing in the black population). There was a man there who was carrying a gallows and had the noose around his neck. He had a placard that read 'Bring back the death penalty'.

It appeared to be a crowd from all walks of life – black, white, coloured, Indian, men, women and children, young and old.

The Emily Williams supporters were very prominent. They had all been given a pink scarf and a pink beanie, because it was Emily's favourite colour. This large block of pink and what it symbolised brought tears to my eyes.

Mike was so good with young people. I could just imagine the two of them together there in spirit, amongst the crowd, and Mike would have his arm around Emily's shoulders, comforting her.

Desmond had done a sterling job of organising the police for security, organising parking all along the proposed route, and areas with large TV screens along the route. I did not see any of the actual marching. It was dismally disappointing as far as the numbers were concerned. People kept coming in very small numbers and gradually gathering in front of the stage. I doubt that there was ever any actual marching through the streets; I think that everyone just came straight to the Union Buildings.

Just before 10am, Desmond had organised a fleet of cars to take his dignitaries and the families involved on a small, slow drive around the block. The first stop was in front of and just below the Union Buildings where there was a memorial statue. He had put large candles there and my three grandchildren were asked to light the candles in memory of all who had lost their lives through violent crime. This they did, but, because of the howling wind, the candles would not stay burning!

Nick, Megs and Annie-Rose lighting the candles at the start of the Million Man March.

From there, we were taken to the stage where the proceedings were to take place.

I no longer remember the order of events accurately, but this is more or less how it happened. It was opened with a prayer by a bishop and Desmond Dube made his speech about crime. He made a passionate plea to the president, who was in the building now in front of us, to show that he cared about his people by coming down personally to receive their memorandum.

Letta, Shimi's widow, made a speech about how the loss of her husband had affected her and her family so dramatically. Two little school girls wrote speeches about crime and how it impacts on the youth. Finally, I was called on to tell my story. I was only allowed four minutes to say what I wanted, as it was all being accurately timed for the TV coverage. I think I just made it!

My three beautiful but broken grandchildren came up to join me on the stage of their own choice - a touching and heartbreaking moment for me.

I had butterflies in my stomach before I was called up, but, as soon as I stood there and saw that sea of faces all looking expectantly up at me, I felt as though a gentle hand was on my shoulder and I suddenly felt quite calm. I started talking and the next thing I knew my little grandchildren had quietly stood up and joined me in front. I know their presence helped to get my message across. How brave was that little gesture of solidarity from those sad little people?

Strangely enough, near the end of my time, I felt a heavier hand on my shoulder and realised it was Desmond. I like to think he was encouraging me, but the truth is probably that he was reminding me I must end!

This is what I said:

"Good morning. Thank you all for taking the time and trouble to be here to unite with us all and to help present our country with a loving and positive energy today. I hope you feel it and take it away with you to help you to be part of a new challenge and movement to change the mindset of our people. We need to eradicate this terrible sickness in our society of brutal, violent crime perpetrated on citizens of all ages, from newborn babies to the elderly.

I am truly humbled to have been asked to say something in honour of our son, Michael, otherwise known as Mike.

Where do I start? Perhaps by asking myself: who was I on 26 September 2007? The simple answer to that would be an ordinary South African mother of four, grandmother to six precious grandchildren. I was very content in spite of the problems that exist for those living in this beautiful country of ours. However, by 8:30 on the night of 27 September, my complacency was shattered. My son, Mike, was murdered in his well-secured home.

I was now the mother of three.

Four thugs found a way to get into the pool area outside their bedroom, where Mike was making adjustments to his pool. He saw two of them, one with a gun, go into the bedroom. He fought the other two outside. They were armed with a gun and a screwdriver. They used both to attack him; he did not have a chance. After a massive struggle, he received a final shot to the head, and was left in the pool; his family was severely traumatised by these heartless men inside their home.

One often reads of murders in the newspaper. If the victim was not a high profile person, a brief mention might appear on the third page. The victim is reduced to being just another statistic. *Shame!* (Common South African word used to describe many varying occurrences.)

I would like to describe to you the kind of trauma that such murders can leave in their wake. Because of my experience, I am qualified to speak on behalf of thousands whose lives have been irrevocably scarred. In some cases, when a person dies, there is a workplace that is now vacant; the benefit of years of training and experience are lost to our country.

Mike was such a man.

That same person could well have been an active person in the community and local school.

Mike was such a man.

He is sorely missed by many. But it gets worse: there is now a grieving wife who was the light of his life and vice versa; the loss to her is without words. She must learn to live without a husband and breadwinner. The effects of the damage have only just started.... In this world, there are fathers and there are dads. There are now three young children who are without their dad.

Mike was the most exceptional dad.

He had so much love and knowledge to give to his children. I am so angry that this has happened to my family. I was made even angrier when I learnt that at least one of these men had already been sentenced to twenty years for murder and rape, and was out on bail at the time. Why was he out of prison?

Mike had a brother and two sisters. They are battling to deal with their loss, but, most of all, we, his mother and father, are two broken people. When you have loved and watched your child grow into the most incredible human being, it is inconceivable that that life should be lost for a mere laptop.

In its wake, this senseless murder leaves nothing but heartache and despair. We will never be the same people again. His laptop has been located. It was bought for a good price. Did the buyer stop to think just what price had actually been paid? Did he even care?

Please, spread the word that this is *wrong*! If there are no buyers of stolen goods, there would be no market!

A further aggravation is the fact that a single murder of a man like Mike can trigger the emigration of so many of our talented families who cannot face bringing up their children with this fear. We have no plans to leave, so let's join hands and hearts and decide today to change the mindset that accepts such lack of human compassion; please! Let us make this event meaningful.

When I was young, a murder was a rare occurrence and I only remember hearing of one. I even remember her name was Bubbles Shroeder. My parents talked about it for days. Let us return to the values of those days and make it our new goal.

I made a promise to my boy at his funeral that I was not going to let these monsters win. We would not allow evil to prevail and I would make sure that some good will be brought about by his death.

It is not by chance that I saw Desmond's first article requesting support.

This is the beginning of my promise to Mike. *Family values will return and good people will set new standards of morality.*

At the end of the speeches, a few people, in my row, including myself, were asked to move to other seats and, in a flurry of activity, some politicians came down like gods from the lofty heights, but not Thabo Mbeki, our president. Criselda handed over the memorandum to Nkondi Balfour, the then-minister of sport. Criselda Kananda had been on the show 3 Talk with Noleen with me. We all thought it a slap in the face for Desmond. Why could Thabo Mbeki not lower himself to receive the memorandum? He was there in the buildings. Where was his leadership? He sent a message to his people that he was not overly concerned about the crime in South Africa, let alone concerned about his people who are the victims. They do not have the luxury of security guards and bullet-proof cars. Sending down one of his minions to receive the memorandum was all the attention it deserved. It probably went upstairs to the minister's offices, straight into the bin!

Perhaps, by drawing too much attention to crime, it could open a can of worms regarding the theft from the state and municipal coffers of his people! We have certainly not had much to encourage us with both of the past police commissioners being suspended and one being jailed for corruption… albeit released on the grounds of having a terminal illness. We are so sceptical. The previous politician who was jailed for fraud was also released on compassionate grounds for having a terminal illness. I think it was the type of terminal illness that we all suffer from and that is the surety that we are all going to die sometime. He is now enjoying his golf and hoping to get back into 'serving his country'!

Desmond closed the morning with another small speech and thanks. My heart went out to the man. He was so visibly disappointed at the turn-out. He had worked so hard to make this a success. In many ways, it was, but the feet were not there and through no fault of his. We estimated about 50, 000 people turned out. However, there was the most awe inspiring synergy that was so palpable. It was a true day of reconciliation and uniting of the

Desmond Dube giving a moving talk at the Million Man March.

different races. It was a gathering of the Rainbow Nation. You could see that everyone there was moved by the day. At the end, Desmond broke down and sobbed.

The stage area was cordoned off by a fence from the rest of the crowd. Someone came up to Lorna and me and said there were two ladies at the fence who wanted to speak to us. We went over to the fence to see what it was about. There were two elderly black ladies, with their hands pushed through the diamond mesh, and one took Lorna's hands and the other lady took mine.

"We just wanted to apologise to you on behalf of our people for what we have done to you. We are so, so sorry. You did not have to come today with peace in your hearts, but you did. Please do not leave this country. We need people like you."

That small act of appreciation from those two simple women made the whole morning worthwhile.

We said our goodbyes and made our way back to our bus. As I got onto the bus, I was quite overwhelmed. As I stepped up to the last step, the whole bus erupted in applause. I was so overcome that, for once, I was speechless. All I could say was a simple, "Thank you."

During the day, Radio 702 had been reporting on the failure of the event and that only about three to five thousand people had bothered to come. That was so unfair, unkind and not true. It was not the million Des had hoped for, but sabotage had played its part in that outcome. Those who were there had a very different perspective.

We will never know why Des' well-intended action for positive change was targeted in this way. In addition to the questions asked earlier, one wonders if it was perhaps anything personal against Desmond. Whatever the reason and whoever they are, may they hang their heads in shame!

Of course both the presenters who had trashed the march beforehand, had a field day gloating about the dismally poor turn-out.

Some people who were there phoned in to say that it was only a failure in numbers. The day was one that none of us would ever forget.

In spite of letters to the station demanding an apology to Desmond, it was not forthcoming from anyone there.

After the march, I invited Desmond and his wife to dinner at our flat. Allan and Sarah, Debby and Carol came too. It was a very pleasant evening, but, sadly, we have not heard from them again. There have been several anti-crime organisations that have been formed from this march.

We are now putting our energies into the Mike Thomson Change a Life Trust, which is doing just that.

With the traumatic events of the march now behind me, I felt I needed to see Laureen as soon as possible. I made my appointment for 18 July 2008 and got across to Alberton in good time for my appointment. In fact, I was about ten minutes early. I sat quietly in the car with my eyes closed, and chatted to Mike and asked him the questions I wanted answered. One minute before my allotted time, I went inside. I was surprised to find there was no one in the waiting room or behind the reception desk. I waited about ten minutes and thought this was most out of character. I went to ask one of the therapists if they had seen her or knew where she was. No one seemed to know anything. I tried to call her, but only got voice mail. After waiting another half an hour, I left feeling very dejected and concerned about her. I could not reach her all day or the next. Eventually, I got an SMS that read: 'Laureen shot in an armed robbery. Please pray for her. She is in ICU fighting for her life'.

"Oh no, please not again!" My stomach lurched and my

heart missed a beat. "Can this really be happening again?" I could hardly believe what I was reading. With shaking hands and racing heart, I called the number of the SMS and Laureen's friend explained what had happened. At ten-thirty in the evening, she heard her dogs barking and went to investigate. She opened the door to go outside and was confronted by this gang, and they just shot her in the stomach. She said Laureen was critical. I prayed for her, but I could not help asking myself, "Why, why, why?" What had she done to deserve this?

That evening, Brian and I were sitting in the lounge watching TV and my cell phone rang just once. The last missed call was a please call me from my gardener, Philip. I called him and he said that it was not him. I checked the time of his call and it was recorded at 9:24am. It was definitely not Philip. I searched on my phone for a record of that call; there was no private number, no record at all. I thought for a while and then turned to Brian and said, "I think it is Mike using the phone again and telling me that he was sorry for me." I had no sooner said that when the phone rang again! Again, there was no record of it at all. Feeling a little better, I said a silent, "Thank you, darling, for the contacts. It is comforting to know that you are still with me."

The next morning, the alarm went off. As had happened before, I did not even have to touch the face; I simply put my arm across to Brian's ear and, as soon as he acknowledged it, it stopped. This was not the first time to experience this; I became more confident that Mike was communicating with me and, in particular, he was using the alarm on his watch.

Chapter Twelve

Mike with his second daughter and youngest child - Annie-Rose Thomson.

Some time before Mike was killed, we had planned a large family get-together over Easter. We had booked for the whole family and some extended family. My cousin, Robyn, and her husband, Derek, and some of her family planned to join us in the bush camp, Bateleur, in the Kruger National Park. Mike was supposed to be with us. So keen was he that he had been the first to pay his deposit to secure the camp. It was a hard decision to make. Should we still go or should we cancel? Though no one really had their heart in the trip anymore, we knew that Mike would have wanted his children to still be part of this, so we went ahead. The camp was in the far north of the park. If we had known just how far, we might have had second thoughts, but the bookings were confirmed, deposits paid and arrangements made. We all set off more or less together and arrived just before the gates closed at the camp. Lorna was very reluctant to come, but she did so for the sake of her children. An icy wind howled, but we were not intimidated; we came to chill anyway. Beanies, scarves, thick jackets and extra blankets saved the day.

It was a very rustic camp, as it was deep in the bush, and the cottages were totally concealed from each other by vegetation. They had been recently upgraded and were very comfortable. We selected one cottage to be the food house and all the meals were held there communally.

We had good game sightings, but the best part was all being together around the fire in the evenings. Having so many members of my family around helped me to cope with that desperate feeling of loss and heaviness in the middle of my chest. It was so rewarding to see all the cousins, first and second, younger and older, all getting on so well together. Lorna, however, kept very much to herself, reading and concentrating on just getting through those few days. Although my own heart was aching, it ached so much more for her.

I had not had any alarm activity for some time and was once again thinking that perhaps it was coming to an end. I asked Mike on the first night there, "Mike, darling, if you are able, please give me a sign that you are with us. I am sure I can feel your presence here!" At 5am the next morning, and the next three mornings, I received my reply! Again, I did not have to stop it: as soon as I acknowledged it, it stopped.

I so wanted to share this with the rest of the family, but the only people I could confide in were Brian and Mike's sisters, Debs and Cally. Robyn would have listened, but she was of the opinion I should not tell people about it for fear that they would think me odd. I know she did not approve. It also made Allan uncomfortable when I tried to tell him and I got the feeling that Sarah was very sceptical. So, rather than have people think that I was 'losing it', I kept this information to myself and the three who believed me and were interested.

It was some weeks later, and Laureen was still out of commission, but making progress in her recovery. My client, Hillary, who had introduced us, called one day to see how I was. She asked if I had heard about Laureen and the shooting. Of course, I told her I had. "Do you still get messages from Mike?"

"Yes. Do you from your daughter?"

"Yes, I do. In fact, I write to her and she has thanked me through Laureen. Only last night, she said hello in the shower with the flickering light. Today, I went to a new medium and she was also amazing. She is quite different to Laureen, but every bit as good."

"That's great. I need to see someone. Who is she?" I asked.

She gave me the details of Lynda Lograsso, who lived in Linksfield in Johannesburg. She warned me that this lady had a long waiting list and it was necessary to book well ahead.

Immediately thereafter, at the end of July, Laureen called to say that she had recovered from her attack and was back at work. As I had not seen her for quite a while now, I made an appointment and got one for the next day.

I set off in good time to see Laureen on the day, looking forward to hearing from Mike. However, at the last minute, I thought I would find out if she was still operating from the same place; no, she was not! Just as well I asked. The new place was easier to find, once you knew how. However, I got very lost leaving there, as my GPS had no clue about all the road works and closures for the soccer World Cup.

We started off by me asking Laureen how she was and letting her tell me all about her shooting and how she was healing and coping. After quite some time, she said, "Your son is here and he is pushing me to start. He wants me to hold your watch."

Of course, it is Mike's watch and the first thing she told me was that Mike said, "Mom, stop being paranoid about the alarm. It *is me* contacting you and I will contact you forever, but the method will change and it will diminish."

She said he was, however, trying to work out another way that I would recognise so that there would be an alternative sometimes. She, once again confirmed that we have a very strong bond and that, although he recognised that my grief was still profound, he thought I was becoming more accepting of his death. I, however, was not so sure about that; will I ever be able to accept it?

I had asked Mike to bring his grandparents from both sides with him. She said there was one set with him and it seemed as though it was my parents, especially my mother. However, there were no 'wow' factors that were that reassuring.

He said that I had done something to honour him recently and that there was another coming up. The one must have been the launch of the trust and the one coming up could be his birthday or the cycle challenge itself, which was to be held at the beginning of September.

I had no sooner seen her when she called again on 1 August to tell me that she could no longer live in Johannesburg and had decided to move down to White River! I could not believe my ears and I could not help but wonder what it was with White River. The only two mediums I knew were both moving there.

Some time later, I decided call Lynda, the new medium

Hillary had recommended to me a few weeks previously. As predicted, she could not see me for four weeks.

It was also about this time when I got a call from the investigating officer of the Parkview Police Station, asking me to come in to see him. Lorna and the children had gone to Plettenberg Bay, a holiday town on the coast of the Eastern Cape, for the school holidays to stay with Rosie, who had been such a comfort to them all in the week following Mike's death. He could not get hold of Lorna, so he contacted me instead.

I met him in his office.

"You will be happy to know we have apprehended your son's killers," said a smiling Inspector Kabiso, very pleased with himself.

My emotions were just so mixed. I was relieved. I was angry. I was grateful and very interested to find out whom, how, where and when.

"We found them in Alex. A man and his girlfriend were having a fight in Alexandra Township." (This is a black township in the northern suburbs of Johannesburg and is colloquially referred to as 'Alex'. It was established before the apartheid era and is still a black stronghold.)

"Her brother was there and he called the police. For once, they came quickly and apprehended the boyfriend, who was wielding a gun in his girlfriend's face. They were then able to arrest him for not being able to produce a license for the gun. The boyfriend then said, 'No man, you can't arrest me. It is not my gun. I am looking after someone's house and there are lots of guns in it. When I go out, I just pick one up'!"

That night, he happened to have picked up Mike's gun. I secretly think that Mike put it in his hand!

Later that night, the police raided this house and, sure enough, there were a lot of stolen guns there and also a lot of stolen goods. Sadly, though, none of the goods were Mike and Lorna's.

They discovered that the house belonged to George Nyembe, who was currently serving a twenty-year sentence in jail for robbery. He was the man out on bail at the time of Mike's killing. I immediately wanted to take on the Minister of Justice for letting the system allow this killer out on bail. I was told I would be wasting my time and my money, as it was perfectly legal to get bail for robbery!

About the same time, Ollie, the private detective brought in by Richard, had traced Mike's laptop, which had been sold already, but that discovery had also led him to other members of the gang.

George was then paid a visit whilst in custody by Inspector Kabiso, who managed to get a confession out of him. George then added that he would not be signing it nor would he admit to it in court, as he was going to claim self-defence! He ignored the fact that he was trespassing and had murdered a man in his own home! What a nerve! According to his confession, Mike did disarm the one attacker, who we believed to be Razor Zulu, and he said that Mike threw him (George) into the pool and was trying to drown him. He did not, however, admit to stabbing Mike. The following conversation between me and a police inspector then took place.

I also have the autopsy report.

"If George confessed all, why did he not confess to stabbing Mike?" I asked.

"There was no stabbing," said the inspector.

"I beg to differ, sir. I personally counted fourteen stab wounds on his body," I replied.

He checked on the autopsy report and he said there was nothing in the report about any stabbing.

I was furious and perhaps he could see the flames coming out of my nostrils in menacing plumes. "Did they actually do an autopsy or is it faked like so many other documents?" I asked.

"Mrs. Thomson, please relax; I will investigate and see what happened," he said, trying to reassure me.

He called me at a later date to say that the autopsy had been corrected and it now did state that Mike had been stabbed. I knew that it was not going to bring him back, but Laureen had told me something of which I could not let go. She said, "Mike says you must please stop telling people that he was killed by that final gunshot. The stab wounds were very deep and penetrated too many vital organs for him to survive. It was the stabbing that really killed Mike; the final shot was just finishing the job! He doubts if he would have had the strength to get out of the pool."

I was not about to allow that to be brushed under the carpet. This man must pay for what he did to my boy!

"Thank you, Inspector Kabiso, I really appreciate your efforts," I said. "I must say that it horrifies me that an autopsy report can be so carelessly put together and then altered when required."

Five years down the line, I am now told that the stabbing is still not in the autopsy report and that it is impossible to have it changed anyway.

Detective Bruce McKenzie, who was part of the team that found and arrested the rest of the gang, gave me the names of the alleged killers and armed robbers. They are:

Raymond Zulu

George Nyembe

Maxwell Kheza (Tabang)

Sibusiso Mashanini

Sisio Manyoni

Elvis Mabusa.

Three nights after Mike was killed, there was another horrific attack. It was on the Paterson family and, as it turned out, it was perpetrated by the same gang – the Razor gang. Bronwyn, the mother, was beaten to within an inch of her life, stabbed with kitchen scissors, almost scalped, her ear torn off and left for dead in a pool of blood. She is a tiny, petite slip of a lady with indomitable courage. The fact that she survived this brutal attack is a miracle. Her husband and young son, Angus, were both rolled into a duvet or carpet and tied up. The daughter, Jamie, who was seventeen years old, was taken into the bathroom and brutally raped by Razor Zulu. Bronwyn was in intensive care for a very long time before she came home. Razor told Jamie that he was HIV positive. She was about to write her Matric and had to undergo Anti Retro Viral treatment. Jamie reacted very badly to the treatment, but, in spite of her circumstances, she was carried into the exams, which she wrote and passed well. Jamie and her mother chose to speak out about this horrific attack. They were not to blame and Jamie showed incredible courage and maturity throughout her ordeal.

Both families were very relieved to get this news, as they had all harboured secret fears that, with these people still on the streets, they may come after them again in case they thought they would be recognised. There were now reportedly twenty-two cases of murder, rape and robbery against this gang, and most of them came from the Sandton and Bramley precincts. The police wanted to charge them all under one umbrella, so Mike's case was transferred from Parkview to Sandton. The new investigating officer was Detective Inspector Baloi. I immediately felt anxious about that. How will they ever get all the witnesses, policemen and victims in one court at one time? I knew it would be impossible.

This was the beginning of our frustrations regarding the court case!

Chapter Thirteen

Mike dodging the eli poos as the river comes down in flood.

Brian was getting quite despondent about selling his incinerator business. He had negotiated with several people who appeared interested, but, for one reason or another, that is where it ended. Business was bad and the Powers That Be were making such ridiculous demands about the emissions allowed from cremators and incinerators that it was becoming absolutely impossible to attain the required results. We were struggling to get business here in South Africa – even though his incinerators and cremators exceeded the overseas criteria. He was tired of losing contracts through refusing to offer bribes. The people who were making the decisions were people with no experience in the field and people who had no knowledge of what was viable, but rather people who had latched onto buzzwords such as 'dioxins' and then demanded unattainably small amounts of dioxin emissions to be allowed from the chimney of the incinerator. This caused untold difficulties in the industry.

Brian had done extensive research on dioxins and always maintained that these extreme limitations were a load of nonsense. He had never found any evidence of anyone ever having died from dioxins or even anyone getting seriously ill. The worst case scenario he could find was that it did cause severe acne, and, even then, it was caused by the person (ex-President Yushenko) being poisoned with a heavy dose of dioxins in his food. He did not die. His research led him to believe that one volcano eruption spewed more dioxins into the air than thousands of incinerators could ever do. His comments and research fell on deaf ears. He was getting increasingly frustrated and worried about our future. We had no pension to look forward to, as it had always been Brian's philosophy that selling his business would be our pension.

One evening, Brian came home from work with the news that he had received a visit from a South African lawyer who said he was representing a consortium of Chinese businessmen. They wanted to talk to Brian about buying his designs. They talked of manufacturing so many units for China that they knew Brian would be unable to cope in his small factory. They hoped he would see them and discuss such a deal. Brian agreed to talk and made a date.

They sat in his office and threw questions at him. He would answer and back it up by showing them something that he had on his computer. He never gave them enough to use, but he did demonstrate that he had everything at his fingertips at the touch of a button.

They told him that they were extremely keen and going to go ahead with it, but had to go back to China to get documents drawn and the go ahead from their superiors. The money they talked about that would be coming to us was just too good to be true; many millions! Needless to say, I felt very excited about it, although Brian was much more cautious in his optimism. He felt that, if it sounded too good to be true, it probably was.

The lawyer kept in touch and said all was going well. He and his Chinese lady partner took us both out to dinner, and they were very friendly and encouraging. They said it was all going ahead.

About two weeks passed and we started getting calls at night from Chubb, the security company, to say the alarm was going off at the factory, but they could never find any problem. This happened three nights in a row, and the fourth night, a Friday, there was no alarm. On the Saturday morning, we received a call to tell us that there had been a break-in at the factory. The thieves had not just pulled the burglar bars off the wall; they had pulled the entire window out! The only item stolen was the computer in Brian's office. All the other computers were left. Why only that computer, and an old one at that, and no others? Was the Chinese mafia responsible? We never found out.

From leading a sheltered life with no crime connection, we suddenly found ourselves being battered from all sides by the horrific crime scenario in South Africa.

In addition, we never heard another word from the Chinese and, surprise, surprise, the lawyer never answered his phone and neither did he call! While the disappearance of the Chinese from the scene was a huge disappointment to us, it was not the disaster it might have been. Brian had always been meticulous in the backing up of his work and always took the storage discs home. He had, in fact, lost nothing except his office computer and our chance of retiring rich! The Chinese market was so huge that the chance of them taking business away from us was negligible. However, what it did do was sow the seed that his intellectual property was a saleable item. If he could not sell the company, perhaps he could sell his designs.

I am unsure if this theft triggered my road to depression

or if it was just the straw that broke the camel's back. I had to force myself to get out of bed in the mornings. Escaping to the warm confines of my bed was what I really wanted to do. I cried at the drop of a hat and I lost all my enthusiasm for the new house and going out to the dam. I was worried about finances; I was worried about Brian's health, as well as my own. I worried about my girls living on their own and driving home at night to an empty house. I was worried about Lorna and her children and their future. I could only see a half empty jar and, of course, my grief was still profound. I was missing Mike so much that it physically hurt.

I was also beginning to find the flat too small and claustrophobic. I started looking at houses for sale and, when I saw something that I thought I could live in, I would take Brian along with me. Of course, he was totally disinterested and would find fault with everything I showed him.

I was also feeling very alone in my grief, as Brian was burying himself in the house design as an escape from his worries and his own grief. I was resenting the fact that he was terrible company! I felt he was not listening to me and that made me feel even worse. I always had to put on a brave front when with other people. I frequently had people telling me how brave I was. If only they knew!

One day, when I was at a client's house, he asked me how I was getting on; I just broke down and sobbed. He was so kind and said that he understood, as he had just been through a divorce and had needed to talk to someone. He recommended a man, Dennis. I thought that a man might be a good idea, as maybe I was being selfish and he would see my problems from a masculine viewpoint. I had found counselling useless for me in the beginning. As nice as the lady who I consulted was, I would sit there and think, *Lady, you have absolutely no idea. You have never walked in these shoes. You cannot possibly tell me what I should or should not do! You cannot even begin to understand – no matter how well qualified you are. You cannot possibly know what I am going through.*

It was a good decision to see Dennis. He was an excellent listener and was very understanding of most of my problems. I thought him wise; he wanted to see Brian as well as myself. I was unsure if Brian would go, but he did. Dennis was able to make Brian see that he was neglecting me and that it had made me feel unimportant in his life and, by the same token, he made me see that designing this house was *very* important to Brian. Brian had been through a lot himself in his workplace and, on top of all that, the loss of his son. It could have major repercussions for Brian if I was to take the designing and building of our house from him. The design thereof was proving to be his 'Linus Blanket'. He explained to both of us that losing a child puts an enormous strain on any marriage and that, unless the marriage is a strong one to start with, it frequently ends in divorce. We both came away with food for thought. I am unsure of what decisions Brian made to change, but I made up my mind that I would go to the new house at Hartbeespoort Dam and make the most of our time there – a decision I have never regretted.

I decided that I would start to count my blessings and live for the *now*. Every evening before going to sleep, I would think of five good things that had happened that day, no matter how trivial. I slowly started to get stronger and deal with my life in a more positive manner. I decided to put my energies into making our promise to Mike that his death would not be in vain become a reality. I found myself crying a bit less, but still unable to talk about him without the tears welling.

For many years, I had, from time to time, suffered from anxiety attacks. I had always been a good organiser and was not afraid of hard work or tackling any project. I appeared to be very calm and relaxed about things on the outside, but, hidden inside me, I took strain. The fight or flight syndrome would manifest with a build-up of adrenalin in my body and, when whatever I had been organising was over, I would not be able to breathe.

This occurred with gaps between episodes varying from three to five years apart in the early period and getting more frequent as the years went by. My GP always treated them with what I understood to be a mild calmative called Xanor. It took some time to kick in, but, when it did, my breathing would return to normal and I would gradually come off them with no problem or side effects. I certainly did not find them addictive at that time.

A few weeks after the funeral, I recognised the familiar build-up of not being able to breathe again. Straight away, I was put onto Xanor again. It helped at the time, but I was not ready to go off them quickly like I had in the past.

While Brian and I were dealing with our own issues, Lorna had taken the children down to Plett to visit the pillar in her life – Rosie and her husband, Paul Deans. As I have mentioned previously, they live in Plett and this was the perfect place for Lorna to take her children in the school holidays to escape from their continued stress and trauma in Johannesburg. Night after night, even the slightest noise outside put them all into a terrified state and they spent many a dark hour huddled together in a cupboard until they thought the offending sound had moved off.

In July 2008, Rosie called from Plett to say that the family had improved so much while staying with them. They were all sleeping in their own rooms again and had developed rosy cheeks and were actually having fun like children of their age should be doing.

"Di, how would you feel about Lorna and family moving down here?" she asked. "Lorna is quite keen on the idea and it would be a far more relaxed life for them. She has already been offered a part time job at Kurlands Hotel."

Kurlands is a boutique hotel that caters for the international polo fraternity. Guests come from all over the world for polo tournaments on a regular basis and Lorna would be required to run a children's programme. This was right up her street.

I spent no time at all in thinking about my answer.

"Rosie, this is, for us, a far better option than Scotland. I have been so worried about their current lifestyle up here that this is, to me, a perfect alternative. It is far, but nowhere near as far as the UK; it is small town and the children will lead a far healthier life than they would up here in Johannesburg. In addition, it will help them to move on and there are no reminders of what happened to them all in Plettenberg Bay. It will all be new. To add to it all, you and Paul will be there to help and guide them. Thank you so much for your love and support to them all."

The decision was made. Lorna found a house in Plett, which was perfect for their needs, and her offer was accepted. She would stay in Johannesburg until the end of the year for the children to finish school and for her to give her little pupils enough notice for their parents to make other arrangements.

A major step in the process of moving on had begun for Mike's family.

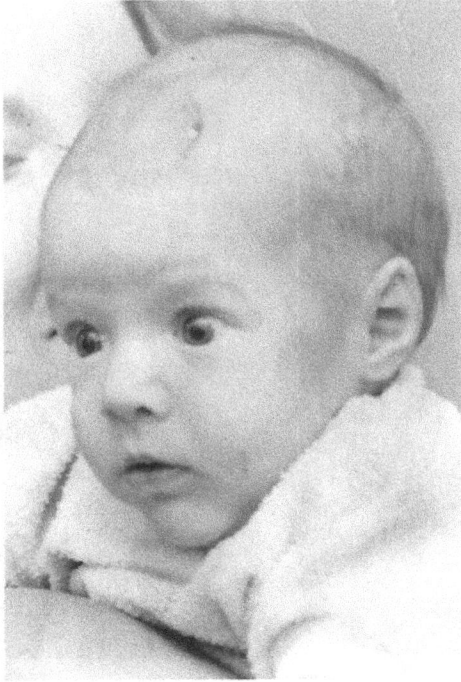
Mike as young baby.

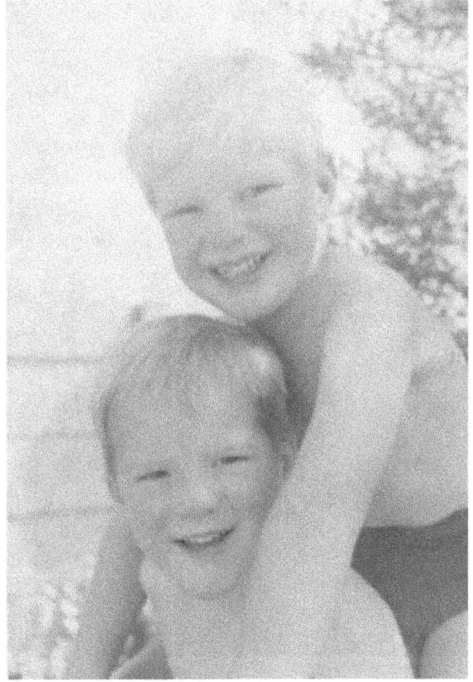
Mike (below) and his older brother Allan.

Mike and his two sisters, Debby & Cally on Cally's first day at school.

Mike in his brand new white Honours Blazer at Bryanston High School- the first boy to ever receive this honour in the history of the school.

Mike and his two closest friend from University - Richard Moss and Peter Upfold.

Mike at his 21st with his late godfather Brian Heeley.

Mike & Lorna on their wedding day.

Mike and his family on holiday at Ntsiri.

Dale Goldschmidt, Mike, Lorna, Allan and Richard Moss on Mike & Lorna's wedding day.

Mike as a game ranger at Tanda Tula during his 'gap' year.

Mike up his tree for the last time.

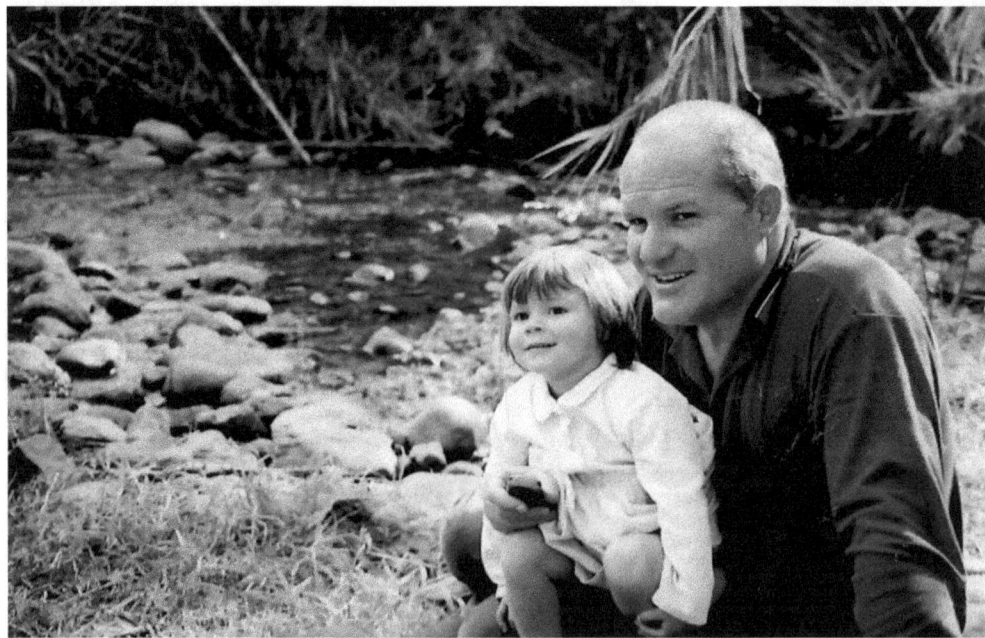

Mike and Annie-Rose enjoying a picnic on father's day.

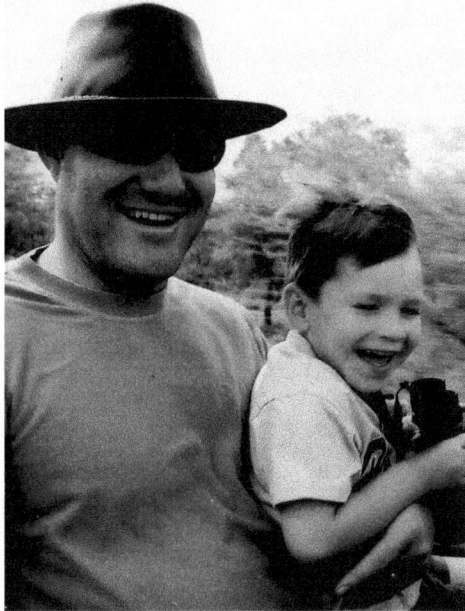
Mike and Nick enjoying the front seat of a game drive vehicle.

Mike and his little family enjoying one of the many great holidays they had at Shelly Beach.

Mike in his Black Belt and coloured Gi during a grading session.

Mike cooking Christmas lunch in 2006 - our last Christmas with him and as a full family.

The collage of Mike, and his family and all their happier times together.

The special corner in the garden with some of the soil where we scattered Mike's ashes, as well as the ashes of his faithful dogs. I often sit there in solitude and think of my son.

Mike as a young man loving the bush - where he met the love of his life - the then Lorna Shields

The stain glass doors that Mike initially made and almost completed. We have now installed in pride of place at the main enterance in our new Hartbeespoort home. The Thomson crest sits above the doorway.

Mike and his siblings. The last photo all together.

Present day Meg and Annie-Rose - They are a very close knit family and are remarkable, supporting and loving siblings to each other.

Megan, 17, Nick, 15, Lorna and Annie Rose, 14.

Chapter Fourteen

The week before my appointment with Lynda, the new medium, was another low week for me. I was once again very emotional and just so incredibly sad.

I had quite a few alarm calls in the past few weeks. I am sure it was in response to my emotions. I was beginning to rely on my 'SMSs' from Mike, which, deep down, I knew could not last, but, while it did, I would treasure it.

The night before I went to see Lynda, I asked Mike to please tell me if he was going to be there. I also hoped that my parents would also be there for me. The next morning, there was nothing; the phone was silent. I tried hard to avoid reading anything into it, but, at the back of my mind, I was a little apprehensive and disappointed.

I should have known better! Mike was saving his energy for Lynda and me.

Getting there was easy. I had no drama in getting lost or being late this time.

At first, I was a little sceptical and thought perhaps she may not be the right person. Verna, my sister, would definitely have described her as 'woo woo'. Her consulting room was huge and she sat at one end of the room and I sat at the other. She sat on a lonely chair in the middle. It was decorated with crystals of all shapes and sizes. I think I recall incense and soft gentle music in the background.

Lynda started the reading by talking about chakras and how she was going to concentrate on my chakras and then heal them. Not having had any experience with that, I was interested to hear what she had to say about me.

She started at the bottom and said my root chakra was well grounded, which meant I was earthy and well balanced. So far, so good. She said I was a child of the soil – very true. She picked up that my solar plexus, heart and throat chakras were very 'flat', which meant they were disturbed. I was amazed to hear her say, "Your crown chakra is wide open and you really don't need me. You have the ability to connect yourself."

"Yes, I do have an open mind to this and I do feel a connection, but I don't know how to make it without a medium," I replied.

Lynda began by stretching out her arms and resting them on her lap, with her palms upwards and open. I saw her touching her fingers with her thumb one at a time. Something I had not seen Laureen do, so I became all the more fascinated.

After some time, she began, "There are a lot of people here in the room. In fact, it is quite crowded. I think all of them are family in one way or another. There is a lady here who has a basket of flowers and secateurs in her hand. She has a lovely straw hat on. She says she is your mother. She has a balding man with her – your father.

"There is man on your level who had passed from a sudden chest problem. He is not coming through for you, but sending a message through you. Please pass on the message to my wife that I am fine and happy with the family on the other side. Tell her I am proud of her and how she has coped. Tell her I will always love her and be with her." I assumed it was Sandy, Verna's husband, as she never came up with any names, but validated it by saying he had a connection with Zimbabwe (his son, Ralph) and family in Cape Town (his daughter, Barbie).

Sandy had gone out deep fishing with his son, Ralph, and two grandchildren while on holiday at Shelley Beach about ten years ago. While at sea, he had caught a large fish and was struggling to bring it in. He had handed it over to Ralph and said, "You do it, son." Then he smiled and was gone. He'd had a massive heart attack. The shock for Verna was earth shattering. Her whole world collapsed in that moment. He went out fishing hale and hearty and came home dead! Sandy had only just semi-retired and they had so many plans for the future.

I passed on this message to her, but it did nothing to encourage her to go herself. I felt so sad that she was not willing or interested in having the opportunity to connect with Sandy, who she was missing so much. He obviously wanted to connect with her.

My mother could not have been better described. She loved her gardens and always had a bowl of fresh flowers from her garden in her house. I have inherited her love of flowers and nature. It was also a repeat of what Jacqui, the first medium, told me. My father was balding, which Mike had inherited.

Lynda was not as quick as Laureen. She was quiet for some time, her head tilted to one side, and she listened very intensely before she spoke. "You have lost a son who was in his late thirties. It was a violent death, but not a car crash."

Her head went to one side again and she listened. "He was shot! He felt no pain and was very, very angry. He put up a huge fight. In hindsight, he says he may have done things differently." All this endorsed what Jackie and Laureen had told me, except that Jackie said he would do it all again and was powerless to change the outcome. Were these different interpretations of the same message, perhaps?

One might think that this is old news and need not be repeated. No! It confirms to me over and over again that the connection is there and Mike is communicating. How could it possibly be that three people come up with the same story?

Lynda continued, "Your son says he is very angry at being taken too soon, as he had unfinished business. At this point in his life, he was very happy and achieving his goals. He loved his wife and children. I am getting the feeling that he and his wife came from very different backgrounds. In spite of that, they loved each other and were very happy, even though there was the odd issue that cropped up, as it does in all marriages."

This could not have been more accurate if I had written it all down for her!

She reiterated something Jacqui had said. "Your son says he has no intention of reincarnating for a long time. He wants to be around to watch over his children."

She continued to stun me with her accuracy. "You always had reason to be very proud of your boy. He was a high achiever and very active in his community. He wants to thank you for the small, pretty garden you made in his memory. It has a water feature in it that was meant for him."

When she said this, I nearly fell off my chair! Lorna and I were going to give him the water feature for his fortieth birthday and have it installed in their Craighall Park home while Mike was away on business. He was due to go to London on the Monday after he was murdered. The water feature was ordered, paid for, and about to be delivered when he was killed. I was going to do the garden around it. As Lorna had moved out the house that same night and had no intention of returning there to live, we decided to donate it to Craighall Primary School, where Mike had been such an active parent, and had it delivered there. The grounds man installed it, but I hated seeing it in this very bleak and neglected little garden. I decided to take my team of gardeners to the school instead. We created a pretty garden to enhance the water feature in memory of Mike.

How could Lynda possibly have known anything about that?

Mike then responded to one of my requests. She said, "You have honoured Mike in some other way. I see a crowd of people and a stage. He says he was very proud of you, as well as his children." (He was with us at the Million Man March.)

She was by no means finished. "Your son is worried about his family, but especially Nick. He knows that Nick is missing him so much. They are going to move to a new home in a holiday town. He is happy with that decision and feels that the children will do far better there."

Mike told her that he and I have always had a special bond and it will always be so. That was so comforting and made me feel good, but, yet again, inordinately sad.

He told her that I do a lot of writing and that I have even written letters to him. I do and I did. He thanked me for them. Mike also said that I am thinking that one day I may write a book about my experiences and he thinks it is a very good idea. This message was to be the start of what you are reading today!

This is how I responded to Mike in my thoughts. *Mike, I will write to you some more. I do not know, however, just how to put all my writings into a book! Thank you for coming through so strongly today. How could anyone have even the slightest doubt after an experience like I had today with Lynda?*

Mike talked about the fact that Brian and I were having difficulties with agreeing on our future at the moment. We definitely were! However, he did not say how to fix it, except that I must find my true self and listen to my inner voice. I thought, *I have voiced my thoughts and fears and I will now wait to see what unfolds.*

He said that there were two visits to the bush planned and the one did not happen, but the second one did. The first one was a weekend we had planned with the family at a small intimate bush camp, Zebanine, in the Timbavati nature reserve. It was run by his old boss, Pat Donaldson, and his wife, Eileen. As I have mentioned earlier in this book, they had introduced Mike and Lorna. We had to cancel it at the last minute. Lynda even confirmed that it was the Kruger Park. Both true! He said he was with us and he knows that we often talked and cried over him and that he knew we were missing him. He said he was with each one of us when we were missing him. He appreciated that.

She asked, "Was your son cremated? I am really very confused; I see a small box, but, at the same time, I see the ashes being scattered in a holiday place."

At the time, I had no answer for her. It only occurred to me when I was driving home that Lorna still has some of his ashes in a small wooden box, which they still keep in their 'Daddy corner' they have created in their new home and, of course, we had scattered the rest of his ashes at Ntsiri. She had it spot on!

By this time, she knew his name was Mike and she then said, "Mike says to tell you that it was him who made the fan work in Allan's fireplace on the day of his funeral…. He says that you flashed pictures of him at his funeral and he thanks his family and friends for that." This was yet another validation of Mike communicating with us.

She paused again and listened hard, head to one side. He said that I had recently cut some flowers and put them next to the photo of him in the lounge. Amazing, because I had!

He said his dad was having problems with hearing and he wants him to go and have something done. That is the second time that he has said that... two different mediums. We have complied with his wishes and been to a hearing clinic. They say that Brian must return in a few years' time. His hearing in the higher register is bad, but not bad enough for a hearing aid yet.

Mum came through again and she said she has always been with me; she wished she had been able to comfort me. Lynda said, "Your mother says that you only have a few pieces of jewellery and you look after them. One of the pieces, you wear a lot. It looks like a chunky brooch, which you wear in the middle. It used to be hers."

This took my breath away, because I do have just a couple of pieces of jewellery that I have looked after and wear a lot. "Yes, that is correct, but it is a necklace," I replied.

She interjected before I could say any more. "Yes, it is a gold locket; it opens and you have photos in it. You have a photo of your son in there." It is the locket that was Mum's and I wear it almost constantly. I do have a picture of Mike in it, as well as Brian and both my parents.

She said, "You have some sort of award that he was given for his sport and achievements at school, but it is not a cup." Lynda could not pick up what it was, but she repeated, "Definitely not a cup." She said I have not always had it, but it was given to me after his death.

This was so true. I have his white blazer that was awarded to him in his Matric year for all his achievements. He was the first boy to be awarded this blazer of honour.

The memory of that occasion is very precious to both Brian and I. We were invited to go to the school assembly that day. Mike took nearly all of the prizes in his year, as well as the Victor Laudorum cup for athletics. The final accolade in recognition of his achievements was to be awarded this white blazer. Spontaneously, the whole school body just stood up and gave him a standing ovation. Our chests were bursting and the tears flowed copiously, but that time for a very different reason! Lorna gave the blazer to me when she had the strength to go through his clothes and possessions and dispose of them. She gave me that and the lovely blue and white striped shirt in which I always thought he looked so handsome when he wore it to Robyn and Derek's wedding celebration, which was the last time I saw him alive. I treasure both of those items.

She told me that most of the people who come to her are distraught over guilt or regrets during the loved one's lifetime. They come to her to try to repair the relationship with the one who has passed. She said she has never had such a full room of family who only radiated love. She said my grief was profound because of the love that we shared. According to Lynda, we have been together and very close in past lives.

Although there was so much more I wanted to hear, my time was nearly up.! The only thing that she brought up that I could not identify was that there was a brown, medium-size dog with him. All the mediums have told me this and, for the life of me, I and the rest of the family cannot identify it. We had black dogs, great Danes, little maltese and miniature collies; no medium brown dogs. I often wonder if he has picked up a spirit stray, which would not be out of character!

I was super impressed with this lady and came away from my reading with a newfound respect for these gifted people who have honed their ability to communicate with the other side. I wonder if they know just how much comfort their messages give and, in addition, how much they do to contribute to the healing of the grieving clients who come to them.

When I was going to sleep that night, I spoke to Mike. "Mike, thank you, my darling boy, for coming through for me.... I really felt that I had a long chat with you and thank you for bringing Shanny and Dan Dan (my parents – his grandparents). I had hoped that Gaga and Bompa (Brian's parents – Mike's other grandparents) would be there, but it did not seem so. They were always somewhat retiring and not pushy, so perhaps they were there with the family, but did not push themselves forward."

Below is the letter I wrote to Mike just before I saw Lynda.

My darling Mike,

Tomorrow, I am going to see Lynda in the hopes that you will be there to meet me and make contact – I need it so much.

First, I want to say I am so sorry that I got into a state about the watch alarm calls ringing during the period we were at the Kruger National Park. You made contact on so many days that I started to doubt myself again and think that I had not been hearing the alarm occasionally, but only hearing it when I wanted to hear it and that, in fact, it goes off every day. Because I sometimes have ear plugs in because of Dad's horrendous snoring, I was worried that I have not heard it. I then asked you to not call for a while so that I could re-establish my trust in the alarm. I'm so sorry to have done that, but it is so hard when I cannot speak to you. I get overwrought about it and then, when I asked you to stop, you have been quiet for so long.... I cannot get it right, can I? I am so sorry, darling. I miss you so much that I cannot bear the fact that I may be imagining all of this. However, I do know for sure now that it does not go off every day. Please do not stop contacting me unless you have to. If you do have to, please tell me through Lynda what I should expect.

Were you with me at the march? Will you say something about it? I did feel that you were with me when I had to speak. Thank you.

I would love it for you to validate that you were with us in the park.... I missed you so then and so did your family.

Can you suggest how we go about helping your children and in particular Nicky? I think the girls also need help, but perhaps Nicky Toms is the top priority at the moment because of him losing the same sex parent. He misses you so much and, although Allan is trying so hard to be a substitute dad, he can never fill your role.

What do you think about the family moving to Plett? I would be so sad to lose them, but it is preferable to them going to Scotland. What do you think?

Am I right that there seems to be a small breakthrough with Lorna letting me have the children and letting them go out a bit more? She did such a wonderful job of Annie's party. I was sure that you were there as well. I must admit, I do not like going to your home anymore. It is just too much for me to handle. I have been sad since Saturday. It was so brave of Lorna to have it there. There is such a huge hole in my heart without you being there.

Seeing that tree house that you built and had only just had the official opening right up there with Annie was so painful. Remembering the 'tea party' hoisted up in the basket by the pulley you made them made me want to cry. I also thought of Megs, who liked to use it as an escape when all of Lorna's charges were bugging her, so she would climb the rope ladder and go up there with a book and then pull the ladder up! The children have been robbed of so much!

Jackie told me that you were working hard to sort things out for Dad and I think you are doing a fine job. You were so right when you warned him about Rob and thank you for making him at last see the truth. Each day, something unfolds and perhaps we will land up fine in the end.

Will anyone ever buy his intellectual property?

Hope you can do this for me. I sometimes expect too much, don't I? No harm in trying and it helps me to write to you anyway. I love to look at your lovely smiling face every time I sit at my computer.

I will always love you and I will have no fear of myself dying anymore, because I do know now that I will see you and Shanny and Dan Dan again. I have learnt that there definitely is life after death and that communicating with that life is so very comforting.

If you can, try to bring a message from Gaga and Bompa for Dad and, of course, for me from Dan Dan and Shanny.

Have you met either of my grannies? Have they returned to Earth?

Have you found peace and what are you doing in the spirit world? Is it like I have read in the last three books? Do you have a job there yet?

My love to you, darling, and I hope and pray that tomorrow I will hear from you once more. Your loving mom.

Many of my questions, but not all, were answered for me. Lynda was so accurate and I cannot stress enough how rewarding it has been to put aside my earlier prejudices that I had about connecting to the other side. Death is so final. Without that contact, I would have had Mike one day, gone the next and then nothing but memories and this never ending void. The situation now is that I do not have Mike physically, but I do know that he is still with me and those messages from him are what keep me going.

I have been told on so many occasions by the sceptics that I should let Mike rest in peace and that I am forcing him to be Earth bound.

First of all, I loved Mike so much that I would never do anything to cause him harm or problems on the other side. If that is what is required of me, then that is what I would do. However, I have read extensively about this and I have asked Laureen on many occasions. The reality is that it has nothing to do with me at all. Mike wanted me to make contact and doing it in the future will not prevent him from moving on. He can remain Earth bound for as long as he wants and, when he is ready to move on, he will. He can return whenever he wants for as long as he wants. There is no such thing as time in the spirit world and, as far as I can understand, there is no such thing as eternal rest. He will have things to do wherever he is.

Of course, there is no way of proving this until we get there ourselves. However, there are so many people who are able to communicate with the spirit world who corroborate what I have repeated that I have no reason to doubt them.

It was 10 August 2008 when we collected the family from their stay with Rosie and Paul Deans. Rosie was so good to them and good for them. They all came back looking so well and happier than I had seen any of them since Mike died. The children were booked into the local school and the purchase of the house had gone through.

Last night, when I was in the bath, I told Mike that I was happy about that and that I knew the children would have a much better life down there and a better chance of growing up well balanced and well mannered. Rosie can say things to the children and Lorna that I am unable to. I am too close and worry that Lorna would take any suggestion as a criticism. The last thing I ever want to do to is hurt her.

I wondered just how much influence Mike has had on the development of this or is it just chance? The next morning, the alarm went off again and it refused to stop when I touched the face as I usually do. This time, I had to push the button!

The live show, *Mama Mia*, came to Johannesburg. Mike would have taken his children to see the show. The children had the DVD, and they loved to sing along and knew all the words. The whole family went and we had to sit in two rows. During the show, little Brian crawled over the seat to sit on his mother's lap. That empty seat in front of me made the absence of Mike so poignant. The next morning, I got my message: "You may not have seen me, Mom, but I was at the show with you all! I had the empty seat!"

These contacts through his watch mean so much to me and I get quite uptight about them. If they come too often, I worry that I am just not hearing it daily; if there is a long gap, I worry that he has stopped.

If only I could get a written confirmation or just hear his voice.

Chapter Fifteen

The annual Old Parks Club had their dads and sons soccer day in August 2008. This was to be Nick's first time to play without his dad. I was so heart sore for him, but he insisted he would be there to play. Lorna would be there for him. Lorna had recently taken a young boy under her wing, as his mother was an alcoholic and never at home. His father was also seldom home for reasons unknown. This boy used to go home to an empty flat and go to school functions day and night on his bicycle until Lorna got to hear about him. She brought him home every day to her Craighall home when she had other children as a kind of aftercare. This was so typical of Lorna and it was one of the traits that Mike had found attractive. The boy was a few years older than Nick, so he volunteered to stand in as 'Dad' for him and play in his team. I am sure Nick felt so much better having someone there for him and I am sure this lad enjoyed the experience of being needed. The next morning, Mike let me know that he had been there with Nick.

It had been about a week without the alarm going off. Both Brian and I were awake at 5am on Friday after my visit with Laureen, and we were both waiting for it. There was nothing. Later, while we were making the bed, I said to Brian, "It is strange, but I get as much comfort from the days when I do not get the alarm as I do when it does ring. It makes the days when I do hear it that much more validating. Does that make any sense to you, darling?" Brian agreed that he felt the same.

That night, Pete Black, a very dear friend of ours, came to us for supper on his own, as his wife, Ronnie, was away. We got talking about how Mike makes contact with us and he was interested and totally intrigued by what we had to say. The following morning, the alarm woke me. I put my arm next to Brian's ear and he heard it.

He said, "Morning, Mike." Then it stopped without any touching at all. It did not even go on for as long as usual. As soon as we greeted him and acknowledged him, it stopped. I am sure he was telling us he heard the conversation with Pete, and that made my day.

My goal in sharing these snippets with you is to try to help other parents who are grieving from the loss of a child. I want them to not be afraid of travelling this path. There is nothing to be afraid of and oh so much to be gained. I hope I can pass on the wonderful feeling of connectedness and the comfort that it brings me. It will never bring him back, but to still feel connected is so rewarding. I also wish to stress that you need to be open to signs. If you are open to them, they will be there. There are so many occurrences that we cannot understand and so often just dismiss. Think about it. Could it be your loved one letting you know 'I am with you'?

It makes me think of years ago when I was a child; a cousin of mine's mother-in-law had lost her husband. She used to tell us that he used to visit her and she used to talk to him and keep his chair in the lounge for him. How we mocked her and thought she was out of her tree! I want to apologise to her now, even though she has been dead for many years. We did not know and did not understand. How do I pass on this knowledge without people thinking that I have lost it? When both Brian and I together have witnessed his messages to us, it cannot be our imagination. I have to say again and again, I will treasure it for as long I am able to receive it and as long as he is able to make the connection.

13 October 2008 dawned, Megan's thirteenth birthday, and we all had a lovely braai (South African barbeque) with Richard and Louise Moss. Of course, there was a huge gap without Mike. Megan looked so lovely and I think she enjoyed her party. I gave the three children the next instalment of my history of Mike. I had started writing the previous year when it was his birthday. We could not give him his presents, so I wrote down random memories in no particular order, with the intention of adding to it every year, and gave these to his children in honour of his memory. I hoped it would help to keep his memory alive for them. I think his children will appreciate it in time, as they

each have their own copy.

The next morning, we got a call from Mike. I expect it was to acknowledge the history I had given his children. The following day, there was no connection. I wrote another letter to Mike, now knowing without a shadow of a doubt that he 'receives'.

Wednesday, 15 October 2008

My darling Mike,

Perhaps now that you are back in your spirit form, you may remember when we first saw each other, a few hours off forty-one years ago? You had already decided that I was to be your mother: I suppose about eight months before that. You will never know just how grateful and privileged I feel that I was chosen to be your mother. You were deliberately conceived (on the night of Dan Dan's birthday)! I know because all of you, except Allan, were planned... even the sex was planned! We were out to dinner to celebrate his birthday that night. I had read a book on how to plan babies' births when Dad and I we were first married and it made sense to me, so not only did I get the baby I wanted, but the sex that I wanted as well! We always said we wanted four children and, if we could wing it... it would be two boys and then two girls! As you know, we were successful: fluke or not.

Although I am heartbroken that I have lost you now, I would not wish away one day of being your mother and having you as my son. You never gave us any cause to worry about you... I do know that if I had known half the things you were up to, I probably would have never been able to 'calm down to a panic'! (Mike used to tease me because I have always been a worrier about my children and their well being. Often, on his arrival home, he would tell me that I could now calm down to a panic!) *However, whatever they were, they were never BAD things... just what young people do! That is why parents worry about their* children so much, because they remember what they used to get up to! Somehow, today, the children get up to and experiment with far more dangerous and risky activities.

I know you were with us at Richard's home for Meggie's birthday. She is growing up to be such a beautiful young lady. Did you read the letters I wrote to them about you?

Thank you for the call this morning. I hope that I will hear from you again tomorrow, just so that I can say happy birthday. I know you will be with us at the theatre tomorrow night.

I was sending on some of your Ntsiri photos to this guy in Switzerland with a very heavy heart. He is very serious about buying the place, but he has never seen it. I wish that we did not have to even contemplate selling Ntsiri. I wish that I knew what the best thing would be for us to do. I am very heart sore at the thought, but I have to keep telling myself that you will always be wherever we are and not left there. I will remember your words that it is only symbolic. It is so hard, my darling, to think sensibly and rationally about it. However, I am the one who is being left to do the photos. Dad just does not get around to doing it. Is it the right thing to do?

It looks like things may be coming right for Dad business-wise. Please keep pushing for us in the right direction.

Before I go to bed, I just want to say that not a day goes by that I do not grieve for you, but I think that a present for you will be that perhaps, in the long run, I am a little stronger than I was and I am trying very hard to learn to live without you and your teasing and your lovely warm bear hug. If only I could have just one more!

How can I wish you a happy birthday tomorrow? All I can say is that I will be holding you in my heart the whole day and celebrating the start of a very special relationship that I shall cherish for the rest of my life. Thank you, my love.

Goodnight
xxxooo Mom

On the morning of Mike's birthday – 16 October – we had an unusual call. Brian and I were both awake when the alarm went off – perhaps about the letter – and I acknowledged the call and said I wish I could hug and give him a kiss for his birthday. A little later, it went off for the second time. This had *never* happened before. How I appreciated that added contact. I thought of my boy all day and, when I got home from work, I lit a candle next to his picture and I had it burning all day. Robyn, my cousin, just came without invitation and brought some lunch, which was wonderful, as it was just great to have family there and company, as Brian was still at the office.

Leading up to this day had been very difficult for the family. We obviously wanted to do something special to remember Mike on his day; however, Lorna was very insistent that it must not be anything depressing or morbid and it was important for her that the children were able to remember and honour him in a positive and happy manner. With that in mind, it was decided that going to the theatre to watch *Beauty and the Beast* was a good option. Mike loved the theatre and he and Lorna had taken the kids to just about every show that came on at the Barnyard Theatres or at Monte Casino. Thus, this would be a perfect way to remember him and to do something that he would have enjoyed.

So, on the night of Mike's birthday, we went to see *Beauty and the Beast* together with Lorna, the children and Carol. This is something Mike would definitely have taken his children to see. At the last minute, Shanny, my other granddaughter, decided that she would like to join us as well. I then immediately went to try to book another single ticket; however, I was informed that the entire theatre was booked out and there was not a single seat anywhere in the theatre available. Thus, poor Shanny could not join us. As we had already booked later than we should have, we had to get separate seats, in two separate groupings, but we were in the same row. Brian, Cally and I sat together, and Lorna and the children sat at the end of our row. At interval, we met in the foyer. Lorna said to Megan, "Tell Didi about the seat."

Meggie, with eyes glistening, said, "There is one empty seat next to me and it is number sixteen!" Bearing in mind that the theatre was fully booked, without a single seat available for Shanny to join us, what are the chances that the one seat that is left empty is number sixteen and situated next to his family?

We all knew without a shadow of a doubt, Mike had organised his own seat to be there and chose his birth date number so we would know it was him. How clever is that?

After watching that wonderful show… Mike told me the next morning with my usual 5am alarm: *it was me; I was there!*

Later that day, I received a call from Debby, which validated this a hundred percent. Debby had an appointment with Laureen, who had, by this stage, moved to White River – her own move to escape the crime of Johannesburg after her incident. During Debby's session with Laureen, Mike asked her to pass on a message to me. Mike said to Debby that she would not understand, but 'please to pass it onto Mom and Lorna'.

The message was: "Yes, it was me; I booked the seat."

As Debby lives five hundred kilometres away from us and was not aware of what we were doing on a daily basis, she had no knowledge that we had booked to go and see *Beauty and the Beast,* let alone what had transpired that evening, and thus, at the time, the message made no sense to her. However, she duly passed on the message to me and, of course, I knew *exactly* what she was referring to.

Chapter Sixteen

After the Razor gang had been arrested, Lorna, Meggie and Nick had to go to the Hillbrow Police Station to attend an identity parade. They had to go in individually, as the police needed to prevent one witness from influencing another. Meggie was extremely traumatised the night of the attack, as they were being told all the time 'don't look at me' by the robbers. The result was that she was unable to identify anyone. Lorna was able to positively identify one man; I think he was called Stoffele. Nick, who was only ten, was also able to identify one. (I think also Stoffele.) I was told by the officer who went in with him that they were very impressed with him. He studied them all and, in a very serious, mature voice said, "Please, can number four step forward?" He looked intensively at the man.

Nick then asked, "Please, can he turn sideways?" Then he asked, "Please, can number six step forward?" Again, he looked intently at the man. "Please, can he turn to the left?"

Having studied them carefully, Nick made his identification. It gave the family a small measure of relief and safety to know that some of those evil men were behind bars and would not be coming back for them.

A little while later, they were asked to go to the Sandton Police Station, as another member of the gang had been arrested and held. The first identification parade had been traumatic enough for them, but they were assured that they were behind one-way glass and could not be seen. The light in the room was good and they could see the suspects well.

The Sandton session was a different story. It was far worse for them, as there was no provision for the family to be hidden and they had to enter the room with the suspects through the same door and pass them in the passage. They were terrified and worried that the killers would come after them if they knew they had been identified. They came home in a really jittery and disturbed frame of mind. I was very angry that they had been treated without compassion or sensitivity.

Once we were told that they were now all arrested and in jail awaiting trial, we felt somewhat relieved and optimistic that justice would be done. How naïve and unprepared for the judicial system we were!

Imagine our disbelief and disappointment to hear news over the radio a few weeks later that the Razor gang had escaped from custody! We were afraid this would happen, as they were constantly being transported to the court in Alexandra, only to be remanded again and again and again. It is so easy to bribe one of the guards or warders to look the other way and leave the leg chains unlocked or the van door unlocked.

This had a detrimental effect on both Lorna's and my slow roads to recovery. We were warned that one has ups and downs in the journey of recovery, and we were both once more on a downward road. I worried so about Lorna and the children and their safety now that the gang knew that they might have been identified.

I was very surprised and glad to hear from Lorna that a friend had recommended that she go to see a healer in Magaliesburg, a small rural town just outside Johannesburg. This man was a spiritual healer. He told her as she walked in that she was being accompanied by a big man. It was comforting for her to know that Mike was with her. On her return from her healing session, she came straight to visit us and tell us all about her time with this healer. She said, "He has a son who runs a self-awareness course, which is run over three days on weekends. Didi, I would really like to do it. Please, can you have the children for the weekend?"

I was overjoyed, not only for her, but for the knowledge that she was again asking me to have the children. This was a very big step forward for Lorna and perhaps it would be just what she needed. I believe that she has not yet, since the first night, had a really good cry. It is all bottled up inside and she had to keep going. I am fortunate in that I have had no problem with crying. I often wonder just how people cope when they have to deal with multiple losses at the same time. I have a friend, Sugs Smith, who lost her husband, two daughters and her mother-in-law in one car accident. She was left with her son and her father-in-law. I so often think of her with such admiration of the way she has handled her tragedy. She is an inspiration.

Talking about crying, Meggie had not yet had a good cry either. She had taken on the adult role of being strong for her mother. One afternoon, she and I were sitting on a couch and we were talking about various things, and she put her head on my shoulder and the tears just flowed. I held her close and we wept together. Bless her; she was so concerned that my blouse was all wet. I hope that the little weep did something to help release her pent up emotions.

Lorna went off to her self-awareness course and the children came to stay with me. I have always kept a box of Lego since my boys were toddlers, and Nick loved to get the box out and make things. Shortly before his dad died, they had come to visit us in the flat, and he and Mike made a red aeroplane complete with a pilot in it. Nick asked me to keep it safe and not to break it up. This aeroplane became an ornament in my crowded lounge, sharing space with Ladro china and Waterford Crystal. Over a period of time, it was accompanied by all manner of recognisable and unrecognisable Lego creations made by little boys visiting us. I was checked on a regular basis to see that their creations were still there. Interior decorators would not have given me any points for style!

This time, when Nick came, he asked, "Please Didi; may I have the aeroplane to put next to me while I play?"

He gently took it from me and just laid it down next to him while he played. Thus, a regular habit was started and, every time he came to visit, he asked for it. It must have provided him with some sort of comfort of a happy memory with his dad. Once they were settled in their new home, I carefully packed it up and took it down to him. It is now in his bedroom.

Lorna returned on the Sunday and came to fetch her family and tell us about her weekend. I was delighted to hear her say that she had gained a lot from her experience. She realised that she is really loved by the Thomson family for herself and not because she was 'Mike's wife', as she had always considered herself. She realised that their friends also loved her and not only Mike. She said she had so much more self-confidence. I later met the lady who was Lorna's roommate on the course and she said that everyone there had loved her. She told me that, on the first day, the flood gates had opened and Lorna just sobbed and sobbed. Lorna had made a new friend of her own.

Lorna said, "In one of the sessions, Mike came through to me through the healer's son, who was leading the group. He was also a medium. He told me that Mike was holding a little brown dog. I think it must have been Meggie's little dog who Charlie killed."

Charlie was their beloved golden labrador who killed this little stray puppy that Meggie had acquired. Yet another medium telling us about a dog, but the others had described it as a medium-sized brown dog. In my mind, the mystery had not yet been solved!

The following week, we were all very relieved to hear that the Razor gang had been recaptured. While out of jail, instead of lying low, they were continuing to ply their trade with impunity. They were caught by the Douglasdale police from a tip-off. The chase and recapture resulted in a shoot-out between them and the police. During the shoot-out, Maxwell Kheza *aka Tabang* was killed. This was predicted by both Jacqui and Laureen. My new belief and confidence in mediums was vindicated.

Before this incident, it was thought that it was Razor and George who were in the swimming pool area with Mike, primarily from the confession made by George Nyembe, but, now that one of them was dead, they shifted the blame of killing Mike to Tabang. That made it impossible to prove, as he could no longer speak for himself!

This new blame has continued through the case until present day and has created new challenges in successful prosecution. It will not make any difference to the outcome for Mike, but I hope the truth will come out and we will be able to bring the real killers to book.

Chapter Seventeen

Both Lorna and I were still finding it very difficult to come to terms with Mike's death and were grabbing at anything that might help the healing process. The knowledge that Laureen had left for White River did not help me. I would have to look again for another medium to assist me in my contact with Mike.

Lynda was good, but the wait for an appointment was just too long.

Rosie took Lorna to a friend of hers who she called the 'Bach Flower Lady'. Her name was Bridget. She had a very large following of patients who visit her for healing of all sorts of complaints, and she treats them with Bach flower drops and other alternative treatments. Lorna thought she had improved since she had been taking the drops and visiting Bridget. She encouraged me to go and see her, as I was having serious breathing problems, which are related to the anxiety attacks that I mentioned earlier.

The Xanor tablets I had been taking since Mike's death were no longer working. I had been to see my doctor and she confirmed my suspicion that I was hooked on Xanor and must be weaned off it. She wanted me to take another anti-depressant, which I was reluctant to do. I thought that I must get myself back to normal without the aid of medication. I slowly decreased the Xanor tablets until I was not taking them at all. I did not take the other pills either, but the difficulty with breathing was getting worse. The worse it became, the greater the anxiety, and it develops into a vicious circle. Maybe Bridget could help.

I called straight away and went to see her. She was a lovely warm person and I liked her immediately. She gave me drops and said that I was definitely experiencing withdrawal symptoms. I realised that she was correct and I had to see it through in order to get rid of the problem altogether. Could I do it? Please, let Bridget be the right person to help me.

I took the drops for the first week and I think the breathing did get easier, but not better. I went again the second week for more. After my consultation, Bridget took me around her garden, which was very pretty in an English countrified sort of way. My best was seeing her lovely silky bantams and their babies wandering freely around the garden. When I had my family home in Bryanston, I too used to have silky bantams in my garden. I loved them. On her veranda was a man with lovely, large penetrating brown eyes.

She introduced me to him. "Di, I want you to meet Peter, who is the most wonderful medium."

Was this a coincidence? Am I being led to these people? When one goes, along comes another! I asked his price and was delighted to hear they were much less than the others I had seen.

"He is here every Tuesday and Wednesday and he does his

readings here on the patio," said Bridget.

I immediately made an appointment for the next week when I came to get more drops. Was it Mike sending him now that Laureen was moving away?

The day before I went to see Peter, Brian came home with a smile on his face and so much tension gone from his demeanour! He had succeeded in selling the intellectual property rights on his cremator and incinerator designs and it was signed, sealed and he had proof of the first down payment. For the first time in over a year, we drank some champagne and it felt so good. The relief was just fantastic. Things were starting to look up!

The following day, I went to see Peter, once again feeling excitement mixed with a little trepidation. Would he be as good as the other mediums I had seen? We sat outside on the veranda that spans three sides of Bridget's house. The tranquil setting and the bantams in the garden, together with the homely atmosphere, boded well for my chat with Mike. I had spoken to Mike on my way there and asked him to come through and, if possible, to bring Mum and Dad and Brian's mom and dad.

Peter started by asking me to hold a pack of cards and said it was just to get my energy and nothing else.

Without hesitation, he said, "You have lost your son. He was not a child. No, he had children of his own. He died suddenly, unable to say goodbye."

After a slight pause, he said, "He was shot. Your son is saying that you both had a very strong bond. He is communicating with you, but he is looking for ways to change the methods of communication. He is doing much better with being able to get through to his wife."

Again, I was blown away by the next comment. "He is holding a little brown dog."

There he was again with this little brown dog. Who is it?

Peter described what my life had been like this past year. He said how my personal problems had impinged on my relationship with Brian. He assured me that, after my birthday, things would start to improve.

He said that there were new changes to Brian's life and, when I confirmed that he had just sold his intellectual property and had come home with the deal signed and sealed, he bowled me over with the details of the contract and exactly what the terms of the sale were. He correctly stated that we did not get the down payment that we wanted, but he assured me that, in the end, we would be fine.

"You have other assets that you must not be afraid to realise. I do not understand what Mike is talking about, but I will repeat what he is saying. Mike says that the place is not what it used to be, as the ethos has changed and, if the decision is made to sell, do not feel bad about it."

How could Peter possibly have known about Ntsiri and that we had talked about the possibility of selling? We needed the money to retire and we were finding it very painful to go there without Mike being part of it all. He and Brian had always shared the maintenance of the home and bush vehicle. Allan, Carol and I were the 'landscapers and garden fixers'. Debby looked after local things that were needed. As much as the family had their own ideas of how we could keep it and how it could be managed, Brian could not face the future at Ntsiri without Mike's help. There were other issues complicating the inheritance of Ntsiri, which also contributed to our decision to sell our much-loved bush home.

Peter frowned and looked directly into my eyes for some time and said, "Again, I cannot make any sense of this, but I can see a watch and a silver bracelet."

Wow! I knew immediately. The watch was obvious to me, but the silver bracelet is what Mike asked me to buy for Lorna for the first wedding anniversary that they were apart. It was soon after his death.

I did not write about it with my first visit to Jacqui, as I wanted to include it here. Jacqui had said that there was a wedding anniversary coming up. Mike asked her, "Please ask my mom to buy a silver bracelet for Lorna. I was going to replace her ring that was stolen a while ago, but now I can't. Please tell her it is a symbol of my eternal love for her." She recited a little poem, the words of which I cannot find anymore.

Debby and I went shopping together to follow Mike's wishes to get Lorna a bracelet, and I am convinced Mike led us to the shop where we ended up. It only sold silver items and we explained what we wanted. The jeweller brought out the perfect bracelet. It was a solid silver band, but had three medallions in the middle, all linked together. They symbolised their three children. Mike acknowledged the purchase and his approval in the usual way at 5am.

When I gave the bracelet to Lorna, she was in Scotland with her dad. I did not see her reaction when she opened the present.

Peter asked, "Did your son do a lot of charity work?"

"No, not official charity work. Why?"

"I see him doing work with children less privileged than his own. I also see him doing a lot of work in his community."

I replied, "Yes, he was on the governing body of his children's school. He also brought his domestic worker's little daughter to live with them during the week, as she could not afford the daily taxi fare for the two of them. The little girl shared a room with Annie Rose. In addition, the child came to Lorna's playschool for free. I remembered there was another family who had an alcoholic mother and the children often used to go to Ntsiri with them. Other times, Lorna would let them sleep over when the mother forgot to fetch them."

Oh, what a loss to the community his death is!

Peter then told me that Mike is still working with children. He said that he helps children who have died in traumatic circumstances to cross over. I agreed. "That is just what he would have chosen or been chosen to do. He was always so good with children and, in fact, people in general."

The hour passed so quickly for me. Peter closed the reading. "Your father is here waiting very patiently on the side. He said he was very proud of you and of your family."

I was thrilled. He described my dad perfectly. "Your father is a large man with watery pale blue eyes. He is balding and has a very proud and distinguished character. He has been with you throughout your trauma."

Peter then described my mother in almost the same way that Jackie, Laureen and Lynda had done. She had secateurs in her hand, a basket of roses over her arm and she was picking roses. So typical of my mother! My mum comes from a long line of very keen gardeners. It has been rewarding to observe that my children have also inherited that gene from me. At long last, I really feel that Mum and Dad are coming through to me and are watching over me In life, Dad would have sided with Verna and been very disapproving of my 'meddling', as he would have put it. I bet he has changed his mind now! Peter is the fourth medium who had described my family in the same manner as the other mediums. Their connections are irrefutable.

On this occasion, I came away with such a good feeling that I was once again in real contact with Mike and my parents. I had found another medium I could trust.

I was feeling a lot better with regards to coming off the Xanor and was also determined to get myself off sleeping tablets. I wanted no more pills or dependence on any substance to keep me going. In particular, I wanted to be able to control it in the future without having to resort to medication. But how? I spent many late nights researching on the internet when sleep eluded me. I found someone in the USA named Joe who had sorted out his own anxiety issues. He, too, had become addicted to anti-depressants and wanted to get off them. After much research and trial and error, he devised a method of controlling his mind. He taught me to recognise the symptoms, to relax and accept the condition. I learnt to tell myself that I have been there before and had come to no harm. I must face it head on and tell myself I can cope with it. He had written a book and held workshops. He had had remarkable success with it. I sent off for it and started working on his programme. At first, it sounded very theoretical and I was wary that it would not work. Nevertheless, I threw myself into it and believed that it would work after reading how many others he had helped. I was able to successfully wean myself off all the pills and, when I now feel an attack building up, I can put it off with his method!

There have been several times since we lost Mike when I have had a stressful time and have felt the symptoms building up, which manifests in not being able get enough oxygen and having to take deep breaths all the time. This actually ends up in too much oxygen and then the anxiety kicks in. As soon as this begins, I go back to Joe's method and, without me realising it, I find myself breathing normally. Thank you, Joe!

To add to my relief, he would not accept any payment for his book, which he sells in the USA. It really worked, so what a win!

I have passed on his book to a number of people, but only one person has been able to achieve the desired result. I am so grateful that I was the other!

Chapter Eighteen

The Mike Thomson Change a Life Trust

Before the first cycle challenge was to take place, the trustees met to discuss the beneficiaries. It was decided that the money would only go to organisations where the founder was still actively involved. No figureheads or large corporate offices where the people running it were salaried individuals would be considered. The organisation had to be run by people with passion.

The second criteria would be that the cause had to be working in a positive fashion to fight or combat crime in South Africa. Activities such as protests and demonstrations would not be acceptable, but a good productive and constructive process would most certainly be considered.

The primary beneficiary was to be the DNA Project. If we could assist to get this project up and running, laws changed and passed through Parliament, it would be a massive achievement. It would also bring us in line with other Western countries with their success rates in solving crimes through DNA. There is no crime committed without DNA being left behind. This would result in killers such as Mike's being found and convicted with far greater speed and ease than currently occurs. I would urge interested readers to Google the DNA Project South Africa and follow the progress of this amazing initiative of Vanessa Lynch and the success so far. Also click on the link 'Sponsors' to see our connection. It is the 'Change a Life' link.

The second selected recipient was Martin Dreyer. Martin Dreyer who was also participating in the cycle challenge, and who had auctioned off the back seat on his tandem bicycle at the launch of the trust, lived in the Valley of a Thousand Hills in KwaZulu Natal. He applied to the trust for funding, as he had a dream of starting an academy that would take in youngsters off the streets and train them in canoeing. At the same time, he encouraged them to pursue their education, taught them the value of life and instilled in them a set of morals, ethics and a belief in oneself. It was agreed that this would prevent certain youngsters from becoming criminals, so he was given the go ahead. He named it 'The Martin Dreyer Change a Life Academy'. In his first year, he and one of his protégés actually won the 'Dusi' canoe marathon. This is a very famous canoe race equal to the Comrades Marathon in prestige held annually in Natal, starting in Pietermaritzburg and ending in Durban. It is held on the Umsindusi River, affectionately known as the 'Dusi'.

Another beneficiary was Carole Podetti, a French lady who had started an organisation called 'I Choose to Change a Life'. Carole visited the courts and 'rescued' youngsters who had fallen foul of the law with petty crime such as cell phone theft,

theft of food and other misdemeanours. She did not address perpetrators of violent crimes. She took these children and put them through a very intensive life skills programme and, when she felt they were rehabilitated, they became ambassadors for the group and returned to their community to teach others that crime does not pay. She requested help and it was granted.

The last beneficiary was a man who had started a rape crisis centre. A much needed asset in South Africa, where rape is almost a national past time!

The cycle challenge was a resounding success, and a very impressive sum of just over three million rand was raised. What a fantastic start! Mike must have been in awe of what was being done in his name!

Shortly after the challenge, Computershare organised a report back and again we were invited to attend the function hosted by the JSE. What a professional gathering it was. Drinks and cocktails were served of the very highest standard. The camaraderie that was created by the competitors and the organisers of the whole event was so humbling to observe. These men and women, who were at the peak of their careers, had all got on so well and made permanent bonds and business networks. The humour coming from so many was really infectious. It was obvious that they had the most wonderful experience and, almost without exception, they booked their places for the following year in spite of the destination being kept a secret. I could not help shedding a few quiet tears when I saw all this going on and hearing them reminding themselves of the real reason for the exercise. They would not lose sight of the fact that it was because Mike had been murdered.

It was such an uplifting experience to be part of an event of this calibre.

For more information of the trust and its achievements, as well as the current beneficiaries of the trust, please see the appendix.

Chapter Nineteen

Digging for water like an elephant at Ntsiri.

I was not particularly looking for another medium, as I was happy with Peter, but my friend, Pam, told me of a man whom her son, Mike, visited now that Jacqui had moved away. She said Mike thought he was excellent, but the thing that attracted me was the fact that he gave classes to teach you to make the connection yourself. Remembering that Lynda had said I could do it myself, I thought I should find out what it was about and, in fact, if I was capable.

I made my appointment and went to see him. On the way, I chatted to Mike in my head and asked him to please come through for me.

I did not know what to expect. He was slightly built, wore loose, ill fitting jeans and had long hair tied in a ponytail. The impression I have is that he wore earrings, but I cannot be sure.

He talked a lot about my past lives and that I still needed to learn life lessons on Earth. As he talked, he was drawing my guide on a page he held in front of him, who was apparently a person called Anne. Verna would have had a field day with me and this medium, thinking him very 'woo woo'.

I cannot say that I was over impressed with the appearance of my guide. Maybe I was being too critical? She just looked odd! He seemed to be drawing without looking at the page: he said my guide was assisting him. His hand was moving in circles. The outer layer was blue, the next layer of circle was yellow, then blue with a narrow strip of white, then blue, then white, the circle constantly decreasing. Then came her face. Oh dear, where did she come from and how old was she? The blue circle he created gave the appearance of Anne wearing a habit like a nun or being covered like a Muslim woman. She had piercing dark brown eyes with extraordinary eyelids. It seemed that there were three folds on the eyelids and no eyebrows; her nose was flat and broad. Her skin colour was very light coffee colour and, to my mind, she had an unsmiling mouth. Sadly, I did not feel any connection to her at all.

However, a very strange thing happened. I brought the drawing out to look at it in order to describe it now while writing this. I had not looked at it since I first got it. As I was looking at her, and the longer I looked at her, her mouth began to smile a bit and her eyes became softer. Was I being too harsh to start with? As I looked at the drawing it, it seemed to change before my eyes: it may have. Was she trying to communicate with me as I was describing her?

I was rather disturbed by some of the things that he said, such as, "By me enabling you to be aware, you will be opening up a Pandora's box." What on earth did he mean by that? He told me that sorrow and loss were part of my life lessons that I had to learn. That upset me, as it made me think that it may be my fault that Mike had to die and that his family had to suffer so much pain and trauma because I had a lesson to learn. I did not want to believe that and could not have lived with that knowledge had it proved to be true. I still have the consultation tape and I do not want to listen again.

I was also told that Mike chose to die, as it was his time. I also do not want to believe that. Why would he do that when he had such young children whom he adored and who still needed him? No; I cannot believe that. It was *not his time*! That theory would then absolve the killers of any blame, as it was planned and not their fault; they were then merely the instruments. I don't buy that. They must face the consequences of their actions.

Since seeing this medium, I have had it suggested to me by Lynda that we do not choose our time to die, as she has had so many people in spirit, including Michael, who told her that they were not ready to go. She maintains that some people who are ill or old may know their time is over, but not young people who die a sudden death. I am far happier with that theory than the other one.

The medium said in a questioning tone that there was a young child there. When I said 'not that I can think of', he fumbled and blustered about it. In hindsight, I was reminded by Debby that I had lost a baby between Mike and her. Perhaps I was too harsh?

Feeling uncomfortable for him, I added, "I did lose my child, but he was no longer a child."

He said, "Oh yes, yes, yes, that is it and he is here, but he is not communicating with me. He is using the guides."

I immediately lost some confidence in him, as Mike has never done that before. Suddenly, he said, "Wait a minute, he is shouting at me really loud. *I am here! I am here!*"

I had to smile; I could actually hear in my head Mike's voice, and I sensed that he was really irritated with this man. I asked him what he thought about the alarm from Mike's watch and, before he could answer my question, he said, "Mike is shouting at me again: *it is me!*"

I did not get any more information that I thought was helpful. I resolved that I was certainly not going to open up any Pandora boxes, so I left there feeling that Mike did not like him at all. Neither did I. He is one medium I will not be seeing again.

The members of Allan and Mike's dojo were feeling the loss of Mike enormously and one of the students had a charcoal portrait done by a friend for the dojo. Dee Knight organised a special unveiling of the picture after one of the grading sessions. Brian and I were invited to attend. It was a very moving little ceremony and Dee read out a letter from her daughter living in England.

Time passed and it was soon time for Lorna to pack up her house, pack up Richard's granny flat, call in movers and take herself and her family down to Plett.

Debby drove down from Hoedspruit to help. Between Debs, Carol, Sarah, Brian and I and sometimes a friend, we went across to Buckingham Avenue to help Lorna sort through the house and pack up her things. She had started on her own, refusing our offers of help, but I think the task became just too overwhelming, heartbreaking and emotional. It was impossible to do it alone.

Brian and I started on Mike's workshop. That was a very painful exercise, as he had inherited all of my father's woodworking tools and had also bought a lot of my late cousin, Adrian Parnell's, tools as well. He had such an organised and well-stocked workshop. Even now, it pains me to think of it and that it is all gone. Mike made beautiful furniture and a stunning grandmother clock, which Lorna has. Trying to find a home for all these tools was not only difficult, but very heart wrenching. As well as bringing back memories of my son, it also brought back memories of my father and one of my favourite cousins. We kept a lot for Nick for when he grows up and he now has it all stored in their new home. My dearest wish is that he has inherited his dad's creative genes and one day decides to use his dad's tools.

29 November was the date that Lorna had set aside to bid farewell to all her friends and family. A week before she left, she organised a picnic in her Craighall Park garden, which was still looking good. We had retained the services of their gardener, Sandwell, who also became the caretaker of the property. I had continued to look after the garden with the help of Sandwell. This was a task I hated with a passion, as Mike and I had put that garden together. It had been landscaped with so much love, and the emptiness that I felt when I went into the garden was almost more than I could handle. However, I continued to go there because I knew the house had to be sold and I have always been so aware of what a huge plus it is to have a lovely garden. I did it for my boy.

Mike had built this beautiful tree house in one of the biggest pin oaks I had ever seen. The house was very high up, with access by rope ladder only. The children had hardly had a chance to use it before he was taken from them. However, just prior to loosing Mike, they had all had the chance to commission the new tree house with a tea party up in the newly completed structure. All the party goodies were hoisted up in a basket by pulley.

At the farewell party, Lorna had various meats on the spit and she made salads and bought all sorts of lovely breads. Everyone in the family chipped in with desserts and cutlery and crockery. All the guests came with picnic blankets and chairs and settled in her garden. It was a lovely day; the weather was perfect and the children had such fun playing in the garden for the last time. It was the first time in a year and would be the last time that we heard the sound of laughter and love in that garden. The children adored that tree house! One little baby girl went scampering up the rope ladder so fast that her dad was unable to keep up with her. When she got to the top, she point blank refused to come down! With much cajoling, bribing and pleading, which all fell on totally deaf ears, her dad eventually went up the ladder himself. He scooped her up and stuffed her down his shirt, much to her disgust. She was squirming and wriggling to get free while he gingerly made his way down the rope ladder with his little girl, who was protesting with gusto.

I know Mike was there and he would have loved that little scenario. I bet he would have longed to be able to let us know that he was with us. He might have tried, but, that day, no one noticed. I knew he was there, and I wished I could have seen him and hugged him. In spite of the sadness surrounding us, it was a successful day and Lorna made a lovely speech to thank everyone for their love and support over the last year. I was proud of her. I also made a little speech by virtue of being the matriarch of the family! I wanted to wish her well for the future. I think this was validating the start of Lorna realising and knowing that she was loved by so many in her own right and not just because she was Mike's wife.

The morning of 9 December 2008 was not a happy one. Lorna and the family were leaving. Debby had remained in Jo'burg to help her pack up and then to travel down to Plett with her to help Lorna unpack at the other end. I was so grateful to Debby. She made a big effort to be there for Lorna and her family.

Lorna was very tearful, now doubting the wisdom of her decision. She suddenly realised what she was leaving behind, but the die was cast; she had to go. I was feeling desolate and very apprehensive for them all.

Tearfully, we kissed and hugged our goodbyes and Mike's family nervously set off on their journey and their next step to recovery. Most of all, it was to make a new life without a husband and a dad.

I was left standing, trying to cope with the gut-wrenching pain and knowledge that not only had I lost my son, I was now losing the close contact I had enjoyed with his family. I could not hold back the tears.

Chapter Twenty

2009. The Razor gang had been in prison for over a year and still we had received no information on the court case. It was a useless exercise calling the investigating officer, because, every time I spoke to him, he would say he was going to court on Wednesday and he would call me on Friday. Needless to say, I never, ever, got a call on Friday, and, if I made the call, I was told the same Wednesday/Friday story again!

I had been chatting to Pat Tarr, whom I have already mentioned lost her son, Ian, in an armed robbery in their shop at Broadacres. Her son's killers had been found through their own private investigator. They had already been caught and prosecuted. She gave me the name of a retired magistrate who had helped bring their case to court. I called him. He visited us and seemed very keen to help. He went to the Alexandra courts and was horrified to find that the amount of cases to be heard was a huge pile heaped on the floor of the office and that Mike's case was not even on the court role. He pulled some strings and managed to get it located and onto the court role. However, there it stayed with the prosecutors, who were still trying to have all these cases lumped into one and getting nowhere slowly!

I did not hear from the magistrate again and he no longer answered my emails or calls. I struggled to understand why there was this change of attitude. In addition, I have still not received any bills, three years down the line. Feeling very let down, I had to give up on that line of help. I have often wondered if he knew something that I did not and thought it a waste of time. Perhaps he did not want to upset me?

I wrote letters to Parliament, I wrote to the shadow Minster of Justice and numerous others to try to get them to separate the cases, but, if I got a reply, it was always the same: it is impossible for them to intervene with the courts. However, most of my correspondence was ignored.

One morning at home, I heard a lady, Bronwyn Paterson, speaking on a Radio 702 talk show. She, too, felt frustrated about their court case. Her family had been attacked in their home by the Razor gang three nights after Mike's murder. I had heard about it on the news, but, at the time, I was still in shock myself and we were unaware that their attackers belonged to the same gang, so I had not followed the story too closely. I knew that none of the Patersons had been killed by the gang, so, in time, there would be hope for that family, although they, too, must have been pretty devastated. However, Mike was dead, there was no hope, and the pain and grief would be with us forever.

I heard how Bronwyn had been beaten and stabbed with kitchen scissors to a bloody pulp and also that her seventeen-year-old daughter, Jamie, had been raped by Razor in the bathroom. Bronwyn said that she, too, was frustrated by the complete lack of communication from the police with her family. There had been no progress reports at all. She also mentioned that she thought that combining all the cases together was a bad idea – I felt the same way. We wondered if we would ever get those vile men behind bars forever so that they could never do this to other people. We both wanted just punishment and sentencing for the heinous crimes the Razor gang had committed.

We had a lot in common.

I tried to phone 702 in order to respond, but without success. I wanted to meet this lady and see if we could combine our resources and try for justice together. I did some super sleuthing and managed to get her phone number. Bronwyn was very happy to meet me so that we could work together and do everything possible in order to stop this gang. We met for coffee one morning. I was quite taken aback when I first saw her. She is a beautiful, extra petite lady who looked so fragile that she could easily snap in a breeze. It was impossible to imagine she could survive such a beating and stabbing and all that she had endured. How wrong can first impressions be? She turned out to be one of the most courageous and determined mothers I have met.

We spent the whole morning together and, in spite of us being very different people, we got on so well. She was a retired ballet dancer (hardly me!) and she told me her story. It was horrific! Considering that these were the same men who killed Mike and attacked my family, we had reason to be very thankful that Lorna and the children escaped being badly beaten and raped.

Bronwyn felt, after hearing our story, that it was a miracle that they had come out of this alive. We determined to do everything in our power to put a stop to these evil men.

Over the years, we wrote to newspapers, called radio talk shows and contacted whatever media we could, but there was little response from those who were supposedly in charge of our cases. When one is placed in a situation like this, the media is truly the only weapon one has, but this takes courage and perseverance, as the last thing one wants to do is to expose oneself constantly in this way. Both of us called the various police stations involved in our cases every few weeks, but we were constantly fobbed off and never kept informed from their side.

Three years later, the Paterson's case finally came before the court. It was to be held at the Alexandra courts, also known as the Wynberg Magistrates Court.

At last, we had confirmation that the cases were to be split. This was some encouraging news.

By now, our families had become firm friends, so Brian and I decided to go to the court with the family in order to support them through this awful ordeal. A book could be written about that fiasco alone! The trial was due to begin at 9am.

In order to get to the courts, we had to drive through derelict streets lined with pavement hawkers, pavement hairdressers, and dubious fast food outlets. This made progress so much slower than we had anticipated and we were concerned about being late. We were worried about having to park in the street, for, if we had had to, there may have been a strong chance that the car would not have been there when we returned. Thank goodness there was a parking lot a few 'shops' down from the courts with a security guard on duty. Hastily, we then picked our way gingerly across the broken pavers, litter and the odd rat scuttling past and other unmentionable obstacles.

As it turned out, we need not have been too concerned about

the possibility of being late! Firstly, we had to go through the security and then find our way to the court allocated to the Razor gang trial. Grey, grubby, depressing corridors led to the court where the Razor gang was to appear. In the passage outside the court, there was a row of benches where those waiting to go in could be seated. On the one side, the windows looked down onto a bare cement courtyard where one tree battled to survive. The rats, however, had no problem!

The prisoners were brought in through this courtyard. They would look up to the windows frequently to wave or shout arrogantly at the victims, using cut-throat gestures. In the corridor, there was a stream of supporters of the accused coming and going, and they looked for all the world as if they were about to attend a show. Some of them were blatantly wearing leather thongs around their stomachs or necks as they paraded past the Paterson family, making sure that this was seen. It looked very much as if this was an intimidation tactic. These amulets are often worn by the African people as prevention of evil or to indicate that they have magical powers.

There was a sad old lady who clearly set herself apart from all this. She appeared to be a victim of abject poverty and she was obviously in distress. She had alternated for over an hour between pacing up and down and sitting with her head in hands in despair. Bronwyn went over to her, put a hand on her shoulder and asked her if she was a mother of one of the prisoners. She was, in fact, George Nyembe's mother. Bronwyn told her that, as a mother herself, she was very sorry about her grief. The old lady shook her head and said, "I don't know why he had to do this terrible thing to your family and I hope that he is punished."

I was again in awe of this diminutive lady who had been through so much. The fact that Bronwyn could identify with this mother and offer her sympathies when it was, in fact, this woman's son who had inflicted so much harm and pain on her and her family was truly humbling.

For a very brief moment, I allowed myself to ponder her situation. She was obviously a caring old lady. Had George become this hardened criminal through lack of guidance as a child growing up? Was it due to abject poverty or was he influenced by his peers? Was he perhaps an untreated psychopath? I, too, felt sad for her, but that is where my sympathy ended. Her son had stabbed my boy fourteen times and I felt no sympathy for him. I, too, hoped he would be punished for his crimes, but I did identify with her as a mother and understood her anguish.

By 11am, we were still waiting for a lawyer representing one of the prisoners. The entire court was kept waiting, doing nothing, and we imagined that the lawyers who were working for the justice system would still be paid for not doing their jobs, as all the accused would be, being represented by lawyers from the legal aid society. It would seem they were quite unconcerned about the time and money that was being wasted. At about 12:30pm, we were told to go and have lunch and to return to court at 2pm.

Immediately after we returned, Jamie was called in to testify about the attack on her family and her rape. The family was not allowed to go into the court and Jamie was sent in alone. Once on the stand, Jamie could not identify any of the prisoners and she could not identify anyone in any of the four identification parades that were held. As a result, she could not be cross-examined by the defence.

Standing before us was a young slip of a girl, who, at the age of seventeen, had been just about to write her final Matric exams at school, when she had been raped by Razor Zulu. She had been callously taken to the bathroom, locked in and raped. Razor Zulu had finished off by glibly telling her he was HIV positive! She related her story calmly and with such maturity that it was heartrending.

We knew that DNA samples had confirmed that Razor was the rapist, which meant that at least he would be found guilty! She was questioned by the prosecutor thoroughly about the attack for over an hour. Jamie told her story as it had happened, in great detail, with poise and inordinate composure. All the while, her rapist sat in front of her. At one point, Razor actually had the arrogance to wink at her. This was when Jamie told the court how she had told her brother not to look at their faces in order to prevent him becoming vulnerable to attack from them at a later stage if they thought he would be able recognise them.

Brian and I were so glad to have been there to support Jamie, for I am sure that being able to see two familiar, friendly faces in a sea of impassive strangers must have been of some comfort to her. Then, too, we were able to tell her parents that they could be very proud of the way she had handled yet another ordeal.

The court dismissed Jamie and it was adjourned until the following week.

The following week, Bronwyn had to give her testimony. The court then learnt that, during the course of the attack, she had been separated from her family and ordered at gunpoint to escort the gang leaders all over the house so that they might have access to their valuables. They would ask her questions, and then pistol-whip her, swearing profusely and making derogatory racist comments every time she answered them. They threatened to kill her and her family constantly for an hour and a half.

At this point in the trial, one of the accused decided he wanted a new lawyer, so it was postponed yet again. This is apparently a human right, and prisoners abuse this to prolong the process.

Just when progress is being made, a prisoner decides that he is either gravely ill or wants a new lawyer and so it goes on. It appears that they are allowed to get away with this with impunity! Fortunately, the delay did not turn out to be too lengthy and we were back in court a month later, thanks to Michelle Bayat, the very determined prosecutor.

Bronwyn was put on the stand first for cross-examination. What a brave performance! As she was being cross-examined, the lawyers tried to bully her and she responded with polite firmness. She was unwavering in her convictions and answers, and Brian and I were both so impressed. After Bronwyn's dismissal, an hour later, she was allowed to sit in court to witness her husband, Alan's, testimony and cross-examination. Alan was bullied in much the same way. Both Alan and Bronwyn identified three prisoners, and each prisoner was represented by his own lawyer. Each lawyer had a turn to cross-examine the victims.

Brian and I were unhappy with several aspects of the trial. One in particular concerned us a great deal. Upon being sworn in to testify, the Patersons were forced to reveal their address and car registrations. These were repeated out loud for all to hear. This was disconcerting, as each of the accused had supporters in court. The Patersons have been unable to move since the attack, or change their cars.

This is a disgrace. How can this be allowed to happen when it could put the lives of the victims in jeopardy? Fortunately, there have been no repercussions yet, but the Patersons are extremely unhappy and nervous about it. In addition to this, one of the lawyers representing one of the gang made the accused stand up and walk right up to Bronwyn and face her, inches away, the very face he had beaten. This was in order to prove that, because he was roughly the same height as her, he could not possibly have been able to beat or stab her. Clearly, this was a tactic used by the lawyer to break her down. Bronwyn kept her cool.

One year after the trial, Bronwyn and her family had heard nothing. Suddenly, one day, out of the blue, a friend called her to say that she had heard on the 702 news that Razor Zulu had been sentenced to thirty years and George Nyembe had been sentenced to twenty years. They had never been informed about the sentencing and neither were they called to court to hear the verdict. They heard about the sentence the same way that we did on the way home from another visit to Laureen. The remainder of the gang was acquitted due to lack of evidence and some profound bungling of the evidence at the crime scene on the part of some of the police. These people were part of a gang that killed our son. In 2013, we still have no idea if they are still imprisoned or if they will ever come to trial.

Something that really disturbed me was coming face to face with the men who killed Mike. It was totally contrary to what I had expected. I had always visualised evil-looking men and, when I saw them, I was shattered to see that they looked like any person one would see walking down the street. I had always imagined that I would look at these evil men and feel indescribable anger and hate. I thought I would want to lash out at them or scream. I did not. I felt that old numbness that I felt the first night and just an excruciating sadness and desperation. What made these men such heartless killers? Was it drugs, was it drink, was it their past? Perhaps all of it? Have they any idea what they have done to my family and many others? If they do, they obviously do not care. Why?

We managed to chat to the prosecutor one day when we were waiting for the lawyers to arrive, and I asked her if she knew anything about Mike's case. She said she knew of it, but knew no details as it was now at the high court due to the fact that it was a murder case. She gave me the name of the prosecutor there handling the case. I tried to get hold of him for about three months. I always got voice mail and I thought it inappropriate to leave a message. I finally succeeded and was mortified to hear that he had taken Mike's case off the role, as he said there was a lack of evidence and the investigating team must improve their case against them. I was mortified! After all, they had his gun, they had recovered his laptop, they had found his car, surely with fingerprints, and, above all, they had a confession from George Nyembe.

When I questioned the investigating officer about this, he denied it vehemently. I suppose he would! The wait and the lack of information started all over again.

Four years down the line, we were still being kept in the dark. No courtesy call or explanation about the silence on the case. Whatever I gleaned was because I had phoned someone. I called so many people. I got to know the arresting officer, Bruce, who always told me what he knew and kept Brian and I up to date with the gang's other cases. I got to know crime reporters and news reporters, but nothing helped to get the case moving.

One morning on the Redi Direko morning talk show on 702, her guest was the Minister of Justice. The lines were red hot and, as hard as I tried, I just could not get through. However, after he had gone, I did manage to speak to her. The conversation went something like this… "Good morning, Redi. Thank you for taking my call even though the minister has left."

"Good morning, Diana. It's a pleasure. What did you want to ask him?" she asked.

"I wanted to ask him if he could find out why my son's case was taking so long to be heard. The accused have been in custody for four years now, but still there is no court case. Is it unreasonable to think four years is a long time to wait? I have become very disillusioned and bitter, as there have been many high profile murders since my son was killed and their killers were caught and tried within a few months, yet Mike's case is still unheard. Is this fair to any of us ordinary citizens?"

"I am so sorry for your loss, Diana. Of course you cannot get closure while this is hanging over your head."

"It is not even that, Redi. For me, there will never be closure. I believe that word was invented by someone who has never experienced such grief. Whilst there will never be closure for me, nor for his wife and children, there must be, for them, acceptance of his death and a chance to move on. With this case hanging over their heads all the time, they are being held back. Also, when the lawyers do eventually start their bullying tactics, which we have seen firsthand, how can people who were so traumatised at the time be expected to remember all the details after so long? In addition, my grandchildren were very young and, I am sure, will struggle to remember details," I said.

"Diana, I cannot imagine what your family have been through and are still going through. It is unacceptable. Mava, my producer, will take your details and we will see what we can do," she kindly assured me.

"Thank you so much, Redi. You are the first person who has bothered to listen to me. I have tried so many times to get on the radio. I really do appreciate your effort."

She finished off by saying, "We will do our best."

Later that day, Mava called to say that the *Star* newspaper had heard my call and would I talk to one of their crime reporters.

Of course I would.

Brian and I were going into Sandton that week, so we met the reporter at a coffee shop. Ironically, it was the coffee shop belonging to Pat Tarr, who has also lost her son. She brought her photographer with her. We had coffee together and I told her our story and that I felt four years was far too long to wait for justice seeing they had already got the gang in custody. My beef was not entirely with the police, as they had done their job in arresting the men. However, the collecting and preserving of evidence was appalling, as well as victim relations.

Currently, though, I was extremely frustrated with the justice system.

Candice, the reporter, was most sympathetic. I often wonder what the other patrons of the coffee shop must have thought about the goings on. While Candice was talking to us, I was constantly wiping away the tears, and the photographer was doing all sorts of contortions to get a good picture of both Brian and I. At one time, he was lying on his back, using the open chair back as a frame! About three weeks later, she called to say that her article had been accepted and would be out the next day. We eagerly went to get the newspaper at the local garage and were amazed to see that Candice had done a full-page story on the case, as well a bit about the trust and how we are turning a personal tragedy into a positive. Her article was headed 'Justice Delayed is Justice Denied'.

So much for that; a year later and nothing has changed! We are now waiting for DNA results to try to get a stronger case for the rest of the gang. There is apparently a strong case for only two of them at the moment. I believe it is for George Nyembe and a Stoffele. George will be indicted, because he made a confession and he was found to be in possession of Mike's gun. Stoffele will be indicted, because Lorna identified him in the identification parade. For the others, it appears that there is insufficient evidence! With no protection of the crime scene and so many policemen wandering all over the house and pool area, it is not surprising that there is no evidence.

The gang was now claiming that Tabang, who had been shot, was actually the man who killed Mike. This, of course, is a very convenient accusation to make, as he is no longer able to speak for himself. That now puts doubt on the assumption that Razor was the one who pulled the trigger. The fact is that Razor seems to be the one who rapes his female victims, and Lorna and Megan were not raped. To me, it therefore makes sense that he was unable to rape her, as he had been fighting with Mike and was either injured or too tired. Will he now get away with his crime?

Chapter Twenty-One

Another Christmas at Shelley Beach came and went. It will never be the same, but we do try for the children. We have still not had another Christmas with Lorna and her children. I think it is too painful for her, so she makes sure she is working over Christmas at Kurlands Hotel. I live in hope that it will one day happen again.

After Christmas in 2008, Brian, Carol and I went to Ntsiri. The bush was looking quite beautiful. The rains had been good and the lush green grass was interspersed with the summer wild flowers, which had always been my passion. The impalas were everywhere, looking fat and sleek, and each female had dropped her baby. How I loved to see the nursery of lambs peeping over the heads of the wild white forget-me-nots. The babies looked picture box beautiful in the gentle drizzle and it made me so aware of Mike's absence, as we were always enjoyed identifying the flowers together. It made me sad to think that many of these dear little creatures would land up as the lion's supper!

Elephants were plentiful and the old bulls loved to visit our house and just hang around there all day. Although I did not weep quite as much this time as before, I still found it very hard to be there. The memories were very painful.

Mike was such an integral part of our time there. He, of all of the family, embraced the life and the bush. He was so knowledgeable and shared his knowledge so willingly. Seeing elephant or lion always evoked some sort of memory or story about Mike and his escapades in the bush with his friends and family. Perhaps, in time, this would become a joyful memory, but, right now, it just brought pain and deep sorrow.

There was a manager's office, little shop and members' swimming pool on the top of a hill a few kilometres from our house. We could get odd emergencies there, but the main reason to visit the shop was to have a swim and to buy cold drinks and ice! None of our gas freezers could keep up with the demand in summer. One relaxing hot summer's day, we went up to the pool for a cooling swim. There was not a cloud in the azure blue sky; the temperature hitting 38°C. The pool overlooked a huge plain below. While sitting in the water on the top step with an ice-cold G&T in hand, we could see herds of impala, zebra and a large family of giraffes. They were quietly grazing on the lush vegetation resulting from the good rains that summer. An old elephant bull and his two askaris were making their way to a water hole in the plain. The scene was printed indelibly in my memory I was chatting to our farm manager, Carl, and said to him, "Brian and I are thinking of selling up here, but a scene like this below us makes it so hard to do."

He asked, "Are you serious; after so many years?"

"We are talking about it, but have not made any final decisions yet. It is a very emotional decision for us."

"Let us know when you do and what price you will be wanting," he said.

I took it no further, as I was not enthusiastic about selling our share at all in spite of Brian insisting that we must.

I had several mornings where Mike let me know he was there with us and then it happened! The watch battery died and with it my contact! I was desolate once again. I had been warned it would not last forever and that Mike was figuring out another way to contact me. Even though I was prepared for it, it was still devastating to me. Once again, I started feeling despair that I would never get over this grief.

Once home, I took the watch in to get a new battery and asked the jeweller to please not change any settings. He said he did not! However, when I got the watch back, the alarm went off at 9am every day until Brian managed to stop it. It was no longer sporadic and, therefore, no longer Mike. I tried to be sensible about it and rationalise that I had been warned and I must now look out for other signs, but I still felt completely gutted.

During one of my visits to Laureen, she described to me a clock that she could see. It was a grandmother clock and it perfectly fit the description of the clock Mike had made in woodwork classes at school in his Matric year. She said that he was trying to figure out a way that he could contact Lorna through this clock. He said he was not sure if he would be making it chime at the wrong time or make the chimes wrong, but he would find a way.

I asked Laureen, "Must I tell Lorna this?"

"No, he says not yet. You will know when he has done it," she said.

Mike's Clock that he made at school and now sits in the main room of Lorna's new home.

When I returned home, I recorded it in my journal and told Brian, and then forgot about it.

When Lorna and family finally moved into their new house and started unpacking, she told me one day, "I can't understand it; I have put a new battery into Mike's clock and I have reset it and put it on the wall, but it must have got damaged in the move, as it keeps chiming wrong!"

Of course, I knew why and I told her.

Some months later, Brian and I went to look after the children in Plett so that Lorna could come up to Johannesburg to see to some business affairs. It was irritating Brian that the clock was wrong and I think he had forgotten the reason. He changed it so that it was chiming correctly. I was upset with him, but I need not have been; it was only correct for two chimes and then it went back to chiming wrong! Lorna wants to keep it that way.

While Lorna was up in Johannesburg, she went back to the Bach Flower Lady. While she was there, she went to see the medium, Peter. He told her that Mike was there. Mike said that he was taking care of her and that he had saved her life twice while she had been driving and not concentrating. Lorna said that she was aware of both of the times that she had narrowly escaped having a serious accident. I could only say, "Thank you, Mike."

However, she only told me about one of the occasions. It was on one of her journeys back to Plett after visiting us here in Johannesburg. It is a long trip and it goes through several types of countryside, including the Karoo, which is semi-desert. The road is straight ahead for miles and miles, seeming to have no end. She said that, ahead of her, she saw a picnic spot where there is always a table, benches and a rubbish bin. It was dark and she did a very unusual thing for her, which was to stop and throw rubbish that had accumulated in the car into the bin. That probably slowed her down by a minute or two. She started up again and had not gone very far when she came across another car where they had had to swerve for three kudu crossing the road. These are very large antelope. The males have huge twisting horns. Had Lorna not stopped, she would have driven right into the kudu, which, in her little car, could have been fatal.

In South Africa, hitting animals on the road at night it is a very common cause of accidents. At the time, she said she did not know why she stopped to drop off the garbage, but she did. After Peter told her that Mike had saved her, she said she knew then that it was Mike who made her stop.

Some time after we had returned from Ntsiri, we had a phone call from Carolyn, Carl's wife and the game farm admin manager. She said we had an offer for our house from someone in France.

"He is very keen to get a river frontage; what is your price?"

We had not actively started marketing it yet and, in fact, not even made up our minds if we were going to sell. However, this move jolted us into action and it started a flurry of correspondence and sending photos over to France. He made us an offer that was difficult to refuse. Now the word was out: 'the Thomsons are selling'.

In no time, we had two other parties offering more and upping the price. As nothing had been signed, I notified the French man and he agreed to improve on the original price discussed. I was so unhappy about the thought of leaving this special place and, in particular, I felt I was deserting my son, having scattered his ashes there. Brian was still resolute that we had to sell in order to retire comfortably. I had to let common sense prevail, but it was with huge heartache that we finally accepted his offer.

I had not seen the medium, Peter, for at least six months and I wanted to go again, as I was missing the watch contact and had not recognised any other signs. I also wanted to see Peter again about selling Ntsiri. I needed to know how Mike felt. Mike came through very strongly and he said that I must not worry about the decision to sell. Peter said, "Mike says he has told you long ago that you must not fret about his ashes being there; they are long since gone with the rains. It is purely symbolic. If you make the decision to sell, he has no problem with it. It will be hard at first, but it is the right decision."

I left there feeling heavy hearted, but somewhat more at peace with our decision than I had been before. I had always seen this as a legacy for our children and grandchildren. In reality, because of the strict rules of ownership there, it could very well have become a vehicle for discord amongst family members and that was not what we would want.

I got home and told Brian of my time with Peter, and we decided to accept, with sadness, the French offer. One property sold to someone… sight unseen!

Not long after we had got that sale in motion, we decided it was time to try to sell Lorna's house in Craighall. For a while, she had a friend who had separated from his wife who was living there. Lorna had chatted to a mother from the primary school who was an estate agent and just mentioned that she was going to put the Buckingham Ave house on the market. Out of the blue, without a show house, she got a call to say that this lady had a buyer for her house. He had not seen it, but he owned the house behind Lorna's property and he had already bought Perry's house next door to hers for his mother. Perry was the wonderful friend who had come to her aid that awful night. He now wanted to buy Lorna's house as well and talked about demolishing the house, re-building the pool and keeping the garden for the children. He was willing to pay the market price. We could not believe her good fortune. This was an old house and, apart from the garden, had not been lived in or maintained for nearly two years since that fateful night. The property market had dropped drastically and we had visions of trying for months to sell this house and having to accept a much lower price than she got. In addition to the state of the house, there would, of course, be people who would not want to buy a house where someone had been murdered. Naturally, Lorna was only too pleased to sell it and have the responsibility taken from her. Another house in the family sold – sight unseen!

Chapter Twenty-Two

It was April 2009 when I got an email from Laureen to say she was coming up from White River for two weeks and, during that time, she was going to be holding two courses on how to learn to become a medium.

Again remembering what Lynda had told me and remembering my bad experience with the disliked medium , I was very keen to do it with Laureen, as I trusted her. It would be over two days, all day. I accepted and was looking forward to it.

I arrived in time to have a cup of coffee and a chat with the other people on the course and get to know them a little. There were four women and a young man. They were all very ordinary people and not at all 'woo woo'. Only one had experienced a personal loss. She was an Indian woman who had lost her brother. The others all thought they had the ability and wanted to expand on it. The one young man was the son of the hostess and he was there purely out of curiosity. At that stage, I had not told them about Mike.

The first day was very general. Laureen gave us exercises where she gave us photos of her family and her life and we would have to breathe deeply for a bit and then hold the picture and write whatever came into our heads about the picture. It may or may not have had a deceased person in the picture. I found this very difficult and it seemed to me that what I was writing was absolute garbage. I just wrote down, as instructed, whatever thoughts came into my head. Expecting to be way off beam, I told Laureen what I had written. To my utter amazement, Laureen could completely identify with and confirm what I had written. The other people had the same experience. The next day, we were asked to bring five photos of dead people and a couple of items that belonged to a deceased family member or a gift from them. I took photos of Mike, my mother and father, my late brother-in-law, Sandy, and my maternal grandmother, who had died many years ago when I was a small child. Strangely enough, before I had learnt to believe in communications with the other side, I always felt that I had a strong bond with my grandmother, even though she died when I was only five years old. I always felt very strongly that she was looking out for me. This was confirmed by the medium, Lynda.

For the first exercise, I gave someone a photo of Sandy. She said she was struggling with it. She sat with her eyes closed and was quiet, and then she said, "I am picking up a sudden death." *She was correct.*

"He was not young, but nor was he old," she said. *Correct*.

She continued, "I see sunflowers; I don't know why or what it is to do with this man."

I straight away knew that Sandy had come though. He always used to say that his farm labourers were just like sunflowers. They liked to sit in the sun and have their faces pointing to the sun and, as the sun moved, so the flowers moved. He said that is what his staff used to do when they thought he was not looking. When he died, the grandchildren put sunflowers on his grave and they gave Verna a little ornament of sunflowers. Ten years later, she still receives sunflowers from her family and friends in memory of him. Sadly, there was no message, but the validation was definite.

I was given the photo of the young man in our group as a little boy. I talked about him and I said just what came into my head. I described my daughter, Carol's, life at school, but I added a few other things. I apparently described him to a T, but I was not confident that I actually got a message about him or did I think those thoughts because I overheard a conversation during the tea break talking about someone being ADD. Carol was diagnosed ADD when she was at school, so I was able to describe her and her life. Laureen said I was given Carol as an example because that is what I knew. However, I was still uncertain of myself and not convinced. The latter part of the afternoon was quite different and totally convincing for me. We were each given a photo of someone. I gave the lady opposite me a picture of Mike. I had still not told them anything about myself or Mike's death. Straight away, she picked up things about him, his sudden death, and his three children. She said there was water connecting to his death, a river, dam or pond. *All correct*.

The lady next to me was supposed to read a lady opposite her. She held a photo of the lady's father. She said she had an overpowering feeling of love; she picked up the number twenty-seven, water and a red car. She said that she had a terribly sharp pain in the back of her head. The lady she was reading said she could not identify with anything she was saying. Laureen then said that the message then was clearly not meant for her. She then asked if it meant anything to anyone else there. Feeling a little uncomfortable, I realised, of course! *It was Mike.*

The twenty-seventh was the day he was killed.

The water, of course, was the pool.

The red car. Both he and Lorna had red cars.

The pain in her head was the gunshot.

She, too, was not able to give a message other than the fact she felt that he was sending so much love. I silently said, *Thank you, Mike.*

I was rather embarrassed that my son had dominated the session and I apologised for it. They were all so nice about it and said that he and I must have needed it.

At the end of the course, the other women wanted to make a circle and meet regularly, but I was not happy about that. I did not want to become immersed and more involved in communicating with spirits than I already was. I only wanted to keep in touch with my family and especially Mike.

When I got home, I gave it a lot of thought and came to the conclusion that, even though I may have the ability to connect because I want to, I do not have the confidence to differentiate between messages and my thoughts. Perhaps, as time went on, I might learn to recognise them, but, at this point in my life, I would rather go to someone who knows how to communicate and who does it on a regular basis. I would prefer for them to tell me things that I can identify and validate. I would also then be certain that it is not my own thoughts or wishful thinking. It was an interesting experience and I am glad that I did it, but I resolved to take it no further.

Having got that out of my system, I was happy to rely on one or more good and genuine mediums.

Chapter Twenty-Three

We attended the wedding of Mike Heeley, my friend, Pam's, son, who had introduced me to two of the mediums I have already spoken about. Mike was marrying Angela in April 2009. Sitting next to Brian and I was a very friendly couple. Her name was Vivian. I was standing in front of her in the queue for dinner. After several minutes of waiting, she gently put her hands on my shoulders and I heard a very caring voice behind me say, "You have a very troubled aura. I can sense you are carrying huge grief."

I was so touched by this and told her she was correct. Back at the table, we chatted and I discovered that she was a Reiki master. We had a really good rapport and she said she would be able to help me in the healing process. I went to her for three sessions and I definitely did feel stronger after I had been to her. I had never had Reiki treatment before and was somewhat sceptical about being healed this way, but I was willing to try anything. If nothing else, each session was an hour and a half of feeling relaxed, warm, in caring hands and somehow in another space. I think this was, in fact, a turning point for me. I started to get on with my life and find some sort of purpose for getting up in the morning, albeit always with a lump of lead inside.

As I began to feel stronger, I began to think about the Thomson family contributing somehow to the fundraising efforts for the trust, but I was unsure of how to go about it.

In South Africa, there are a number of theatres called The Barnyard Theatres dotted all over the country and, as mentioned previously, these had always been a favourite venue of Mike's for himself and his family. Each theatre is built like a huge barn, with long wooden tables and chairs in rows, and then single seats around the perimeter of the hall, with a long counter in front. The idea is that one brings along one's own picnic supper to the venue; however, drinks and alcohol are purchased from the theatre bar. After supper, the show starts and it is usually a fun-filled evening.

The Barnyards offer certain evenings of their shows for fund raising, but the fund raiser has to sell the tickets. I had been thinking along these lines when, once again, I was led to another, but even better, idea.

I was offered some tickets to a charity show (not at the Barnyard) called *A Handful of Keys*. This was a show of piano playing and singing originally written and performed by a very talented South African Artist, Ian Von Memerty, which had been extremely successful over the past fifteen years. The original was performed by two people on two pianos, Ian himself and Bryan Schimmel. This particular evening was a special performance celebrating their thousandth performance, with five people who had performed in the show over the years. The show was brilliant with such talent, including piano playing, singing and fun-filled humour. That evening, the funds were all donated to the Actors Benevolent fund.

Ian and his wife were not strangers to tragedy and heartache themselves. Their first two children were born with a genetic metabolic disorder called Maroteaux-Lanny Syndrome or MPS 6. If not reversed by bone marrow transplants, it is a fatal disease. Both children had undergone bone marrow transplants overseas and, sadly, their daughter, Valeska, did not make it. Their son, Oscar, survived, but had a relapse about six months later. He had to have a second transplant and, while on the operation table, his heart stopped. They worked on him for some time and he was resuscitated. Fortunately, Oscar suffered no brain damage from the procedure, but it did stunt his growth. He is now seventeen, but not much taller than a six-year-old. Miraculously, he has inherited his father's talent for entertaining. He may be small in stature, but, in personality and courage, he is a giant.

After the show, we met Ian in the foyer as he came to speak to the organiser who had sold us our tickets. We were introduced and I said to Ian, "We have met. Your daughter, Kasvia, was a friend of my granddaughter, Annie Rose. I met you on two occasions when you were collecting her from a birthday party."

Ian replied, "You must be Mike's mother. I heard about his death and I am so sorry for your loss."

We chatted for some time and I told him about the trust and how I was thinking of doing some fund raising. Ian spontaneously responded by saying, "If there is anything I can to do to help, please do not hesitate. We know tragedy and heartache and are very happy to help with fundraising." The Actors Benevolent fund had sponsored Ian and his family to go overseas for their treatment, so they valued what we were doing.

I went home with my brain working in overdrive. I contacted Ian, who asked me to contact his personal assistant, Charmaine, who would give me dates when he was available. She gave me a few dates, which I, in turn, took to the Broadacres Barnyard Theatre to try to find a matching date. This we did successfully and I booked Ian to do his *Captain Entertainment* show. He was very generous with his price that he was charging us.

I believe Mike had a hand in leading me to go to the *Handful of Keys* show on that day in order to facilitate this new partnership between us.

I then met up with Pat Tarr of the Broadacres Spar to discuss providing food for the show to try to make more money than just the tickets. She came up with really special platters, which we would be putting on the tables, and again I got a very good price.

This came at just the right time for me, as I had to undergo some ankle surgery and, as a result, was to be laid up, unable to get around for at least six weeks. I set to work, leg in a cast and raised on a stool, sending off letter after letter to everyone I could think of, informing them of our intentions and hoping they would support us and buy tickets.

The ticket sales went very well and, by the time the show was due to start, we had a full house. Just at the time we were preparing the programme, Ian sent me a message to put on the front of the programme that he had decided to include his wife, Vivian, as it was essentially a family show. This turned out to be a great decision.

I had managed to get quite a few great prizes to auction, mostly from game lodges where Mike had either worked or from people who knew him in the field. Also, Nicky Rattray of Fugitives Drift donated two days. Her husband, David, a very well-known conservationist and Zulu war historian, was also murdered in the same year, a few months prior to Mike. She was most supportive.

I managed to secure the services of a brilliant auctioneer, Brian Rogers, who did not charge for his time, but added to the auction some superbly made South African memorabilia for which he had a reserve price. Anything over the price he donated to the cause. What a find he was too!

Lorna and family drove up from Plett to be there, which made it such a special night for us all. Debby came up from Hoedspruit and Verna even flew down from Malawi. It was wonderful to have the whole family there in honour of the one we missed

The whole evening was a great success. The Barnyard had never been as full and there was such a palpable energy of love in the room that everyone who attended commented on it. Some people even said it was the best evening they had ever had! The success was due to everyone involved doing their best to make it a memorable evening.

I opened the evening with a welcome speech, followed by Allan, who gave a short overview of the trust and its achievements to date.

My opening speech:

Good evening everyone. On behalf of the Thomson family, I would like to welcome you all here tonight and to thank you for

the wonderful support that you have all given us. In our letter that we sent out about this evening, we said, "What better way could we honour the memory of our beloved Mike than to fill the theatre with friends and family who have supported us and held us up on this very painful journey that we have been forced to travel?" I am so moved and happy to say that, thanks to all of you, the theatre is filled to capacity and then some! Thank you. I think that there is only one single seat left unsold somewhere up there and many tables have more than the recommended number on them. If you have empty seats next to you, it is because of last minute no shows!

Now there are some people here tonight to whom I want to give a very special welcome... they are:

Stan Lorge and the Computershare staff who have been involved in the running of the trust in various ways. Unfortunately, Ursula Du Plooy and Susan Dreyer, who are a major force in the trust activities, are away in Malawi preparing for their next cycle challenge.

At Mike's funeral, we said that we would not let his death become just another crime statistic in this country, that somehow, somewhere, we would make good come out of it. Not in my wildest dreams did I ever anticipate that it would become a reality in such a meaningful way. That is all due to Computershare, their love, their energy and their amazing events.

Of course, I must welcome Vanessa Lynch, who has flown up from Cape Town to be with us. She is the instigator and inspiration behind the DNA Project.

I also want to welcome Lorna and our grandchildren, who have come up from Plett for tonight. It is very special to have them here with us.

My sister, Verna, has come from Malawi to support the family. I really appreciate her presence and support. Debby has travelled from Hoedspruit.

Thank you to you all.

Having completed the business part of the evening, I would now like to ask our son and Mike's brother, Allan, to come up and just give you a very brief resume about the trust and what we have achieved to date.

I hope you enjoy the evening.

Once again, I do not have a copy of Allan's speech, as he always talks off the cuff.

I received a lot of letters and SMSs from people who had been to see the show that evening to say how they had loved the entire event. Brian Rogers was brilliant with his auctioneering and earned us almost as much as we had made on the tickets and meal. All in all, we made a profit close to R140, 000.00. A drop in the ocean compared to what Computershare had raised, but, for a non-corporate function, it was fantastic. We were very happy.

On the back of the success of Ian's show, I decided to book him again for the next year to perform his show, *The Circle of Life*. It involved the beautiful dancing of Ian and his wife, Vivian, and various acts with their children. Kasvia, their daughter, dances with her mom, sings with her dad and performs with the family. Oscar, their son, dances with his dad and also performs with the whole familly.

From the start, the show was beset with problems. It was scheduled for the April holidays and I managed to secure the Broadacres Barnyard once again. However, just as I was about to start selling tickets, I was told that the show had to be postponed, as Vivian needed a knee operation. The date was rescheduled for 2 October. I then had to rebook the theatre, only to find that the Broadacres Barnyard was closing and would be reopening in the Lonehill shopping centre. I later discovered that it would not be opening there after all and I would have to book the Cresta Barnyard, which was nowhere near as big or as nice, but I had no choice!

I followed the same procedure as I had the year before, but found the selling of tickets far more difficult, as the economy had taken a dive and many people could no longer afford luxury spending. We did not do food this time, as it was going to make the tickets too expensive. Costs had gone up too much. Guests were to provide their own food, as is the norm at the Barnyards.

After a lot of hard work, nearly all the tickets were sold by the time 2 October dawned. I was very nervous, but the recipe was just right. Brian Rogers again performed his magic and managed to sell all the items donated. Poor Ian and Kasvia (his daughter) had the flu and were feeling awful, but, as true troopers, the show must go on and indeed it did! Only the family knew and, by interval, so did I. The show was brilliant and, again, that wonderful energy was there.

Brian Rogers was once again a fantastic auctioneer. He managed to get great prices for different donations this year. The only one that was a repeat donation was Fugitives Drift. This time, Brian and I wanted to bid on it. We were bidding merrily against someone from the back of the room. Apparently Sarah, Allan's wife, then pointed out to Allan, "You do realise you are bidding against your dad!" Neither of them could hear above the noise!

Allan finally got the bid, which we bought from him later in the month. One of the donations was for the now-famous private game reserve in Kwazulu Natal belonging to the late Lawrence Anthony, author of *The Elephant Whisperer* and two other best sellers.

In spite of my misgivings, this year, we made R150, 00.00! Better than the previous year.

I discovered that, by not serving food, a huge amount of stress was taken off me and it made no difference to the profit margin.

Once again, Lorna and family travelled up from Plett, Debs flew up from Hoedspruit and Verna came from Malawi.

My brother Malcolm's son, David, came from Natal with his girlfriend and two boys. Sadly, David lost his wife to cancer about six weeks before Mike was killed. I have often thought it just as well that we have no idea what is around the corner. Brian and I travelled to KwaZulu Natal for her funeral. We never dreamt that, in six weeks, many of the same people there would be coming to our son's funeral.

My friend, Bronwyn Paterson, called to say that, as a fellow vicim of crime, she would love to contribute to the evening and the ony way she knew how was to offer the services of her son, Angus, now thirteen. Angus was not only a very talented piano player, but also an equally talented singer. He had finished playing Joseph in the musical, *Joseph and the Technicolour Dreamcoat*, and also recently played a very special classical piece in a competition in Cape Town. All the training was current and he would not need extra rehersal. Ian, not knowing him, was obviously reluctant to let him sing without an audition and there was no time to have one, as Ian was flying up from Port Elizabeth the day before the show. However, he did allow him to play the piano. This young boy played like an adult professional and got a standing ovation! It is a pity that we could not have asked Ian sooner, as he would probably have let him sing as well.

The Paterson family being fellow victims of the Razor gang's evil activities made it such a fitting addition to the show.

When it was all over, I was left feeling very flat and decided that I would not be doing it again the next year. Perhaps, after a break, I may be able to do it again. All in all, it was just too exhausting and emotionally draining, and I was still, of course, working my way out of this dark tunnel I had found myself in since that awful night.

Chapter Twenty-Four

At the end of 2009, we broke ground on the stand where we were to build our new home. It started off on an amazingly traumatic, but 'lucky', break.

Brian had, at last, finished his plans on his computer and they had to be printed in a large scale to take to the builder for quotes and to the local council for their stamp of approval. This we did and made several copies. Our timing was perfect, as, three days later, disaster struck! Brian had been unable to sleep one night; he got up at about 2am to do some other work on the computer. As was his habit, he had his memory stick in the computer and saved his work. He returned to bed at about 3am, leaving the memory stick with all the house plans in the computer. Upon waking, Brian went into the office. His heart sank like lead in a goldfish bowl; his laptop and memory stick were gone!

"Not again!"

In the last few hours of darkness, someone had managed to pull the laptop and memory stick through the burglar bars without disturbing us. The window was right next to our bedroom window and we did not hear a thing! This time, he lost everything! We thought we were living in a safe, secure complex, with all-night security guards on patrol. Had we not had those plans printed the week before, we could not have built our house!

The plans were passed by the necessary authorities. The quote turned out to be acceptable and the builder was selected. This would be the fourth house that Brian had designed and built in our forty-five years of marriage. Brian and I were both warned that building was a nightmare and, to be honest, I was most apprehensive about it. Brian, however, had always concluded the deal with a handshake rather than signing a contract. He had built without hassle and, what's more, had remained friends with the builder to this day. He maintained that this would be no different. Brian again shook hands with the chosen builder and the building ball started rolling.

By the time the builders closed for Christmas 2009, they had laid the foundations.

2010 was a really busy and exciting year, one way or another. It was very rewarding for Brian to see his creation transformed into a reality. All those long hours of designing our dream house had produced something so special. We wanted a 'lock up and go' house with a low maintenance garden. We had fun choosing all the fittings and furnishings. I enjoyed designing the small garden and creating it with the help of one of my men, Reggie Lekgetho, who used to work for me when I operated my landscaping company. Reggie was very creative and particularly clever with rock work. The house had to be designed with a French Provence appearance to fit in with the estate theme. I set out to create a country feel on the inside. Because we had to excavate out of a hillside, we dug out huge rocks when doing the levels. I made full use of these beautiful rocks in my garden and, as a result, it all blended very well into the surroundings.

There is one incident associated with our move that I do think worth mentioning, as it could have been Mike or another of my deceased family members guiding me. Brian and I wanted to buy some good quality wooden desks for our new office. It was open plan with the lounge and has a lovely view overlooking the dam and Crocodile River. We felt that our old desks owed us nothing and had no guilt in ditching them! We went out looking for good second hand solid wooden desks, hopefully matching. We did not want the modern ones with chipboard and veneer. The first shop we went into was a second hand shop in an old northern suburb, Parkhurst. This shop has been there for at least thirty years. We went in, but found no desks, but left our names with the owner in case he managed to find some. As we were leaving, I looked above the door and, to my amazement, I saw a framed photograph that I recognised. I asked him to bring it down in order for me to have a better look with my glasses. Yes, it was a photograph taken in about 1914 of an old corrugated iron house on stilts. Standing on the steps were my grandparents, with their children in front of them. My father was there, aged about four, with his siblings! He was born in 1910. This house was in Lourenco Marques, known today as Maputo. I asked if it was for sale; he said yes, but he doubted anyone would want it. *I did.*

Why was I guided to that shop to have that picture put back

into family hands? Who was it who sent me? Ironically, that second hand shop had been there for as long as I can remember, but, a few months after we bought the picture, it closed down and no longer exists.

It was during this year that Laureen decided to come back to Gauteng. She was struggling to settle and make a living in White River. Perhaps the community was too conservative? It was good news for me! However, before she returned, Debby went to see her in White River. As the reading was Debby's, I do not know everything that transpired, but there were some interesting things that she related to me. She told Debby there was a birthday in the family.

"Yes, my mother's."

"Mike says that he is sending her a birthday present. It will be something small and yellow and will have something to do with a couch and she must not look for it. She will just find it."

When Debby called to tell me, she added, "Mom, Laureen did not say all of what I am about to tell you, but I feel that Mike is telling me this himself. I believe it will not necessarily be an actual gift of sorts, but will more than likely be something you just find, possibly when you sit on the couch. I am getting a vision of something as small and arbitrary as a yellow jellybean. Perhaps you will put your hand down the side of the couch and find a yellow jellybean or something like that. Of course, I am not sure, but this is the feeling I have. I really feel that it will be a matter of 'it's the thought that counts, rather than a specific gift.'"

My birthday came and went on the Saturday and, a little disappointed, I did not find anything yellow. However, on the Sunday, Verna was visiting again; we went to have an afternoon nap after lunch. She got up before me and was sitting in the lounge, but did not notice anything. A little later, when I came in, the first thing I saw lying on its own on the glass coffee table, next to the couch, was a yellow jelly baby. Yes, a yellow jelly baby! It most definitely was not there before, and jelly babies were not something that we kept a supply of in our house. Coincidence? I wonder? Jelly bean – jelly baby – it was close enough for me.

I was really thrilled to find it, but, once I had it, I was unsure of what I should do with it. I studied it thoughtfully for a while, thinking it was from Mike, and then I ate it! The best jelly baby ever and confirmation that it is not the gift, but the thought that counts.

Debby also related that Mike was speaking very strongly about his death. He said he does not want to be remembered as a gunshot victim, although it was the gun that finally finished him off[1]. He said the stab wounds were in vital organs and very deep and, in fact, had already ended things for him. He said he was running on pure adrenalin, as he was aware that some of the gang were already inside and all he wanted to do was to protect his family. Again, she was told he felt no pain, but was just focussed on what he had to do. Laureen kept commenting to

---

[1]Note from Debby: This reading has always bothered me and I could not understand why Mike should have been so concerned with being labelled as a gunshot victim and wanted us to rather focus on the stabbings instead. Mom, too, makes reference to receiving a similar message in one of her readings. I have battled to understand why this should make a difference to him and it has always sat uncomfortably with me. However, in reading through this entire manuscript when helping Mom edit her book, I have come to the sudden realisation that possibly the message was there, but incorrectly interpreted by both Laureen and myself. I believe that possibly Mike's concern and insistence on focussing on the stabbing as opposed to the gunshot was his way of trying to get a message to us that the autopsy had been insufficiently processed and that the report did not contain any information on him being stabbed, and he wanted us to know so we could try to get it corrected in order to assist with successful prosecution of the case. His unhappiness of being referred to as a gunshot victim was not in reference to us talking about the event, but was in reference to the actual autopsy report. In putting this in writing here, I suddenly have this incredible sense of peace and knowing that I have not had when talking about or thinking about that aspect of this reading, which further allows me to believe that this is the correct interpretation of the message.

Debby with total awe that it felt as though she was experiencing a Hollywood scenario where the hero, against all odds, with fatal wounds, was able to fight to the very end.

Laureen repeated to Debby what she had told me years before: that Mike had a very strong energy and was very easy to read and, in fact, very often dominated a reading and assisted weaker souls in coming through with their own messages too. His reference to the final shot was that it was a formality, as Mike thought that, even if he had been able to drown George Nyembe, he would not have had the remaining strength to climb out of the pool. All this was a repeat and reinforcement of what I had been told before by other mediums as well as Laureen. Is it not interesting that not only do I get the same message from different mediums, but that the same message can be told to two different clients? How can anyone question the validity of this in any way?

Mike also mentioned to Deb that he was with us at the Ian Von Memerty show. He asked her to tell me that he was there and he was very proud of me. He confirmed that I was getting stronger, but he was concerned about his dad, who tended to bury his feelings rather than confront them.

Debby, like me, went to see Laureen on a number of occasions and always came away feeling she had had a lovely long distance conversation with him. It gave her as much comfort as it did me.

We moved into our new home in November of the same year and we were both thrilled with the final result. In spite of my earlier misgivings, I was very happy that I had decided to move and enjoy the environment there for as long as we're able. For the first time in my married life of forty-seven years, I had a home with everything I had ever wanted, albeit smaller. To boot, I even had a small selection of wildlife and my own bit of 'veld' (South African word for natural grassland with wild flowers).

On our estate, we have dassies (rock rabbits or hyraxes), spring hares, porcupines, cane rats, which look like dassies with a tail, vervet monkeys on occasions and baboons in the mountains in front and behind us. There are many leguaans (monitor lizards that grow to the size of a very small crocodile) of all sizes seen all over the estate, as well as in the water. We have seen both the slender mongoose and the water mongoose. The bird life here is exciting to observe. We have a wonderful variety of water birds, as well as eagles, kingfishers and other bush birds.

It was time for me to see Laureen again, as I had not been to see her since she returned and I was getting those compelling thoughts again that I must go. I again had my breath taken away by her validations. She said, "There is either going to be a move or you have just moved." *We had been in our house for two months.*

Mike is saying, "You have honoured him three times in your new house, one outside and two inside." *I have.*

Firstly, I was given a beautiful charcoal portrait of Mike done from a photo. It is large one of him in a bush shirt with a herd of elephants in the background. It was done by Adie Parker, the daughter of a very good friend of mine. Adie is a bourgeoning portrait artist now residing in France and doing very well. It was a gift from her and I truly treasure it. She knew Mike at school and I can see the portrait was done with so much love. It has a wall to itself right outside my bedroom door and I see him every time I go into the room.

Secondly, Mike was busy making himself a new pair of front doors when he was killed. Lorna asked Brian and me if we would like to have them and use them in the new house. Of course we would! He had only just started to make them and we did not know what his plan was other than he had an open section in the top half for some sort of coloured or decorative glass. We had two beautiful birds done in stained glass. In the one door was a carmine bee-eater and in the other a woodland kingfisher. Both very colourful birds and the finished doors made from Rhodesian Teak are not only special, but turned out to be very beautiful. As Mike was a keen birder, this was a fitting tribute that worked well towards the hand-made front doors he had started.

Thirdly, when we left Ntsiri for the last time, I went across the river to where we scattered his ashes and I filled a packet with soil from the area. In reality, his ashes were long gone, but, for me, it was symbolic. I created a little corner in my garden where I put that soil, as well as some special rocks and stones that I had grown to love and know from around our house in the bush. I felt better about leaving him there, as I had brought some of him back. We also added the ashes of his beloved golden labrador, Charlie, who had lived with Allan and Sarah after Mike's death. Charlie had become very old and we finally had to have him euthanized to join his master.

Vaalie, Mike's rescue dog, who had been so traumatised at the time, had spent his last years with Mike's sister, Carol. He, too, finally succumbed to old age, had a stroke and had to be euthanized. In time, his ashes were also added to his master's spot in my garden.

Quite some time had passed that I had not had any physical messages from Mike. I thought that they had come to an end. One evening, I went into our bedroom and turned on the bathroom light. As I did so, the overhead fan started turning at a very high speed. The two switches are not connected and, when we do use the fan, switched on by remote control only, we do not use the high speed.

Was that Mike? Was that to be our new method of communication? I was hopeful.

Time would tell.

Chapter Twenty-Five

The year 2011 was a very sad one for me. My beloved brother, Malcolm, lost his very brave battle against cancer. We used to talk often about my visits to Laureen. After he had lost his son, Bruce, he had tried to see a medium in Cape Town and, sadly, that person was not of the same calibre as some of the people I had seen. He was put off and never went again. A few weeks before he died, Brian and I visited him in his home in Howick, and I was able to have a very meaningful conversation with him. We both knew that the end was near and I asked him if he was afraid.

He said, "No, I am not afraid of dying, but I am afraid of where I am going."

I tried to reassure him that he would be joining all of our loved ones who had passed before us. I told him that I would be in touch and he must promise me that he would come with Mike. He gave me a wry smile and said, "That would be nice."

He was worried that he was going to Hell, as he said had done some things that he was not proud of in his life. I tried to assure him that everyone had done things in their lives that they would like to wipe away. I told him what my belief about Hell is. I said that Hell is a man-made concept and that, in fact, Hell was here on Earth and that we had both been there when we lost our sons. I do not believe that, when one reaches the other side, one will be judged or condemned for one's sins on Earth as we are taught through religion. We may have to return to 'hell' on Earth one day and improve on the last time here. I acquired these beliefs through many of the books that I have read. They have always made more sense to me than my old school indoctrinations.

Since coming to this conclusion about reincarnation, I have recently read a book about a British lady, Betty Shine, who is a medium and a spiritual healer. She has been hailed as the world's number one spiritual healer of our time. She has sown a small seed of doubt in my mind, as she says she and her church have done a lot of research on reincarnation and she can find no convincing evidence that we come back to Earth. To confuse me even more, I later read her third book, *Mind Waves*, written when she was very much younger. In this book, she is most convincing in her belief in reincarnation. I do not know how she came to change her mind.

Dr Brian Weiss has written equally good books about his experiences in past life regression sessions he has had with patients. He is convinced there is reincarnation. Who is right; who is wrong? The jury is out; the debate still wide open? For my money, I would rather not come back, but enjoy being reunited with my family for eternity!

I do believe in a higher power or creator. One only has to spend time in nature and work with plants to see the magnificent markings and designs on birds, flowers and animals, as well as how all of nature is linked, one dependent on another, to think along the lines of a creator. The belief that one has to go to church, be reborn or any of that dogma that is purely related to organised religion is the only path to salvation is, in my opinion, far too prescriptive and egocentric. I believe that having to belong to a single group in order to get to Heaven is not the case. I have always found, when in a garden or in the bush, a certain calming of my inner being. What has, in my mind, been confirmed for me is the fact that, at no time since we have been getting messages from Mike has he said to me, "Mom, we got it wrong. You better get to church quickly, because I am having a tough time here."

I believe he would have done so if that was the case.

I saw Laureen in April 2011, four months after Malcolm's passing. She started by saying that there was very new energy there.

"Have you lost someone recently?"

How could she possible know if he was not there?

"Yes, I have; my brother."

"He is here and he wants you to pass on this message to his wife, Naomi. He says to thank her for all she did to help him when he was so ill. He said there were lots of ups and downs in their marriage, for which he shouldered a large amount of responsibility, but he said she had been wonderful to him at the end."

This was so true; Naomi was a star!

"Your brother wants to thank you and everyone involved in his funeral. (I did his eulogy.) He said there was lots of humour in it and that it was just what he wanted." Laureen had never heard of my brother before and there was no way she could have known about the humour. Malcolm had an unstoppable sense of humour and there was not a day that went by that he did not bring a smile to someone's face through a practical joke or prank phone call. This was portrayed at his funeral; there certainly was plenty of humour.

He said that he had been shattered at Mike's death and this is true. I mentioned earlier how he had sobbed and sobbed over the phone when we were eventually able to reach him in Mozambique. He confirmed he was with family.

For the first time, she told me something with which I could not identify and nor did it happen. She said that I would see a top, warm, white and fleecy, and not be able to resist buying it. It would actually be a gift from Mike. There was no sign of it then and I am still awaiting its discovery more than two years later.

I listened unbelievingly at what she had to say next. "You are taking his son on holiday with you. I see a lot of water, not a beach holiday, but never-ending water. Mike said he is over the moon about it and says thank you. He says he will be with you every inch of the way."

I was gob smacked, to say the least! We were about to join Allan and Sarah and their family on a cruise across the Atlantic (never-ending water) and we were indeed taking Nick, Mike's son, with us. We thought he would benefit from some male family company.

Mike was definitely with us. One day, I knew with a deep conviction that he was there. Nick and his cousin, Shannon, and Allan and Sarah went to ballroom dancing lessons on the ship, and Brian and I went to watch. As much as I would have loved to join in, as we used to love dancing when we were young, my fused ankle made it impossible. We were sitting on the side watching them and I turned to Brian. I don't know why, but I just knew and said, "Mike is here; I can feel him."

Brian said he did too.

Although Brian was at no time sceptical of my visits to Laureen, he had never accompanied me, as he always felt he might somehow spoil my connection with Mike. He was afraid that, by coming, his presence would ruin it. I managed to convince him that it could not and would never happen like that and I knew Mike would appreciate his visit. With Brian's consent, I called and made our appointment.

This visit was in October 2011, shortly after the second Ian Von Memerty Show and the 2011 cycle challenge. I am sure that Laureen did not know anything of the show, as it had not received any publicity and I did not approach her to buy tickets. I doubt also that she would have known about the cycle challenge, as she is not interested in cycling. Her passion is horses.

Laureen said, "I see a very large gathering with some very well-known people there." (I thought it must be the show.) "Michael is asking if you could feel his presence there that night."

Through Laureen, Mike said, "Mom, I am very proud of you, but you have done enough now. It is time for you to have some *you* time." I was grateful to hear this due to the stress the last show had put me through. I had found it very difficult to sell all the tickets, as I did this more or less on my own. I did not have the luxury of a booking agent or anyone else taking on the responsibility with me. In the end, I did have a full house, but it was hard going.

Laureen carried on, "He is telling me about another large event to raise funds. (The cycle challenge.) He is saying that it will get large TV coverage and that it will, in time, become international."

It did get large TV coverage and, at that time, Ursula was busy planning the next challenge to be in Egypt. This, however, had to be cancelled for various reasons, mostly political. We will be watching out in the future to see if it does go international.

Laureen then said, "Mike is concerned about Nick. He is very emotional at the moment and struggling with his school work. He is, however, doing well in sport at school." (That was true.)

"Mike says he communicates with Annie and she with him. He said that Megs would travel again overseas to her friend." (This did happen in July 2012.)

Laureen sat for a while listening intently and then said, "Two of the killers are going to be sentenced to life very soon, but not for Mike's case, but for two other family attacks. Mike's case will not be heard for a long time."

Mike says he knows that I write a lot. He likes that.

He said that his family has moved to a place where there is water and that they have a house with two levels. This is true. Their house in Plett is double storey. He says Lorna has different beliefs to our family, but she is slowly accepting things that she had rejected in the past. However, she may find it difficult to talk about it to some people. I believe this to be true.

Laureen surprised me again with the following statement. "His oldest daughter (Megan) is going to have teeth issues. She will be seeing an orthodontist and it will be a lengthy procedure."

This is true. Megan does have teeth that have not descended correctly, as not all her baby teeth have fallen out. She will need intervention when she is sixteen. There is no way that Laureen could have known that. It is also possible that Laureen got the siblings muddled, as it is Annie Rose who is currently having orthodontic treatment, which is going to be a very lengthy procedure.

"Megan is very bright and she will one day be a vet."

Time will tell, and I hope she is correct, because that is precisely what Megs would be brilliant at, as she has always had an extraordinary way with all animals from a very young age. However, not five minutes after writing this, I had a call from Megan. She had been invited to go and spend the afternoon in the theatre at the local vet with one other girl. They were allowed to watch some surgery. The other girl fainted and Meggie was enthralled and watched the whole operation! Is this the start of her career; helping out at the vet?

Laureen said that there is a karate connection and said someone will get an award in his name. She got the karate bit right, but, to date, there has not been an award given that I am aware of. However, perhaps the purpose of that statement was to plant a seed, as I have since donated two trophies in Mike's name; one for seniors and one for juniors.

She said that Mike said I have a wall of family photos and that the tree was an integral part of it. His words to Laureen were, "Tell Mom that I love her wall of family photos in her new house."

Laureen could not have known that I had insisted that Brian plan a wall specifically for my collection of family photos. They range from my great-grandparents on both sides and going through generations up to today. Included is the photo he was talking about, with the tree being an integral part of it. This collage was put together by Debby for Lorna. This is the tree that Mike always used to climb when he got to our house at Ntsiri. It is where his ashes were scattered and the plaque is attached to that tree.

Laureen asked us if we had any questions.

I replied, "Yes, please ask him if he was trying to contact me last night, as, when I went into the bedroom, I switched on the light and the fan started again. Was this his new method of telling us he is there?"

She replied, "Of course it is. He told you he was going to find another way."

Brian and I just looked at each other knowingly and felt a deep sense of comfort.

She ended off by asking if he had a receding hairline and demonstrated with her hands how it was. It was exactly as his hair grew. To my knowledge, Laureen had never seen a photo of Mike.

We were discussing the reading on the way home in the car

an hour later. Imagine our surprise when we turned on the radio for the news and it was announced that two of the gang, Razor Zulu and George Nyembe, had been sentenced to thirty years and twenty years respectively for the attack, rape and armed robbery of the Paterson family and another family where the husband was a pastor and his wife was raped. The pastor and his family had emigrated to New Zealand immediately after the attack. I bought the morning edition of the *Star* newspaper from a newspaper seller at the next convenience store at a filling station to see if by some chance she had seen it there; it was not reported. The sentence had been passed down that morning. I sent her an SMS straight away to tell her how 'spot on' she had been.

Many books that focus on angels and messages from loved ones often refer to the use of white feathers as gifts and signs of love and support, specifically when they are found in places that are not likely for one to find a feather. Our experiences have been no different.

In November, Lorna was busy upstairs wrapping up Nick's thirteenth birthday present. She left what she was doing to answer the phone and, when she returned, there was a white feather on top of the present. She called me immediately to tell us that Mike had left a present for Nick.

Just before we left our flat to move into our new house, Carol came to visit us. Prior to opening the front door, a white feather came floating down in front of her. It was a perfect white feather with no marks on it and also no line on the shaft where it would have come from the follicle. She was sure Mike had been greeting her as well. We still have that feather.

In early 2013, Debby went to see Laureen and had a

particularly emotional visit with her. On her way out, lying on the staircase in the middle of an office block with no nearby access to windows or an outside area with birds, Debby found a white feather lying at her feet. She is convinced that this was a message from Mike to give further support to the emotional messages she had just received from Mike via Laureen.

In April 2012, I went to see Laureen again. She told me that the gap between visits would become longer. I must never hesitate to see other mediums and that, when I felt I needed to go and see one, it would still be Mike urging me to go.

This time, she said that there was a new energy there from a man who had very recently crossed over. He died from a severe chest problem. I knew exactly what the energy was. We had just returned from KwaZulu Natal from one of our closest friends' funeral. We went to be with Gloria, as her husband, Duncan, had just had a massive heart attack and was not expected to recover. After undergoing a nine-hour operation, he sadly did not survive. Duncan came through and thanked us for all we had done for his family.

I could not in a million years have had more validation than I had received in the past few years that there is life after death and communication with loved ones is possible if only one is open to it.

When it came to question time, I asked what Mike thought about me writing a book. She said, "Oh, he says that is old hat. You told him long ago that is what you are planning, so he thought it unnecessary to comment." Then she blew me away. She said, "You are writing this book with the help of someone else." This was correct; my cousin, Graham, who is a journalist and author, is helping and guiding me with this exercise. How on earth did she know that?

The year 2012 was a difficult year for Allan and his family for a number of reasons. One morning, he and I had coffee together and it was a very special morning for me. We spoke openly like we had not done for many years, and it rekindled that bond we had when he was young. He admitted to me that he had never really dealt with Mike's death and that he had been burying it. I knew that, but had been unable reach him until that day. He had not liked me talking about going to see Laureen, so I had not told him of all the amazing contacts I had with Mike.

Allan looked at me with tears in his sad blue eyes and he asked me, "Mom, how do you deal with something like that?"

"I cannot tell you that, son, as I don't know the answer myself. What I do know is that I have had so much comfort from seeing a medium and having a 'long distance chat with Mike', which I would never have had, had I not gone to see one. I find it so comforting to know that he is still with us and that he is, to the best of his ability, still influencing his family through their thoughts. I can only explain it to you like this: one day you have a son who is so important in your life and the next day, without warning, he is gone. Without that contact, he would be gone forever with nothing but a great big, desperate void ahead. At least, this way, I am comforted by the knowledge that he is with us and he is commenting on what we are doing. It does not compete with having him here in person, but it sure competes with nothing but memories. I would love you to go and have a reading with Laureen and see for yourself. I hope that, by doing so, you will in some small measure understand why I do. Would you like to go?"

"Yes, I think I would. Will you come with me?"

Of course, I agreed to do so.

I would have liked Allan to go in without her knowing his surname, but if I was to be in with him that would not be possible. I called Laureen to see if she minded if I sat in with him, as he wanted that, and she said it would be fine. While we were making the appointment, she interrupted me and said, "Sorry, Di, is there a birthday today or in a few days' time?"

"Yes," I replied. "It is Brian's birthday today."

"Well, as you were talking, Mike came through to me and said that there was a birthday and he wanted to say 'happy birthday'."

Brian was sitting at his desk in front of me and I immediately told him before we rang off. He became very emotional and said what a special wish that was!

The night before we had our appointment, Brian and I were preparing for bed and, once again, the fan switched on, moving very slowly. I knew it was Mike endorsing all of the previous conversations and arrangements.

The next morning, we were both still in bed and we heard a 'click' and the light in the middle of the fan came on. Again, this can only be switched on by remote control or by pulling a cord on the fixture itself.

I said to Brian, "That must be Mike again. He has definitely found another way to tell us he is here."

Brian got up to find the remote in the drawer and switch it off, which he did and returned it to the drawer. He was still sitting on the edge of the bed when I said to him, "Look at the fan." It had started to rotate very slowly and then built up speed slightly and then just kept moving. We both acknowledged it to Mike and turned it off and it stayed off. It has not happened again. I am sure Mike was telling me that he would be there for Allan.

I drove in from Hartbeespoort Dam to Sandton, where Allan lives, in good time to collect him and get us to Laureen for the reading. Allan was very apprehensive and asked me what was likely to happen. I explained to him that there is nothing hocus pocus or 'woo woo' about it. Laureen would be sitting in a chair in a little room and we would sit opposite her. She would start by telling him how she works. He must not say anything unless she asks him to validate the messages she is getting.

We arrived early and did not have to wait. She was ready for us. Laureen explained to him that it was going to be harder than usual, as she knew Mike's story now and she would not be able to use any of the validations that she had used in the past, but Mike would come up with something if he came through. She explained that she has no control over who comes through and it does sometimes happen that no one does. She said that she would not look him in the eye, as seeing his expression can sometimes influence her thoughts. If she faced to her left, she would be listening to her and Allan's guides and, if she faced to the right, she would be listening to whoever had come through.

This was Allan's personal reading, so I am not going to repeat it in detail, but just outline some of the prominent and less personal issues that came up. Suffice to say, Mike did come through and one of the validations she gave was a strange one. She said that Mike was showing her a very feeble moustache, not a full-blown one. We could only think of my brother having a moustache, but not Mike. She was adamant that it was

Mike and she said it was a fun thing he was trying. She also spoke of a five o' clock shadow. It suddenly dawned on me that, in my garage, I have a bookshelf against the back wall and on the top shelf is a photo of Mike with a very feeble moustache and the five o' clock shadow. I see it every time I go into the garage.

Laureen told Allan that, very soon, he would be starting a new business with a new partner and that they would be very successful. Neither Allan nor I could think how this was going to happen under the current circumstances. We both tended to dismiss this information. However, it was not too long before Allan did get a new partner and his prospects were starting to look very promising.

As soon as I got home from our visit with Laureen, I found the photo, scanned it and sent it to both him and Laureen.

At the end of the hour, Allan said he was glad that he had come. I hope that he will now be more understanding and supportive of my continued visits to a medium.

Chapter Twenty-Six

2 0 November 2012 was selected to be the date for the report back of the 'fifth' annual cycle challenge that had just been held – now established as a regular and successful annual activity. Every year, the annual report back on the success of the cycle challenge is also combined with a detailed report back

from each of the Change a Life Trust beneficiaries. It is always an inspiring evening where the cycle challenge is reviewed and the various beneficiaries come from Cape Town, Natal, Port Alfred and Johannesburg to report to the people who have raised the money. They inform everyone there as to what they have achieved in the year, how the raised money is being spent, the successes and challenges, as well as what they are planning for the coming year.

This particular year, we invited our dear friends, Pete and Ronnie Black, to join us. We got there timeously for the allotted time of 6:30pm. As usual, it was sponsored by the JSE and held within the JSE premises. We walked into the foyer and registered our arrival at the registration table, and were all given our corresponding name tags. The drinks and finger snacks were being offered by smart waiters in their black and white attire.

Di, Brian, Pete and Ronny Black.

We were very warmly welcomed by Ursula, Stan and the organisers of the trust. Many cyclists came up and greeted us with a hug or kiss. The beneficiaries were there to give their unstinting support to the evening and they too came to greet us. There was such a tangible energy of love and enthusiasm permeating the room. I could feel Mike's energy with us.

After some time of mingling and chatting with different people, we were ushered into the auditorium for the proceedings to begin.

Gerald De Kock, the well-known in South Africa sports commentator and cycle challenge participant, as usual, opened the evening by welcoming everyone and reminding us all of the reason for the trust and its anti-crime activities. This was followed by a DVD of the cycle tour through the Waterberg reserve and mountains, which turned out to be very gruelling exercise, but apparently everyone loved it, riding through game areas and tackling steep mountainous roads and magnificent scenery to compensate for their pain!

After a short outline of the next year's plan was explained, the report back started.

Vanessa Lynch from the DNA Project opened the session with the news that she has, at last, got the draft Bill, which she waved in her hands and said that nearly all their requests were included in the bill and that, early in the New Year, 2013, they hope to have it ratified in Parliament. The DNA database would become a reality! This will make a huge difference to the solving of murders such as Mike's in the future, as well as other crimes. June 2013, the Bill is to be put to Parliament and they are calling for submissions from the public. We have embarked on a huge internet campaign asking for support. I hope to be able to report on the result before the book goes to print.

She reported that, last year, she told us that they had trained two thousand seven hundred policemen, security guards and rescue personal to secure the crime scene with the express intention of protecting and being able to collect viable DNA and, this year, they have now trained approximately seventeen thousand people! She showed us a clip of a very impressive and hard-hitting TV commercial they made on the Cape Town Station, where a large face was made on the ground with white river sand and a face cleverly sprayed onto it in black. When the train arrived and commuters started walking over it, it was steadily destroyed – exactly what happens to an unsecured crime scene. To Vanessa's joy and amazement, it had a tangible effect on the people, who suddenly realised what was happening and showed so much interest and interaction.

The university degree specialising in the forensic use of genetics, which was initiated by the project, was at first only available at one university – the University of the Free State – and is now available at another four. Vanessa has made wonderful progress and she acknowledges that, without finance from the trust, it would not have been possible.

Three other beneficiaries told of their progress, and they all brought young people who stood up and told their stories and how they had been either given a second chance or how they had their lives changed and were so grateful to the Change a Life Trust for the opportunity granted to them. Carol Podetti's I Choose to Change a Life organisation was one beneficiary whose ambassadors made an impact on me and reconfirmed what amazing changes are happening in my son's name. She brought in two youngsters; one was a young man who said that he had lost his way and was headed for a life of crime and prison and, through the Change a Life programme, he had been given a second chance and he was not going to waste it. He thanked Change a Life for his new opportunity to turn his life around. The second youngster was a young girl who had also taken a wrong turn in her life and fallen foul of the law. She also thanked Carol and the Change a Life a Trust for also giving her a second chance. She thanked them for showing her that there are people who care and who would have confidence and faith in her to turn her life around. She said that she had learnt through Change a Life that crime does not pay! One of the amazing coincidences with regards to this beneficiary is that the very first ambassador brought to a report back event within the third year of the challenge's existence was a youngster by the name of…. Michael Thompson! What are the chances? This was solid confirmation to us, as the Thomson family, that real benefit was being achieved as a result of the heartache and trauma we had had to live through.

Martin Dreyer, national canoeing and triathlon champion, showed a DVD on how his Change a Life Academy in the Valley of 1000 Hills had grown in Natal. Their activities had spread from canoeing to cross country running in the local schools. He now has some of his protégés working for him and helping with organising the running meetings in the schools.

Jan Blom spoke about his Change a Life Project in Port Alfred in the Cape. Jan's project focuses on taking care of children after school. He helps with homework, math and sport. In particular, he has developed a rowing team. He explained how it has grown so much that he desperately needs more ground and accommodation. This, he is trying to get with the funds from the trust in spite of difficulty with co-operation from the local council.

All through the evening, I was on a roller coaster of emotions. One minute, I would be sobbing inside, then the next, weeping openly, followed by laughter mixed with bursting pride, suddenly to be dropped to heart wrenching sadness again.

Finally, Allan, Mike's brother, spoke about the dojo and the project he had developed to honour his brother, and how it has progressed and grown in strength from year to year. The Kushido Change a Life project has brought in a pre-selected group of youngsters every week from the squatter townships of Drummond and more upmarket suburb called Cosmo City. These youngsters are being trained in the arts of Kushido. The reasoning behind this is that karate gives a person an extreme sense of self-confidence, as well as instils in them a belief in self and a goal to work towards. By working through the various stages and gradings, they are also learning the simple process that hard work and personal commitment bring rewards.

This simple lesson is vital if one is to aim to improve one's life and to avoid the usual pitfalls such as crime that poverty brings. Kushido karate, as a style, is a very non-aggressive style and is based more on defence than attack. One of the requirements when working towards your black belt within the Kushido style is to actually become a healer and to be able to heal people. Allan had two young men who had been with him since he started bringing in young boys from the squatter camp. They have now progressed to a green belt and were both inordinately proud of what they had achieved. They described how they had come with no knowledge of any life skills whatsoever, and they have learnt to respect themselves, and to persevere and make something of themselves. One young man was now at a media college on a scholarship and the other was at a local university studying to become a mechanical engineer. Both admit that these developments would not have been possible without the lessons, confidence and stability they have gained through their participation in the project and the vital life lessons learnt. All thanks to the trust.

What finished it for me was when Allan stood up he said, "This is a very bitter sweet evening for me, as, whilst I am so proud of what has been achieved in Mike's name, I would give it all up in a heartbeat to spend one more hour with my brother."

Good has triumphed over evil, but that short sentence said it all.

The fact that this was all happening because our Mike had been so loved in his lifetime and was brutally taken from us was very humbling. Ronnie and Pete were so thrilled to have been part of the evening and they said the whole event was inspirational.

Some time after the report back evening, the CEO of Rand Merchant Bank (where Allan was employed some years ago and who so kindly supported the family with a midday meal every day until Mike's funeral) contacted Ursula with a proposition. He had been at the cocktail evening and he was very inspired. He requested that Martin Dreyer expand his academy to Johannesburg. He then committed the bank to donating R1.5 million every year to the trust. This will ensure that they now raise a minimum over R4 million every year. It is awe inspiring how the Mike Thomson Change a Life Trust just grows and grows.

How does a mother translate the enormity of her personal grief to the sheer awesomeness of the good that is being generated in his name?

Chapter Twenty-Seven

I was well into my fifties when I lost both my parents, through natural causes and in their old age. I was devastated, but accepted that it was their time. I had one brief encounter with a medium I had seen on TV. She was promoting her book in a store and, at the same time, taking group bookings for a group session on the Saturday. I thought it would be nice to communicate with Mom and Dad, as I did miss them very much. Carol and I went on the Saturday afternoon. It was a disaster! I thought her a total fraud and never gave it another thought.

If I thought then that I knew what grief was, I was in for a big surprise. I had no idea. I have been to funerals of my friends' children and I felt for them and tried to understand, but trust me, I had no idea what they were going through. The grief one experiences with the loss of a child, compounded by the brutal manner of the death, has no words of description. The numbing, searing, agonising, crippling emotions that take over, you can only know if you have experienced it yourself. Only then can you begin to understand. It is a deep, dark hole that you think you will never be able to leave. It feels as though someone has thrust a jagged, blunt knife into your solar plexus and is slowly turning the handle.

One's mind cannot get beyond the fact that your son is gone; it cannot be true. This happens to other people. Slowly, it sinks in that it is true and does not happen to other people; it has happened to *you*.

You have to somehow find a way to continue living without him and go back to being the wife and mother you were before. The flashbacks of the scenes of Mike lying on the side of the pool, cold and dead, his weeping and traumatised family seem to permeate my brain no matter how hard I try to erase it. The sound of Allan's voice telling me that Mike was dead continues to haunt me in the dark, lonely hours of the night when sleep eludes me for one reason or another. It is now five and a half years since it happened, but, still, it does not go away.

Since leaving school, I had made my choices about life and religion. I did not find comfort and solace in the confines of a church. I do, however, acknowledge that, for many people, that is their way of dealing with life and the problems it throws at us all, and I would never argue the point. If I can have a real contact with the spirit of Michael, I see no reason why millions of people should not have a contact with the spirit of Jesus and find that inordinately comforting. To each his own. Something Deepack Chopra once said on a *Larry King Live* show that struck a chord with me. Larry asked him if he was religious. "No," he said. "Religion is for those afraid of going to Hell. Spirituality is for those who have already been to Hell." That is me.

Long before we lost Mike, I learnt to find comfort and my spirituality through nature and have always been happiest and at peace when in the bush or a garden. I was not exposed to the afterlife in any sort of way. However, my mind started to open by the TV show with John Edward and his readings. I was so impressed with him and his authenticity. Mike and I used to stay up to watch it; mostly not together, but we would share our thoughts on it later. Gradually, I found myself thinking that there may be more to life than death; there may well be an afterlife.

Some of the books I have read say that your life is planned by you before you incarnate. I am not yet convinced that I agree with that, but the thought has crossed my mind that, should it be the case, then was Mike subconsciously preparing me for what he felt was coming? I have often thought in my life about coincidences that have led to certain outcomes that have made me wonder if it was a coincidence. I now tend to think not.

Soon after Mike was killed, I started reading books about death and the afterlife, as I desperately needed to know where he was and would he be okay. (Once a concerned mother, always a concerned mother.) I learnt that there were many people who had found themselves communicating with a deceased loved one. We had already been getting our messages; I realised that I was definitely not imagining things and I was not losing it. I was led to the various mediums as I have described to you, and my story of growth began. It did not take me long to know it was real and decide that I would not heed all the people who were either sceptical or naysayers. I will forever be grateful to the friends and family who encouraged and believed me and to those who gave me phone numbers.

I realised that we were not alone with our experience when I read a book on my Kindle called *Quit Kissing my Ashes* by Judy Collier. It is about her son, Kyle, who died in a car accident I think. She, too, had messages from Kyle and she used to go to John Edwards' readings and others. I just so identified with her story that I would urge anyone who wishes to validate what I have been saying to read her book as well. You will be rewarded.

By communicating with Mike, I have been able to channel my energies into positive activities rather than wallowing in my misery. To all those who grieve, I am guided to share my experiences with you in the hope that you, too, will take the steps to make contact with your departed loved one. I have read in many books written by people who have far more contact and knowledge than I that our loved ones actually want us to communicate with them. They possibly have and still do try in the many ways I have mentioned, but, because we are not open to it, we do not see it or we attribute it to some other earthly or inexplicable reason, and, eventually, they give up. I treasure my contact and I am so relieved it has not stopped, although it is not as frequent now as it was when I first started.

I do need to add, and, as many a true and valid medium will tell you, they are unable to guarantee that the loved one you want to contact will and can come through. We all have different energies both in life and, it seems, in death. All the mediums I have visited have stated in the beginning that some spirits have a far stronger energy, they come through more forcefully and are easier to communicate with, and others do not necessarily have the energy to do so. We are exceptionally privileged that Mike has such a strong energy and connecting to him has been so easy and, in fact, once again, just about every medium I have seen has commented on the strength of his spirit energy and that not only is he able to dominate the energy in a session, but he uses his energy to assist others to come through and communicate as well. Knowing the man Mike was in life, the deep love and intense energy he had in everything he did and everything he was, this comes as no surprise to us at all. Of course he would be continuing this energy in death as well.

The concept and understanding of energy has been an enlightening journey for me. When we pass on into the spirit form, we still remain an energy, but on a much higher frequency. Spirits find it much easier today to make contact through electronics and electricity, as they, too, are a different frequency of energy. Our lives today are surrounded by electrical energy waves and it is apparently much easier for spirits today to connect with this energy. They have to lower their energy to make the contact that we can recognise. This is one of the reasons that so many people who have experienced communications or messages from their loved ones have done so via electronic means, whether it be the lights, the TV, cell phones, computers or other electronic devices.

When we were visiting Lorna and the children in June 2012, we were all in the kitchen one Sunday evening and the lights flickered; not once, but twice. In a different time, I might have brushed it off and said it was just power surges, but, under the circumstances, I was sure it was Mike, because we were all together and he knew I would acknowledge it. We have recently come to suspect there is another method that Mike is using in our home. We have a light in the lounge that, every now and then, we switch it on and it just does not work. When we first moved in, we called in the electrician who installed the light and he could find no fault at all. When he was there, it worked. Twice since then in the two years, it has done the same thing. The last time, I said, "Mike, if it is you, please make it work again the next time we turn it on." It did.

That is where an open mind is helpful.

We all grieve differently and we should not judge others if their methods of coping differ from what are considered 'normal'. In more primitive peoples and in days of yore, it was a part of man's culture to communicate with their ancestors. Over the years, through religion and other means, it has been stamped out from Western cultures. It is my hope that we return to those days. Not only for ourselves, but for our loved ones who have crossed over and wish to stay in touch. I cannot stress enough the comfort it has brought me knowing that Mike is with us and that, at any time, if I ask him to come through for me, he will. It is so comforting to know that those I know who have passed are all right and will be there to help me cross over when my time comes. I have no fear of dying now.

I know that, without Mike's help, I would not have been able to come through my dark, desperate depression. I could not have found the strength that I have, to do the things that I have and, above all, not have had the strength to relive everything in order to write this book with the purpose of helping others to – *have an open mind.*

Chapter Twenty-Eight

It is 23 January 2013 and my book is nearly done. I once again have had this recurring and insistent thought to see the medium, Lynda, again. I called in November 2012 and the first appointment I could get was January 2013. This time, I was prepared to wait, as I firmly believed that Mike was telling me to go to her. Something good would come out of it, I was sure. She told me at the time of booking that she was very tired and needed a break, so she was going away for a while and would not be starting until late in January.

On my way there, I mentally spoke to Mike and asked him to be there and to bring my parents and my brother, but I stressed to him that my priority visit was to have some contact with him.

Lynda has moved to a lovely home in Edenvale east of

Johannesburg. Her reading room is certainly not 'woo woo' anymore. It is totally separate from the house in a lovely peaceful garden setting. After greeting me, she explained to me that she was very tired and had not had her holiday, as urgent requests for readings had stood in her way. She explained to me that, in the past year, her clientele had changed. In the past, it was people who wanted to contact their loved ones who had died through illness and natural causes, with the odd tragedy in between. Lately, it was people coming to see her as a result of losing a loved-one to suicide and to murder, and she found herself emotionally drained from so much tragedy. She felt that sometimes she was too tired to give the client a quality reading.

With that information, I was already starting to feel anxious that perhaps she would not be able to bring Mike through. This time, she said my chakra was a little clogged and wavy. I do not pretend to really understand what and why that should be. Once again, she sat in the middle of the room and I sat on a comfy couch not far in front of her. She sat with her eyes open looking at the ceiling this way and that. She kept saying, "I am not getting anyone." While she was desperately trying to match her energy to that of the spirit realm, I was desperately begging Mike to please not let me down.

It seemed to take forever before she said, "I have your mother and father dropping in." She described them very well, but said they had just come to greet me and tell me that they are with me always. Lynda then said that she was confused, as there were two energies there, each wanting to be recognised. The names seemed to be the same, beginning with M. She then said she was shown the letter C, which she interprets as dying of cancer. She also said that she felt there was a heart condition as well. This was all true and, of course, I recognised it as my brother, Malcolm, coming through. She picked up that he had a good sense of humour. I was amazed when she asked me if his name was Malcolm. Of course it was and that confirmed that my darling brother was also there to greet me. There were some more validations, but no messages per se. She then said, "This other energy is pushing through: is his name Michael?" One must bear in mind that it was three and a half years ago that I saw her. She could not remember any of her readings from so long ago and, in fact, she had not even remembered me. My relief must have shown on my face, as she said, "The dominant member of the reading will always let other family members come through first, but, when he feels that enough of his time has been used, he pushes through."

Once we had confirmed Mike's presence, she proceeded to give validations. Again, she repeated the whole story, including the stabbings, gunshot to the head, fighting in the water and more than one attacker in the gang. She says that he feels that, if he had not fought back, the outcome may have been different, but he says that he could not have avoided the first shot in the side. He says that, by doing what he did, he did save Lorna and the children from a lot worse happening to them, so, knowing that, he would do it again.

She correctly told me of his children and what sexes they are. He said that his son is growing so tall and he is so proud of him. He is very proud of the way all his children are dealing with their loss and how compassionate they all are. This is so true. He said that his wife is doing a wonderful job of bringing up their children and that is why he married her.

As I described earlier in the book, the messages are not fast in coming. She looks up to the ceiling and concentrates hard, then speaks. Through Lynda, he told me that I have created a little corner in the garden in his memory, which has the soil from where his ashes were scattered at the game farm. He said to reassure me that, whenever I go and sit there, I must try to feel him with me, as he is always there with me. I do.

I did have a very surprising validation. She asked if one or more of his siblings had been to the coast for a holiday. Of course, we had all gone down to Shelley Beach for Christmas. She then asked if we had gone to a water sports park while there. We all did. We spent a whole day at the Water Park at the Wild Coast Casino in Port Edward. Mike's two sisters, Debby and Carol, Sarah, and her three children, Brian and I spent a lovely fun day there. Mike then said he was there with us. The strange thing is, we talked about him and said how he would have loved to bring his family to the park for the day.

To my huge disappointment, I missed out on a big message due my own lack of thinking beyond the box. She kept telling me that I am doing charity work and, when I said 'no, not really', she insisted that I was. But, because I was thinking along the lines of actually doing charity work on a daily basis, I kept saying no. At the end, when we were just chatting, I told her about the trust and she said, "That was the charity he was talking about." Oh dear, I did not pick up on that and I lost an opportunity to hear what he thinks of it all.

I had to smile, as, several times, she said that Malcolm wanted to say something and then she would say 'no, Mike is dominating', and, at the end, I hardly got what Malcolm wanted to tell me. I cannot control it any more than she can. However, I think he wanted to tell me something about one his daughters. He linked it with horse racing. This daughter was recently in a relationship with a jockey. I realised it was his daughter, Robyn. As soon as I recognised the validation, she said he had faded away. By this time, Lynda was really tired and felt she was not able to give me enough, so the reading ended. I was disappointed.

Whilst the reading was not as powerful as the first one, it was good enough for me. The interesting thing about the meeting was that I discovered she has recently written and published a book about mediumship called *Butterflies and Umbrellas* (which I bought there and then) and she was able to give me so much information and advice with regards to publishing this book.

Is that why Mike sent me there?

I have read her book, and what has come out so strongly is that my spiritual journey, while being unique and new to me, is, in fact, not. There are so many people who have lost loved ones and been to see her and have come away so incredibly comforted. They are convinced that their loved ones live on in spirit and that they are still part of their lives, although not visible or huggable.

If my book has failed to persuade a sceptic or a grieving person who is afraid to go this route, I suggest you read further and Lynda's book would be a good recommendation.

Epilogue

The Court Case

I was recently told that, as no DNA evidence was found on the scene, there is not enough to convict the gang that murdered Mike and robbed and traumatised Lorna and the children. The investigating officer had then said that they were examining a brown jersey for DNA; however, they are not quite sure who the jersey belonged to. I was, at the time, highly sceptical that, after five years, the police should find a jersey that could incriminate the accused. Subsequently, my scepticism has been proven correct and, in fact, it has now been confirmed that no DNA evidence is available.

I was concerned that Mike's laptop that was found by Ollie – the private detective we had hired – was not mentioned in the evidence as far as I know. I have contacted Ollie again and asked him to follow up on that

Ollie called Brian and me to his offices and, before we got there, they would get Mike's case from the archives and follow up on what has happened. He was able to tell us that Karl, his assistant, recently had a meeting with the investigation officer, whom Karl assured me is doing the best he can to get the case on the court role. Karl, however, gave us the bad news that there is just not enough evidence to indict the rest of the gang, so only two may be indicted. I believe that I have reached the end of the road as to what I can do to make sure the case is not lost in the archives and forgotten. I will, however, continue to draw attention to it until there is some justice.

Through Karl's investigations, I have recently found out that there is no longer a strong case against George Nyembe, as the confession he made, which he refused to sign, should have been taken to a magistrate to stamp, which would have made it stand up in court. What actually happened was the policeman just took it back to his desk and wrote his own report about it and put it in the file. This, apparently, will *not* stand up in court. The investigating officer is apparently going to visit George in prison and try to get him to sign it now. I am, however, not optimistic of the outcome of that endeavour!

Razor Zulu, the leader of this terrible group of gangsters, is now denying that he was in the pool area with George, but says it was Maxwell Keza, who was shot and killed previously. Conveniently, he cannot answer for himself and, therefore, it looks as though Razor will get off even though we *know* he was there and the leader of the gang!

There is a chance that Stoffele might be indicted on the strength of being correctly identified by Lorna at the first ID parade. Sadly, at the second one, she did identify four and only two were correct. This is not a good thing, as the defence lawyers will crucify her and try to prove her an unreliable witness. The fact that she had been totally traumatised and told not to look at them all the time is apparently not taken into consideration. I am so concerned about this, as we have seen their bullying tactics and I really do not want Lorna to have to go through this when in court. Our private detective has assured me that, should this case go to court eventually, he will prepare her for the sort of interrogation to which she may be submitted.

With all contributing factors as listed above, it now stands that only two may be indicted and the rest will get off. I have one consolation and that is that Razor is behind bars for thirty years for the rape of Jamie. Apparently, in this country, no one ever serves the full thirty years; they are released after twenty-five years. In my humble opinion, the damage caused by these men remains with the victims and their families forever, whatever the crime committed, be it rape or murder. The perpetrator does not deserve the knowledge that it is, in fact, *not* a life sentence. Razor boasted to Jamie that he had AIDS; with a bit of luck, he has a death sentence anyway.

We hope that, in the future, this sort of injustice will be prevented because of the establishment of the DNA database and the professional collection of evidence and the protection of the crime scene. Thousands of people who could arrive first on the scene have already been trained by Vanessa and her team in preparation for the time that DNA will be used as a tool for conviction and that there will be a DNA database. We are very hopeful it will become a reality in the very near future.

I continue to press for justice. Since being told that there is no DNA, I have heard nothing from the police regarding the case. My information comes from the private detectives and a lawyer who keeps tabs on the case for me.

I was recently in contact with Shelagh Smith, whose husband, Terry, was murdered the night before Mike in the same suburb. She, too, is still waiting for justice and has the same complaint that she is not kept in the picture at all. Terry's children have engaged the services of one of South Africa's top crime detectives, Piet Byleveld, who has now retired from the force. He is of the opinion that he was killed by the same gang. If this is so, it is a very clear indication of the impunity in which Razor Zulu and his gang go about their business. After viciously attacking and killing Terry one night, it bothered them not one iota to go straight out the following night and do the same and then, three nights later, they attack the Patterson family and Razor rapes their daughter. Clearly not one ounce of remorse and concern for what they were doing or whose lives they were destroying. These men deserve to be removed from society for eternity, as they clearly have no ability, nor empathy, to be part of it in a positive and constructive manner.

The Trust

Computershare has made sure that this trust will continue well into the future. It will continue to change lives and, whatever great things Mike achieved in life, they have been surpassed by what is being achieved in his name in death. I can only say that a huge sense of pride wells from deep within and, while my pain will never be assuaged, I am comforted by the knowledge that hundreds of children's lives will have been saved from a life of poverty, hardship or, indeed, crime. Through this great trust, **Mike has indeed *changed lives* and will continue to do so into the future.**

Mike's Family

It has taken the family five years to settle in Plettenberg Bay and begin to thrive. Lorna is facing her future with courage and doing a sterling job of being both mother and father to their three children. Mike must be inordinately proud of his children and his wife, who lost the most exceptional husband and dad, gone through hell themselves and come out the other side stronger, braver, kinder and more loving, and well on their way to success. All of the children are doing so well at school and, in themselves, have become a supportive and cohesive, devoted and protective little group. They have shared grief and trauma together and the bond that they have developed will last them a lifetime.

Megan is now sixteen and a very beautiful young lady. She is bright, works hard at school and is good at sport.

Nick is now fourteen, a tall, handsome young man who has a laidback, strong character. He has his father's love of children and is in demand for helping out at functions where young children are. He is very good at sport and representing his school in the first team for cricket and plays hockey for his school area team. He is following in his father's footsteps without the physical backing of his dad being present. Lorna is giving him all the encouragement and opportunity that he needs and we are all very proud of his achievements.

Annie Rose, who was only seven at the time, has grown into a lovely young lady who is very diligent with her school work and has the results to show. She is also enjoying her sport and, in particular, she loves drama and singing. She is excelling in both of these fields. Annie has always spoken openly of communicating and connecting with her dad and she continues to do so today.

I am sure that Mike is guiding them all through spirit as well.

Mike's Siblings

Their lives have also been irrevocably changed, but they are coping with their grief and, in their own individual way, doing good and ensuring that their brother did not die in vain.

Brian and I

Through our grief, we have grown closer together, stronger and hopefully better human beings. The pain will never go away, but we are learning to cope with life the way it is. My friend, Pat Tarr, described the way she feels, which is exactly the way I do. "Life goes on, we face each day as it comes and there are times of joy with the rest of the family. However, true happiness will never be ours again, as the edge has been taken by the loss of our beloved son, Michael Roy."

We both find joy in seeing him live on through his children. Each one of them has something of their dad that we can recognise in the course of their development.

The journey that we have been forced to take has led me down paths that I never thought I would follow.

When my parents died, I was devastated. However, they were old and ill, so I could not wish for them to live longer. At that time, I was not interested in seeing mediums or communicating with the other side. Whilst I missed them, I found their passing much easier to accept.

I cannot ever explain the depth of my loss and grief when I lost Michael. The desperate urge to find a medium was something I had not experienced before. To know it was Mike asking me to go and to receive the messages that I have has convinced me totally that there is life after death and it is possible to communicate in a limited manner with your loved ones who have passed. It has given me so much comfort and has helped me immensely to reach a point of acceptance (I do not like the word closure). This new knowledge compelled me to write my story in order to help others who are facing unbearable grief to feel comfortable about following the same route. Do not listen to the naysayers; they simply do not understand the need and they also speak from a point of ignorance of the subject.

I would like to add at this stage that, because a lot of what

I have told you of the various visits to the different mediums seems to have always been the same message, you may be asking yourself – why keep going back to get the same message over and over again? What is the benefit in that? I have only outlined and discussed this aspect of the readings with you in order to share with you and show the consistency of validation from one medium to another. Each of the readings was filled with additional and extensive personal messages and information that I have not felt necessary to share and have refrained from doing so for the privacy of our family.

I have been warned with genuine concern from dear friends to be careful of getting involved with evil spirits. I can say with absolute certainty that this will never happen. I only want to link up with my family through a genuine and a reputable medium who has long since learnt to reject the evil spirit, if there is such a thing.

One of the first books that I read after losing Mike was *Reaching Through the Veil*, about death, grief and communication with loved ones in spirit, by Linda Drake. It was inspiring, and she said, "With any type of grief, you know you are on your healing path when you think of your loved one and the previous tears are replaced with a smile as you remember all the wonderful memories you hold in your heart." If that is true: I am getting there.

I also read *Conversations Beyond the Veil, Heaven's Gift* by Jasper Swain. This was the true story of Jasper Swain from KwaZulu Natal, who lost his son, Michael, and how Michael managed to get hold of him. I identified so much with his story, with the following parallels. His family had never met death head on so violently before; neither had the Thomson family. Both children were called Michael and both sons were in their thirties. Both were successful achievers and had a great future ahead.

Jasper had the same overpowering feeling that almost became

an obsession to see a medium: as did I. However, the method of Jasper's message is somewhat more bizarre, but nevertheless just as convincing as my experience was. The day after his son's death, he had this overpowering thought that he must go to Sezela. He did not know where Sezela was and he could not think why he should go there, so he pushed it to the back of his mind. Something kept repeating to him 'go to Sezela; go to Sezela' until he could no longer ignore it. He decided to go. It was on the south coast and about an hour away from his home in Durban. He found Sezela to be a large sugar mill with a large estate surrounding it. At the security gates, to his amazement, he was told that Mr. Merrington was expecting him and he was told where to find him. As Jasper walked in, Mr. Merrington met him with the following words: "Ah, you must be Jasper Swain. Mike told my wife to expect you and, not ten minutes ago, she called to say you were on the way."

This book, more than any other that I have read, resonated with me and convinced me that I was on the right path.

What have I learnt on my journey that I was forced to take? I have learnt that no one is immune to tragedy: it can happen to anyone at any time. I have learnt that death is merely a transition. The body is discharged, but the 'person' we loved and knew is still with us, but only on a different level of energy. It has taught me to look death straight in the eye and no longer be afraid of it. It has taught me that Mike is not 'dead'; he has merely left his body. I have had far too many validations proving he is with us at all times and that he does influence our lives by telepathic thoughts, creating paths for us to follow and learn for ourselves what we need to do.

In spite of all these discoveries, my grief remains profound. The splintering of my heart will be with me forever. I think that my experience has taught me to be accepting of life as it is thrown at me with an inner calmness that was not there before. I just know that, to be judgmental of people, their looks, their religion, their body shape and their behaviour, is wrong: we do not know their story. I have learnt that we cannot change the past and we cannot control the future, so we have to live for now and accept what *is*.

I know that the day to day things that stress us are really nothing that cannot be fixed.

There are far worse things in life and I have been there.

Appendices

The Mike Thomson Trust

"The sad reality is that there are fifty deaths every day in South Africa as a result of violent crime. Many people feel angry and threatened, yet feel apathetic and hopeless due to the enormity of the problem."

Stan Lorge, CEO, Computershare South Africa

Below is a statement taken from the trust website:

Computershare South Africa established the Change a Life Mike Thomson Trust to sponsor anti-crime and crime victim support initiatives following the brutal murder of Senior Manager Mike Thomson at his Johannesburg home on 27 September 2007.

The Mike Thomson Trust commemorates Mike's remarkable community spirit and commitment to children by funding grassroots projects aimed at combating crime, as well as providing support to victims of crime, with a special focus on children. Computershare provides seed capital to the trust and co-ordinates fundraising activities, such as the Change a Life Cycle Challenge, in order to generate additional funds.

The trust is dedicated to a peaceful future for all South Africans. It supports effective grassroots programmes that are judged to be efficacious in dealing with the causes and symptoms of crime.

Victims of crime can apply to the Mike Thomson Trust to receive counselling as well as financial support, if they have no means. The trust also supports programmes aimed at improving the lives of orphaned and vulnerable children whose hopeless circumstances mean that many are drawn to crime.

Change a Life Cycle Challenge

As I mentioned earlier, the first cycle challenge was held in 2008 and just over R2 million was raised. I will take no credit for following information. I have taken it directly off the website, as it is impossible for me to add anything to improve it myself.

Change a Life launched in South Africa with the Change a Life Cycle – an exhilarating three-day cycle along the Zambezi River, which took place from 4 to 9 September 2008. In total, eighty-one senior company executives stepped up to the plate by not only contributing R20, 000 each to Change a Life, but showing the determination to conquer four hundred and fifty bruising kilometres on the saddle in aid of combating crime.

What transpired was three camaraderie-filled days as four designated teams shared thrills and spills, aching muscles, cold beers, laughter and tears as they wended their way from Victoria Falls through parts of Zimbabwe, Botswana, Namibia's Caprivi Strip and Zambia. Cycling past herds of elephants, enjoying sunset cruises along hippo-lined rivers and drinks under star-studded skies was all part of a day's experience. And on the energy-sapping last day, they conquered an exhausting two hundred and twenty kilometres, powering their way along the banks of the Zambezi, from the Caprivi Strip into Zambia, then finally over the famous bridge back to Victoria Falls. This was the *big* challenge of the tour, a bruising ultra-ride that tested the fittest athletes, broke bicycles, brought men and women to tears and highlighted the overwhelming nature of true camaraderie.

When the last group collapsed off their bikes after fourteen hours in the saddle to a celebratory welcome in front of the Victoria Falls Hotel, the real spirit of Change a Life was demonstrated. This three-day cycle and five-day journey had changed the perspectives of the eighty-one participants and forged lifelong bonds of friendship. Importantly, too, it had raised nearly R3 million after costs for Change a Life – the biggest sum raised in any cycle event in Africa.

Computershare matched, rand for rand, all donations raised for the Change a Life Cycle, doubling the funds received from cycle participants. The nearly R3 million was channelled to the Mike Thomson Change a Life Trust, which funds grassroots projects that help to prevent crime in South Africa.

2009 cycle challenge was no less successful.

Faced with a tougher economic climate, and the precedent of a spectacular 2008 cycle tour that collected R2.3 million for charity, the organisers of this year's Change a Life Cycle were undaunted. Sponsors stepped up to the plate and the sixty-two participants didn't blink over the R22, 000 entry fee – although knowing little other than that they would be based on the luxury Rovos Rail train, cycling for four consecutive days on road bikes. This year's *Mystery Tour* really did remain a mystery despite a dizzying pre-calendar of events, newsletters, training rides and a marketing campaign dispensing tantalising hints at the possible location of each day's ride.

Words cannot do justice to the stately sway of a Rovos Rail carriage, and even the most stressed out executives soon surrendered to crystal-clad drinks and the clink of silver on bone china in the dining carriages. Daylight brought a thermometer showing one degree Celsius, and kilometre after kilometre of quiet roads with good tar surfaces leading the cyclists away from a railway siding in *Moerengon*! Road signs pointing to towns like Hopetown, A Hundred Windmills and even the lunch stop at the vast Vanderkloof Dam did not really pinpoint the location. Apart from enjoying koeksisters (traditional South African fare) in the right wing settlement of Orania, much of the day was spent sorting out the pecking order within the three cycling groups on the remote roads of the Northern Cape. That night, the train's journey was interrupted for a spectacular track-side feast on a bed of carpets and brocade cushions under a zillion stars.

Sumbigriver was the following day's destination, which turned out to be the Gariep Dam (Gariep is the traditional name for the Orange River). The Southern Free State brought smooth tar, quiet roads and just enough wind and undulation to keep us focussed, whilst we entertained ourselves with a ghoulish game of identifying the road kill. No expense or effort was spared in preparing the spectacular tea and lunch stops, and, that afternoon, the stand-out moment was the radio broadcasts ringing out from the support vehicles that the 'Boks' had won the Tri Nations series! *Hooray!*

That night's route briefing was again vague about where the next day's ride would be, but the altitude charts said it all: with more than three hundred kilometres already in the legs, two thousand three hundred metres of altitude gain over less than a hundred kilometres was going to hurt! Daybreak left the cyclists anxiously looking up from Maseru into the huge mountains of Lesotho. Tracing the Makhaleng River along the A3 road to the Mohale Dam, they faced the appropriately named God Help Me Pass (2318m), followed by Blue Mountain Pass (2641m). Although the first lot of cyclists reached the Mystery Lodge at the top well ahead of predictions, the real story unfolded in the triumph of determination over gravity for those further back in the field who doubted they could do it, but did!

The last day's riding started among more familiar towns in the Free State, and with 'only' sixty kilometres to ride. The climbers had their moment of glory the previous day; this day's ride was to end in a thrilling sprint against the train to the end point of the tour. It was touch and go, but SA cycle champion Malcolm Lange managed to add another victory to his career tally of over four hundred wins.

At the spectacular gala dinner, there was hardly a dry eye when surprise guest PJ Powers (very well-known and talented female South African singer) called all the hotel workers and support staff, including three of Martin Dreyer's protégés, up on stage to join her in singing *Feel so Strong*. We had conquered mountains, made lifelong friends and raised R3.5 million in the process – this truly was a tour to change lives.

Computershare, the JSE, Kelly Group and Sun International were the primary sponsors of the 2009 Change a Life Cycle.

Route

This year's Change a Life Cycle was a Mystery Tour, so the route was a closely guarded secret. All we revealed was:

- Day 1 will be a full day of travelling as cyclists get to know one another and unwind from the stresses of the office.

- Days 2 and 3 will be long cycling days of 145 km each, but the ride will be gentle and undulating. Click on the links to see what happened.

  http://www.youtube.com/watch?v=JSKSejvAJMo

  http://www.youtube.com/watch?v=eBR1sIqAT7s

- Day 4 is 100 km long, but this is the big hill day and those who haven't trained properly will feel it.

  http://www.youtube.com/watch?v=BjXO4RYPnjE

- Day 5, the last cycle day, is a fun day – only around 60 km long – but there is a twist!

  http://www.youtube.com/watch?v=impnE7pma1Q

The final gala dinner takes place on the evening of 14 September and cyclists will return to Park Station around midday on 15 September.

I wondered how on earth Ursula was going to pull another one out of the bag, but she did! 2010 continued her tradition of producing amazing events.

The Warm Heart of Africa Embraces the 2010 Change a Life Cycle Event

Nearly seventy captains of industry took part in the 2010 Change a Life Cycle Tour in Malawi, raising nearly R3.5 million for the Mike Thomson Change a Life Trust in the process.

Poverty is pervasive throughout Malawi, the 'Warm Heart of Africa', where the average monthly income is just under R300. But so are hope and joy and a warm sense of community spirit that touches all who visit this charming and beautiful country. It was a fitting destination for the executive participants in the 2010 Change a Life Cycle, who set off from the comfort of their homes for six days in the heat and dust of Malawi, and returned having changed the lives of others and, in many cases, transformed their own.

Stan Lorge, CEO of Computershare South Africa, describes the 2010 Change a Life Cycle as: "Brilliant, exhilarating, hugely emotional and a lot of hard work. We are delighted to have raised nearly R3.5 million this year, which brings the total amount generated over the three years since launching the event to nearly R9 million." As a major sponsor, Computershare Australia matches, rand for rand, all funds raised.

The Change Life cyclists take time off each year to cycle together in a beautiful location whilst raising funds to help combat crime in South Africa. Their financial contributions to the Mike Thomson Change a Life Trust help fund crime detection and victim support initiatives whilst providing hope and inspiration for those who lack the resources to transform their own lives.

The 2010 field, as with previous years, was a Who's Who of South African business, with CEOs, directors and senior managers of companies sweating it out in their pelotons as they churned through the Malawi miles. For the sixty-nine cyclists, the gruelling four hundred and eighty kilometre route brought with it equal parts of agony and ecstasy – ecstasy at the surrounding beauty and camaraderie amongst the group; agony at the stomach-churning hills and the excruciating pull up to Zomba Plateau on the final day. As they powered through the baobab-studded landscape, the cyclists were overwhelmed by the enthusiasm of local people, who often ran alongside them on foot or challenged them on thick-wheeled local bikes.

As part of the social contribution made by Change a Life, thirty-five bicycle ambulances, manufactured with steel sponsored by Mac Steel, were donated to rural villages to improve access to local health clinics and hospitals. Malawian Government representatives warmly thanked the tour for choosing Malawi as its 2010 destination and for bringing such benefit to its people.

Route

Our route in Malawi is four hundred and eighty kilometres long; it's not too hilly (except for the last day…) and the individual days are not too long (well, perhaps the second day…). As for the roads, they are in great condition and usually carry very few cars. Add to this smiling and friendly local people and some stunning scenery. It's a sure recipe for success. We will cycle for three days, starting off from the capital, Lilongwe, and ending atop the spectacular Zomba Plateau.

Cost

Each cycle participant has paid R27, 000 to enter, with all proceeds going directly to the Mike Thomson Change a Life Trust. Computershare has again shown its commitment to combating crime by matching, rand for rand, all funds raised.

Below is a sample of some of the letters received from the cyclists.

I am sitting at my desk, sipping an early morning cup of coffee. This is something I have done most mornings for many, many years. Yet the feeling is an unfamiliar one. It might have something to do with the fact that I am wearing a soft cotton shirt and not the figure-hugging Lycra I have recently become more comfortable with. But I don't think that is what it is. It's a wonderful feeling made up of memories. It's a smorgasbord of the crisp clunk of a Campag gear change; the creaking moan of high quality wheels as the peloton stands as one to tackle a gentle rise and to relieve pressured nether regions; it's the ever present, but permanently distant, African haze; the soothing chatter and laughter of children who seem to be everywhere, miraculously and instantly quadrupling in number should you stop for any reason; the gentle and constant buffeting of wind; it's the hour after hour of banter from close friends and soon to be close friends; it's the quiet request from the captain to do duty in the wind or assist a mate taking a little strain; it's the plunge in a cool pool to relieve a too tired and too hot body; the ice cold gin and tonics not normally prescribed as a re-hydration drink, but perfect in Malawi; the painful pleasure of the skilled masseuses' hands as they iron away the knots after every marathon stage; it's the constant surprises of every spoil every day and night – all unique, special and ridiculous in the amount of thought and effort that went into each one; it's the wonder and slow realisation of what a wonderful country

Malawi is, slow because it takes a while to see through the poverty in order to see the wealth of friendliness, the pride, the cleanliness, the resourcefulness, the beauty and the absolute charm that is, perhaps, the real Malawi.

But, maybe it is none of the above that has caused this new feeling. Maybe I just can't put a finger on it. Maybe I don't need to. All I know is that the change is a permanent one and it is definitely good.

Mike Chapman

When we left Johannesburg on Friday, we were on a mission to go and change lives in Malawi for the benefit of the Change a Life project. Little did I know how much it would change my life. The tour in Malawi touched me in such a profound way. To be surrounded by remarkable individuals such as Dale and Linda. Their perseverance and tenacity in dealing with the cards that life dealt them brought tears to my eyes and will be my constant inspiration. It also was very touching to be giving back to the community in Malawi. We arrived there with big fanfare and hopefully the small contribution made by us will also change some of their lives. Thank you very much to you all for an amazing experience. Your immaculate planning and attention to detail was visible every step of the way and appreciated and admired by all. It has been a privilege to cycle to the beat of Africa.

Kobie Hamman

Well done again on a great 2010 Change a Life Cycle Challenge. You, Computershare, your staff, the sponsors, the other support staff, the project beneficiaries and the cyclists keep alive Mike's memory and make a big impact in his name. Mike would be proud to be part of something like this.

Nigel Payne

It really is a great honour to be part of the Computershare Change a Life family and being fortunate enough to be able to contribute to the worthy causes that you have chosen. I sincerely hope that this event will continue for years to come and that you and your team grow from strength to strength.

Granville Rolfe

Thanks once again for getting me involved; you have certainly changed my life!

Gerald de Kock

Thank you very much for what was a true highlight for me. I thoroughly enjoyed the experience from departure to arrival. It was truly world class!

What was Ursula going to do in 2011 to keep up the standard? The final report back was as impressive as ever and the enthusiasm of the participants continued. The fact that the website entry was not as detailed as previous years by no means detracted from the success of this adventure.

Lives were again changed... this time in Malawi as well as South Africa.

Change a Life Cycles to the Wild West

The 2011 Change a Life Cycle event (2 – 7 September) proved to be an adventure of a lifetime – from hot dusty roads to wonderful desert camps, from pain and agony to celebration and ecstasy. The seventy executive cyclists selected to go on the tour travelled across the full expanse of the Namib Desert, explored deserted beaches and towering sand dunes, and partied under star-studded skies. There were the customary surprises along the route, and a combination of exhaustion and exhilaration strengthened the bonds of long-lasting friendships, which have become a key feature of the event.

Route

The five hundred and thirty-kilometre route started in Windhoek on 3 September and headed westwards across the Namib Desert before ending in Walvis Bay on the fourth day.

- Day One was a hot one hundred and twenty-one kilometres.

- Day Two a gruelling two hundred and one-kilometre trek.

- Day Three saw the cyclists enduring sweltering heat over a hundred and eleven kilometres through the Namib Desert.

- Day Four was just a hundred and one kilometres long, providing a spectacular end to the tour as the cyclists pedalled along a well-groomed salt road with the Atlantic Ocean in view.

Cost

The Change a Life Cycle Tour can only accommodate seventy cyclists and, due to its popularity, entry is by invitation only.

The 2011 fee was R27, 000 per cyclist and Computershare matched all funds raised from cyclist entry fees. Sponsors' generous donations funded the costs of the cycle tour, which enabled it to become fully self-sufficient for the first time this year, with 100% of the fees and matched funds channelled directly into the Change a Life Trust for recipient projects.

Below are some of the comments from participants.

Feedback

We at UTi, and me personally, together with Dirk, consider ourselves very fortunate and privileged to have been involved with the 2011 version of the Change A Life Cycle Tour; it was indeed a life changing experience, so professionally organised, in the company of excellent people in an excellent part of the world. I know you strive to offer your demanding riders a different experience every year, which you no doubt did in 2011; the tour was not only different, but certainly was even better than the first tour that I was fortunate to participate in – and that was life changing! A big well done and a big thank you to both of you and that special support team you lead who just get it done so well no matter the challenge.

Gavin Rimmer
President of UTi

Another phenomenal Change a Life Cycle Tour under the belt and another feeling of awe! Every year it gets better and better in different ways, but what remains impressive is the change that is evident in the participants themselves. It's wonderful to ride with old friends and see how the tour has changed and moulded them. And to make new friends. The reputation of the tour itself within the business community and the profile it has achieved directly as a result of the vision and dedication of the two of you is unsurpassed and it is a great privilege to be part of this legacy.

Diane Radley
CEO of Old Mutual Investment Group SA

Thank you again for establishing and running Change a Life. I am so pleased to be part of making a difference in the lives of so many people via the charities we support, and am looking forward to the feedback session. What started as a charity funded by a cycling event has become a community – thanks to your leadership and commitment. Thank you also to Computershare for all you put into the process. Regarding this year's cycle – even though it has already been said – it was magnificent and flawless – thank you and well done. I think we will get a 100% return rate for next year. I look forward to being a part of this special family for many years to come.

Nigel Payne
Chairman of Companies

A quick note of thanks. Once again, an outstanding trip thoroughly enjoyed.

Stephen Horwitz
MD of Central Welding Works

This was, for me, the best tour yet and I express my thanks for the efforts you and your team went to, to make this such a special event. The logistics of creating something special out of a very harsh environment cannot be underestimated and your team did you proud in how they brought this together. Part of the amazing experience is how your back-up teams supported us and here again it is so easy to overlook this. Well done to them all.

Alan Hutcheson
Executive, CEO of Tracker

Thanks once again for what was yet another truly unforgettable experience. I keep thinking that you have set the bar so high that it will be impossible for you to maintain, let alone exceed, the standards that you have set. Yet you do so exponentially each time. The uniqueness of this experience lies in the fact that so many people with disparate backgrounds are united in pursuit of two common goals – their passion for cycling and the great projects that the Change a Life Trust and, indirectly, each participant, supports. The life-changing effect operates on these two levels – the participants and the projects.

Leonard Harris SC
Chairman of Peregrine Holdings

Thank you for another brilliant tour. As always, the Computershare team did an outstanding job and you should be very proud of them. Their attention to the tiniest detail, personal service and intense personal interest in the tour always amazes me. It is something very special. The Wild West Tour was different and is going to quite difficult to top! Ursula, I guess that is your challenge for next year. Thank you for letting me be a part of this very special charity – it does change lives!

Geoff Pinnock
National Audit Leader for Deloitte & Touche

It is very difficult to put into words once again and thank you and the team for the most magnificent trip and organisation. When I had the opportunity to address the people as captain of our group, I don't think people realise how much work and time is put into an event such as this. We were spoilt beyond any expectations and each venue and night superseded the previous one.

The closing night in the desert was unbelievable and not

even the weather could put a dampener on it, and many of us had the after affects to show. Once again, from my side, it was an honour and a privilege to be part of the tour as a participant as well as being able to contribute to the sponsorship through Macsteel.

Granville Rolfe
MD of Macsteel Trading

It is hard to believe that another tour is something of the past. Thank you very much for yet another life-changing experience. It was simply superb – the route, the scenery, the activities, the accommodation, the attention to detail – all leading to the most amazing camaraderie amongst everyone. I am privileged and proud to be part of the Change a Life family.

Kobie Hamman
Branch Manager: Johannesburg of Sanlam Private Investments

Well done to all; what an amazing trip. As you know, I have done many similar events, but you guys top them all.

Stuart Loxton
GM of Retail Affluent Special Projects for Old Mutual

I just wanted to say a massive thank you to you, Stan, and the whole team for staging another amazing event. I absolutely loved the whole experience.

John Dixon
CEO of Draftfcb SA

Thanks again for organising an amazing trip. I am sure you will receive numerous letters thanking you for what is truly a world class event, all of which would still not do the professionalism of the event justice.

Philip Mellor
Commercial Director of First Freight Couriers (Pty) Ltd

Thank you for extending the invitation to be part of the Change a Life Cycle Challenge. At the time of accepting the 'challenge', I surely had no idea of the impact of this unique cycle event on my life. It definitely got me off the couch and onto the saddle. Apart from the health benefit, I am now longing to be out on the road on my bicycle. I feel privileged to be part of this matchless event and its worthy causes. Congratulations on organising such a successful event. Your attention to every detail made it a memorable experience and one I will remember for a long time.

Danie Greyling
MD of IML Interactive

A sincere thank you for a very special Namibian cycling trip. As always, you and your team have produced an outstanding event full of interesting and exciting experiences. The attention to detail, different terrain and incredible camaraderie that continues to grow and will surely keep us all coming back for more. As time goes on, we've become extremely passionate about the organisations that Change a Life supports and I look forward to the feedback session in November. It also amazes me every year how we come together to make a difference in other people's lives and have also ended up making such huge changes to our own lifestyles. Congratulations on a wonderful event. You've certainly raised the stakes for next year!

Hilton Guy
MD of Creative Equipment

A *huge* thank you to and your team for giving me the opportunity to participate in this year's tour! The event was flawlessly and meticulously organised, and it was a real privilege to be able to enjoy the Namibian countryside with all of the logistical support just miraculously taken care of. Every day presented new challenges and fantastic surprises! But I guess the highlight has to be getting to know you and the rest of the cycling team – what a fantastic bunch of people. I have built many new relationships that I will treasure for a very long time. All of this in aid of a really worthwhile cause. So *thank you* again!

Nic Kohler
CEO of Hollard

You must be suffering from post-tour depression like the rest of us! It was an amazing week and thanks to you and Stan for the opportunity to be part of it.

Just a quick note to compliment you and your team on yet another wonderfully successful tour. I am well aware that such events do not just happen and so I complement you for all the efforts made in every respect.

Derek Watts

This was the first year that Derek Watts of Carte Blanch actually participated in the ride.

The Change a Life High Five Tour

The 2012 Change a Life Cycle Tour returns home for an epic journey that will take the Change a Life cyclists through the rugged terrain and pristine landscapes of the Waterberg.

Aptly named the High Five Tour, the fifth Change a Life tour promises the greatest challenge yet, with five days of cycling over five hundred and fifty-five kilometres of undulating roads and through bushveld. Cyclists, riding alongside sporting hero Martin Dreyer and renowned presenter Gerald de Kock, will climb five thousand metres during the course of the tour and may even encounter South Africa's Big Five en route.

Participants who have come to appreciate the challenge and adventure of the Change a Life Cycle Tour will be accommodated at the luxury Legends Hotel with its legendary golf course designed by champions, and will experience dramatic twists, unrivalled in the history of the event.

Of course, the highlight of this annual event, which is supported by South African business leaders, is the opportunity it creates to transform the lives of hundreds of beneficiaries of the Mike Thomson Change a Life Trust.

The Route

The first cycling day will cover a hundred and twenty kilometres of mostly flat road, with a moderate climb over the final twenty-kilometre stretch to the imposing entrance of the spectacular Legends Golf and Safari Resort in the Waterberg. We then cover a hundred and forty-eight kilometres of varied and undulating terrain to Ellisras. Our next day offers the greatest challenge, with a two hundred and fifteen-kilometre undulating ride through bushveld to Vaalwater and then back to the Legends resort. Our final cycling day involves seventy-five kilometres of cycling, finishing with a mad seven-kilometre uphill time trial dash.

When this is over, the trust will have raised close on R15 million in five years. I wonder how many charities can boast that?

What makes these events even more remarkable is that no salaries are paid to the people running the trust from the monies raised. Computershare pays for them!

Mike must, together with his family, be in total awe of what is taking place in his name.

There are no words to describe what these two have done to make the simple statement '*We will not allow Mike to become just another statistic in the criminal files in South Africa. Somewhere, somehow, we will make some good come from this tragedy*' become a reality.

Thank you is never enough!

The Mike Thomson Change a Life Trust Beneficiaries

I mentioned the first beneficiaries in an earlier chapter, but there have been changes and, of course, there has been progress.

Below are current beneficiaries, who have done remarkable work in their field. We have lost one because it is no longer run by the founder and that is one of the conditions of the grant. The one lost is sadly the rape crisis clinic. It is something this country desperately needs, but the trust is unprepared to risk funds being misappropriated by people with the wrong agenda.

The DNA Project

The first and major beneficiary is still the DNA Project.

Vanessa Lynch launched this project in 2005 when her father was brutally murdered in their family home. Vanessa is a lawyer and was horrified to see how the crime scene was destroyed and absolutely no evidence was collected; in fact, it was destroyed by everything being hosed away. This lack of police work resulted in her dad's killers never being found. I have explained how we became involved with her project. The fact that Vanessa was now working with a sustainable financial backing, I am sure, made her task that much easier and encouraging. However, it is her dogged determination that has brought her to the point where the South African politicians have accepted her ideas and the first draft to create a DNA database and to train the police to take DNA from crime scenes is about to be heard in Parliament. It has taken her five to six years to get to this point.

While the Powers That Be were dragging their heels, Vanessa most certainly was not! She and her team have been holding workshops all over the country, training 'first on the scene' on how to secure a crime scene and obtain DNA.

Over a two-year period, ten thousand people who are involved with policing will be reached. That includes security guards, paramedics and, of course, the police. There are, to date, thousands who have been trained and are ready and waiting for the laws to be passed. Mike's sister, Debby, had a hand in training many in Limpopo. Already, state of the art laboratories have been set up, which has already reduced, to some degree, the backlog in the huge queue for forensic work that is waiting. In addition, a university degree in genetics has been implemented in the Free State. The first graduates have already completed their degree. There are now four other universities that will be offering the degree.

"The Department of Genetics at the University of Free State offers undergraduate courses in genetics where the science of heredity is studied on the molecular level (DNA and gene expression), the cellular level (studies of chromosomes) and the level of the organism (population genetics). At undergraduate level, genetics forms part of the introductory biology at first year level and is presented as a complete subject from the second year. At post graduate level, students may specialise in forensic genetics, conservation genetics, population genetics, cyto taxonomy, molecular systematics, behavioural genetics or a combinations of these fields."

When the laws have been passed in Parliament, it will be said that Vanessa Lynch made one of the largest contributions to the combating of crime, solving cases and putting criminals behind bars in the history of South Africa. This is one lady who will go down in history for changing the face of policing and convicting in this country. I hope she is recognised and given her due accolades. Mike would be so proud to be associated with her.

I recently wrote to Vanessa to ask her exactly where they are right now with the legislation and to tell me just how much the Mike Thomson Change a Life Trust had helped. This is her reply:

Hello Di,

Hope you are well.

Thanks for the feedback and I do hope that they are able to find something on the jersey. (Explanation of the jersey was given in the Epilogue.)

Update on legislation is as follows: The Portfolio Committee for Police (PCP) finally accepted the DNA Policy, which will underpin the drafting of the second version of the DNA Bill. The DNA Policy was accepted on Wed, 13 June 2012, with the proviso that, once the Minister of Police has signed off the policy, the state law advisors must be instructed to have the DNA Bill ready for review for the committee by no later than the end of August 2012/ beginning September 2012. The DNA Policy recommended that South Africa establish a DNA database as a criminal intelligence tool, to aid in fighting crime and to enhance public confidence while taking into consideration peoples' constitutional rights. The DNA Project was extensively consulted in the drafting of the policy and we are extremely happy that most of our recommendations have been included. Read here for latest update in respect of the legislation, which will provide you with a very clear picture of where we are at: (the draft bill we are hoping will be ready for review by beginning of September) – http://dnaproject.co.za/blog/ dna-policy-on-new-bill-accepted-by-parliamentray-committee.

I have also attached an excerpt from last year's report given to the Change a Life trustees, which sets out what the trust has done for the DNA Project.

In respect of 2012, below is a brief summary of what has happened to date – there is plenty here for you to choose from to write about. None of this would be possible without the incredible support of the Change a Life Trust.

Take care and lots of love,
Vx

Martin Dreyer Change a Life Academy

Martin Dreyer, who is seven times a Dusi champion and South Africa's multi-sport king, has demonstrated how to change lives. Martin had what seemed to be an impossible dream – to groom ten underprivileged youngsters living in the Valley of a Thousand Hills in KwaZulu Natal to become leaders in the world famous Dusi Canoe Marathon. After competing in the first cycle challenge, his dream came true. He applied to the trust for funding, which was granted. In the space of four short months, eleven of his protégés came in the top fifty and two in the top ten.

Since then, Martin's Change a Life team has gone from strength to strength, competing in top canoeing, mountain bike, trail running and other multi-sport events. They have become well known in their arena. In 2011, they took the first, second and third places in the non-stop Dusi section. Not only have the top performers been able to take home food parcels weekly, but three young men have actually earned enough from their winnings to build houses for their families.

In 2012, Martin launched a cross country Running League in the Valley of a Thousand Hills to encourage hundreds of local school children to aspire to greater heights. His Change a Lifers are mentors and leaders who encourage the youngsters to improve themselves – Martin is confident that a whole lot more young people will become sports stars. They are just waiting for the opportunity and chance to prove themselves!

I Choose to Change my Life

This is also called The Valued Citizens Initiative, launched ten years ago by Carole Podetti Ngomo. It is a turnaround programme that helps youngsters in conflict with the law. In the past ten years, the VCI has trained more than three thousand five hundred educators, four hundred and twenty thousand school children from one thousand six hundred and five public schools across Limpopo, Gauteng, Free State and KwaZulu Natal. It inspires children to respect and adopt positive values, to take responsibility for their civil rights and to abide by the rule of law.

I Choose to Change my Life selects youngsters with leadership potential from the VCI youth diversion programme, which is supported by the Randburg, Johannesburg and Wynburg children's courts.

Of the five thousand young offenders who go through the juvenile courts each month, about one and a half thousand are channelled into diversion programmes such as VCI. These youngsters, between the ages of thirteen and twenty-one, are encouraged to develop a positive self-image, to rebuild the family relationships, learn communication and develop emotional intelligence.

I Choose to Change my Life is a six-month leadership course for youngsters who have shown potential on the diversion programme. When the course is completed, they are awarded their ambassador status and are encouraged to start their own anti-crime projects within their communities.

In South Africa, an average of thirteen thousand children are arrested each month for crime. Without some sort on intervention, and with continued exposure to crime and violence, it is likely that these children's criminal behaviour will become the norm. I Choose to Change my Life has launched a series of clubs in Gauteng to raise awareness and encourage youngsters to deal with issues around crime.

Riverside Kushido Karate Dojo

As I have mentioned earlier, Allan and Mike started this karate dojo, both contributing their different skills, which, as a team, worked extremely well. Michael was good at recruiting new members and he taught the juniors and trained with the seniors. Allan's strength was in teaching a perfect technique to his students, while Michael had infinite patience in helping those who were struggling. In addition, he loved working with the children.

After Mike died, part of the soul of the dojo went with him and Allan found it very hard to remain enthusiastic. He knew that the black belts needed to impart what they had learnt to others, but it was becoming more and more difficult to keep up the numbers.

Once the trust was up and running, the thought occurred to Allan that here was a way to bring in new members to the dojo and, at the same time, to adhere to the motto 'Change a Life'. He consulted with Stan, who requested an official business plan with Allan's application to get funds for his project. Stan wanted to know just how much money Allan thought he would need for his programme. It just so happened that it matched the amount of money that I raised from the shows. Those funds were directed straight to the dojo! Mike would have been delighted.

Allan wanted to bring in children from a local squatter camp. These boys lived in dire poverty and had *nothing*. Many did not have parents or, if they did, they were never at home. He consulted with the local church and fifteen young boys were selected. The ages of those who wanted to come ranged from seven to nineteen. Because Allan realised that many of these children had probably no chance of proper meal that day, or any day, for that matter, he arranged for a nourishing meal to be cooked for them and brought to the dojo. After the training, a good, hot, nourishing meal was brought in by Charity, Allan's housekeeper, who earned extra money by cooking it for them. Each week, this was eagerly anticipated by the boys and girls. Although these children were getting their gis and training and food for free, they were treated no differently from any other student. They were part of the class and taught to persevere.

Transporting these children to and from the dojo was a very costly exercise, as a mini bus had to be hired weekly and then twice weekly as the project grew.

Tracker, who installs electronic devices into cars to detect them if they have been hijacked or stolen, and who are firm supporters of the cycle challenge, very kindly donated to the dojo a brand new Quantum bus. A driver has been employed to drive it. This has taken a huge financial burden off the dojo and the funds can now be used to feed the students, pay the cook, provide gis as well as take the boys on Gashkus (training camps in other towns or countries).

I was present at both the first and second annual grading, and it was gratifying to see how the boys and girls have progressed. There have been negligible dropouts in this time and there have been quite a few additions. In fact, at the last grading, Allan said that one of these students had performed one of the best katas he had ever seen!

I have a very vivid picture in my mind of the first grading. There was a very little skinny boy who was going through the different stances and punches with Sensei Gary and his group. This little chap was standing with his knees bent, back straight and punching the air in front of him one punch at a time. The strain on one's thigh muscles is huge and this little fellow just could not stand any more. He sat down looking completely exhausted. Sensei Gary asked him firmly, but kindly, "What are you doing on the floor? Get up and carry on; you must learn that we in karate never give up! We don't give up on anything. Come on, my boy, up you get."

This little chap got up and started again, and he carried on without stopping until the end. What a wonderful lesson for this young boy, who possibly had no guidance of any sort at home and had no knowledge of the meaning of perseverance, let alone how.

Mike has told me through Laureen just how happy he is with this project.

The information below has been taken directly off the website. I think it was part of Allan's preamble for his application for funds from the trust.

"Kushido Karate-Do Riverside has been a martial arts school practicing traditional Karate-Do since 1992. The school (or dojo), currently situated at Riverside Shopping Centre, Riverside, Bryanston, has occupied these premises since 2001. The chief instructors of the dojo are Shihan Allan Thomson and Sensei Hannes Loubser. The school has had many students pass through its doors and, during its existence, seventeen dan ranks have been awarded to students of the school. The dojo is well equipped with training equipment, a wooden floor on which to train, changing rooms, a healing room and a recreational area for visitors, parents and students pre and post class. Currently, there is a teaching staff of four permanent black belts and two university students who are available to teach on university vacations.

"At present, the teachers and students of the school feel that their art and the infrastructure of the dojo have much to benefit society at large. Currently, it is being under-utilised. The martial arts within the urbanised middle class and predominantly white section of the population are broadly misunderstood and having to compete with other extracurricular activities such as gym, mountain biking, horse riding and scuba diving, etc.

"It is the teachers' wish that the teachings should be brought to a wider community, to individuals with no access to divergent interest in competing activities. Students, who would ordinarily have no access to the teachings and facilities the Riverside dojo offers, could now benefit from attending this school. Thus, the teachers are desirous of making the facilities and knowledge available to those with the least likely access and perhaps the greatest need. Such a situation results in a win-win position for both parties; i.e. the need for senior students to contribute meaningfully to society and give back what they have been taught and the recipient students an opportunity to empower and discover the self. The ability to believe in oneself and utilise what opportunities may come their way, for benefit of themselves and the societies they live in. In a word, they have an opportunity to change their lives.

> *"'Give a man a fish and you feed him for a day. Teach him to fish and you feed him for life.'*

"*LIVES ARE BEING CHANGED.*"

Nemato Change a Life

The Nemato Change a Life project provides severely disadvantaged youths in Port Alfred with the mindset, skills, knowledge and support to become successful in life. Using sport, educational support and skills development as vehicles of empowerment, the project has already had a profound impact on the lives of many young people in the local community.

Now, with valuable support from the Mike Thomson Change a Life Trust, Nemato will develop a Change a Life centre to house its youth empowerment and education project, including an Early Childhood Development centre, homework classes, a skills development programme and a feeding scheme.

This project was started by a young man, Jan Blom, from Holland who has immigrated to South Africa. He lives in an RDP house in the local township. He is possibly the most humble and non-publicity seeking person I have ever encountered. His students think the world of him. He is, without doubt, *changing lives*.

Reviews

Dear Diana!

Hello from Park City, Utah. My name is Trish Walker. I wanted to drop you a line to thank you from the bottom of my heart. I just finished reading your amazing book and I felt the huge urge to send you an email to let you know how much it helped me out. Not for the reason you may think, but for a totally different one.

About six months ago, I started having some crazy life experiences. Fast forward a month or so and I came to the conclusion that I was picking up messages from someone who had died very suddenly and at a young age! Here I was just a housewife from Utah, and suddenly started to think I was losing my mind. It's been an extremely interesting journey that I have been pushed towards writing a book about. Just so you know, I never met the person I am picking up messages from, but have since had the spirit's identity validated by several mediums. I wish I could win the lottery to be able to pay for more medium visits. It makes me feel so much better after a session. :) I would love to know how you may have pushed through any doubts or concerns about how people would react to your book. Thankfully, my husband has been supportive, but there are days where he gives me the look – as in, is my wife losing it.

Diana, I started to type in possible names for my upcoming book (granted, I am only halfway done writing it). One of the names that popped up for me was Soul Connections. Guess what – it brought up your book and I am glad that it did. I immediately downloaded it and read it in about two days. You cannot imagine how relieved I was to see that someone was having the same experiences as me. It made me feel so comforted to know that someone was in the same 'state of mind' as I was. I am now leaning toward a totally different title, by the way.

I just wanted to reach out and thank you again. You have comforted a soul thousands of miles away from your home town. I am so sorry for your loss. I deeply appreciate, though, that you had the fortitude to write down your experiences. It makes my journey validated and, just when I thought I might give up on writing my book, it gave me the impetus to keep going.

Many thanks from the States. I wish you so much comfort and joy as the future moves on!

Best,

Trish Walker

twalker.wellness@gmail.com

Louise Casey Henderson... Victoria Falls

Aunty Di, it made me smile from ear to ear when I read your message! I am so glad you got another little message from Mike. Your book is still next to my bed; I see it every day! I think of you and send you a little prayer when it catches my eye; as I type this message, your book is right next to me. I understand when you say you never get over losing a child, but my hope for you and Uncle Brian is as much happiness as is possible for the future. I hope the pain lessens and just want you to know I think of you often. And my hope is that Mike never stops sending you messages, as I am sure he knows they mean so much to you! After reading your book, I know he was a wonderful man! I know you are so proud of him! And he of you! Thank you for such a beautiful book. At times, I cried, and, at times, I smiled; what a beautiful story of such an amazing family and your love as a mother and granny for all your children. You are an inspiration and I hope if at any time I need to fight for one of my kids I would do half the job you have done, and fighting so much for what you believe in. xxx. Well done and thank you again. xxx.

Wendy Bethlehem.... After the PE book signing, which was cancelled and then revived without any books from the publisher to sell.

Hi Di, thanks for a wonderful talk at your book launch today. I have already lent my copy to the ladies I went to visit after the talk. All those PE people who didn't attend the launch don't know what they missed. Kevin and I wish you well on your path. FROM WENDY BETHLEHEM.

Di, notwithstanding the poor attendance, my friends have phoned to say they were glad they attended the launch. I had a thought you should contact the University of the 3rd Age. They are always looking for speakers and you could certainly sell your books at a talk for them. Please phone me if you don't know about this organisation. Meant to tell you this morning and the time ran away and I forgot. Travel safe.

I received this in my inbox... Dear Diana, this is Biddy's daughter. My husband and I have just finished reading the book and found it absolutely fascinating. I have passed it on to a friend of mine, who lost her husband two years ago and is completely and utterly devastated. I would love to meet you for coffee when you come into town and ask you so many questions. It was unbelievable reading.... Kind regards, Barrie.

From the spiritual councillor for Hospice, Johannesburg

Hello Diana – Thank you so much for yesterday. Your message is so important for people to hear; you saw the impact your story had yesterday on a group that works with death on a daily basis. So yes, people seldom have the opportunity to hear someone talk about living across the veils! People need to hear – so I hope you plan a lot more talks!

I hope too that it was also healing for you to be surrounded by a group of us who honour and work with this part of the soul's journey? Next year, when I put together my 'life after bereavement' monthly support meetings, I very much hope you will be available again to talk to those dealing with the pain and challenge of end of life! Enjoy your trip – and have a blessed Christmas! Cameron.

From Australia

Dear Di,

I have just read your book! I am quite overwhelmed at your ordeal, the courage you have and just how each of you has handled your grief differently. I am just so glad that you found comfort in communicating with Mike and that you have been strong enough to write the book. I learnt a lot about Mike that I had not known and was very impressed by what an outstanding student and adult he was. I guess when we left in Dec. 1979 we were unaware of what a wonderful person he would turn out to be. (Not that he wasn't outstanding then!) It was good to see reference to a few people we knew, like Ernie Sax. It sounds like you have met some incredible people in your quest for justice and for being sure that Mike has been remembered. The DNA testing, charities, bike rides and karate classes, etc. have certainly left a legacy that will benefit so many South Africans. I am sure that you will give inspiration to anyone who reads your book. You are incredible.

Before I had even finished the book, I had a request from Amazon to write a book review of it, so I have just sent one in to them. Needless to say, I did not mention that I knew you! I hope you like the review.

A month or so ago, we saw an English TV travel show with Louis Thoreau as he travelled through SA. He spent a lot of time in JHB, mainly in Hillbrow, where he talked about the gang rule and made it sound totally lawless. It was really frightening to think that that is how parts of SA are ruled. After our years there, when we enjoyed so many parts of SA, it's awful to think that so many people live in fear. I don't suppose that TV show was aired in SA!

Thank you so much for writing your book. I hope that many others will get comfort by reading it.

Much love to you and all the family,
Carol

From my cousin in USA

HI Di,

I just had to email you and let you know that I have just finished reading your book, Soul Connection. What a wonderful tribute to Mike. I was so interested to read about your connection with Mike through Laureen.

I really don't know what else to say, as no one can know what you and your family have been through with the horrific murder of your beloved Mike, but had to make contact, as I so admire the fact that you have put into words all your 'contacts' with Mike through Laureen and also how you and your family are ensuring that Mike did not die in vain, with all your incredible contributions to the charities.

I was so happy to read that you had also managed to make contact with your mum, dad and Malcolm. I miss Malcolm so much. We used to have a lot of chats on Skype and the last time that I spoke to him before he died was on Skype, and he just sang most of the time we were on Skype. I had never realised

that he had such a beautiful voice.
Love to you all,
Sherry

From Beth in UK

Dearest Di,

I finished reading Soul Connection this morning and I want to thank you for opening your heart to us and allowing us into your heart to share your grief, your pain and your slow recovery, and to share in the end the triumph of your achievements, because you lost your beloved Mike so tragically.

I am humbled by this book.

You write beautifully, from deep in your heart, and it comes through to your readers.

Even the sceptics who don't believe in the afterlife connection that you have so clearly achieved with Mike will be inspired.

I salute you, my friend. To have endured what your family went through and to be able to produce such a tribute is a great achievement.

With lots of love.

A friend in JHB, Ness Hills

Morning Di,

Hope all is okay with you and family.

I read your book over the weekend and was really saddened to learn in detail what you and your family have been through. Arthur and I were overseas when the tragedy happened and we didn't hear too much about what was publicised. Thank goodness for your close family and friends.

It was lovely to learn just how much the trust is doing in

Mike's name and I know that's a great comfort to you.

I really admire you for your courage and the fact that you can talk about it. As you know, I find it difficult to talk about my problems, but reading your book has helped a lot. Hopefully I will be a bit more open in the future. I am going to put your book in my book club for all the ladies to read – many of them have their own problems too and I think it could help.

We must keep up our birthday lunches – I really enjoy seeing you all.

Lots of luck with the book sales.

30 November 2013

Hi Di,

Congratulations, oh mighty author!

Am reading your book and thought I should contact you in the more conventional way than you use with Mike!

I was filled with emotion on reading about the funeral for Mike and the tremendous work his murder has triggered.

In a sense, it reopened my old scars from the wrench I felt on leaving SA. I feel massive guilt about what I could have done to help a land I had come to love so much.

No matter the good reasons for emigrating, we all have to deal with that.

Also what great times we had. Growing up in Bryanston, teaching at such an amazing school – generally such talented and good students, with such supportive and appreciative families.

Rob and I agreed that our times with Mike and the lads at Ntsiri were possibly the most enjoyable and gut-wrenchingly funny times of our lives. The sense of freedom, closeness with nature and each other was so special.

Thought much of Mike since – just hope he does not contact

me at five in the morning!

On a different tack, it is great to read of Vanessa Lynch and her work. She was in my form class in my first year of teaching, and both Dave Smith (who taught her geography) and I would not have been surprised that she became a successful lawyer!

Please send my best wishes to everyone.

Regards,

Ian/Fred

Di, your book had such an amazing effect on me. I can't stop reading. Have read it six times and, each time I read it, I keep finding myself drawn to your words and what you all went through and are going through. I think of each and every one of you so much. One day, I would love to visit you and chat to you. I have always been drawn to mediums; I know a few. I will definitely be going to see them soon to find one I have a connection to…. Hope you are all well. lol xxx, Cindy.

Post Script (July 2014)

This book was first published in October 2013 and has been read and appreciated by many all over the world much to my surprise and joy. I have had numerous coffee mornings and mini launches with really meaningful discussions emanating from the book. All have been very successful with many questions being asked.

There have been further developments in all sectors of my story and so in this post script, I will provide the reader with the various updates.

Mike

A frequent question asked is, "Does Mike still send messages to you at home?"

The answer is, "Yes he does, but not nearly as often as he used to".

There had been a gap of about six months since we had last been aware of anything and then in March this year, I was working alone in my office, very late at night, answering my emails. Brian and Carol were asleep in bed. I was engrossed in a YouTube that I came across as a result of watching another one sent to me. It was about a little boy of four living in Scotland. He was constantly telling his mum about his life on an Island called Bara and how he missed his Bara mum. He used to watch the planes land on the beach from his bedroom window. To cut a long story short, after some time, his mom began to take him seriously and found out there was such a place. She took him there and sure enough; the planes did land on the beach! They found the house and he could identify his room and so much of the surroundings. There were some things that did not gel but the conclusion was that he had reincarnated very quickly and still had memories of his past life. I found this fascinating!

The TV had been off all this time. When I had finished watching the clip, I got up to go and turn off some lights in the kitchen. As I passed through the lounge, the TV switched on. I was nowhere near the remote or the TV. I just knew it was Mike saying he was with me while watching the little boy's story. I acknowledged him mentally and turned it off and it stayed off.

Although there were no more physical messages from him, I have received many through Laureen.

Shortly before the first launch, Laureen called me to ask if she could bring her mother and her partner along. I of course said she could. She then said, "Hold on Di, Mike has just popped into my head and he says that he is very proud of you and will be at the launch. He says that there will be a person there who would not normally have been able to make it and she will be wearing blue.

He says that he is concerned because both Brian and you have health issues". She was unable to clarify what they were. She did however, say that he wanted us to go and have O3 (Ozone) therapy. Her words were actually Oxygen therapy. More about that later.

Her parting comment was, "Di, what's this with red takkies? Mike is laughing and asking about red takkies. Who in your family has recently bought red takkies?" I could not think of any but then something dawned on me… I asked,

"Would shocking pink takkies do?"

"Yes that's it. He is nodding and confirming that they are shocking pink."

I was thrilled. I had just bought myself a pair of shocking pink takkies! Mike had seen them and approved.

The night of the launch arrived and I got to Skoobs book

shop feeling very nervous. The books had arrived and my publicist Janine had done a sterling job getting people invited. More people came than we anticipated for which I was not only extremely grateful but also totally overcome. My sister Verna was down visiting with her daughter Barbie. I was thrilled to see her arrive all dressed in blue! I found Laureen and took her by the hand to meet Verna and to show her how accurate and "UN WOO WOO" her prediction was!

The launch was a sell out thank goodness and I had to dig into my own supply to be able to supply everyone with a book.

After the launch, in February of 2014, I had a reading with Laureen. Mike did come through but I have to confess it was not as much of a WOW reading as I have had before. He did however, come through wearing long shorts. When I confirmed that he did like those long shorts, he told Laureen that he only ever wore ¾ shorts: NEVER short shorts. That is absolutely true.

The advice that Laureen had passed on regarding us going for Oxygen treatment was preying heavily on my mind. Many years ago, I became aware of the hyperbaric chamber which is a form of Oxygen treatment that was developed by the Navy to treat divers suffering from the bends. I learned that they had found it amazing for treating wounds, burns and many other ailments. It promoted the healing far quicker than conventional methods.

As a result, I was not against the thought of this and if Mike said we needed it, I was certainly willing to give it a try. I knew that Brian did have some health issues but I was not aware of any serious malady from which I was suffering, except that I was always tired and had developed peripheral neuropathy for which there is no cure. I hoped that if I went, this might get better.

I started making inquiries and came up with two places that did this, one in Pretoria and one at a hospital in Johannesburg. When I asked the price, I nearly fell off my perch! It was well over R1000.00 per session and one was required to go weekly and for several months to have any benefit. Medical aid of course does not cover this. I was mortified as there is no way we can afford this amount of money on a treatment for which there is no guarantee of success! I called Laureen and suggested that when she next has Mike pop in, to please ask him what he is smoking up there because surely he knows that we cannot afford this on an ongoing basis! To my relief, Laureen said, "No, Di. Not that one, this is intravenous and only costs about R60.00 a time". Well, that was much, much better. She gave me the number of a lady who had been cured of Leukaemia with this treatment. She had attended a clinic run by Dr Steve Hansen and was so impressed that she started up her own clinic. I called her immediately and she informed me that she no longer was able to run it as they had experienced an armed house invasion and her husband had been beaten up and hit on the head with a hammer and had experienced severe brain damage. She now had to concentrate on helping him and running their business.

Once again, my life had been affected by the awful violent crime we have to live with in this country albeit quite indirectly.

Thank heavens; she was able to put me in touch with Dr Steve in Sandringham who has a clinic called Natra Heal Nes Health. His fee was not R60.00 a time but R80.00 a time. However, that was still very affordable. I made the appointment for both Brian and I.

Meeting Dr Steve was one of the nicest things that had happened to us in a very long time. He is a very quiet, confident man with very white hair: not from age but from being of Scandinavian descent! He has the palest blue eyes that reflect his compassionate personality.

We started out by having a consultation with him where we explained how we had come to him and what we were hoping to gain from his treatments. I always thought that the peripheral neuropathy that I had developed was a result of being overweight and pre diabetic. He said no, he believed that it was a direct result of the trauma that I had experienced in the loss of my son. He made no promises regarding the return of the feeling to my feet but said it may help. He did however say it would fix other ailments that we may not know about and I would suddenly find myself feeling so much better.

Brian was experiencing bladder problems which were possibly connected to a prostate problem. Although he was not aware of it, I was becoming very concerned about his cognitive memory. He has a history of family having Alzheimer's or dementia and I was very aware of this and becoming more and more worried about him as was the family.

Steve did not bat an eyelid when I told him how we had arrived at his clinic. He asked if I was still experiencing the physical pain associated with grief. I said I was. He then took me into another room and took me through the most painful sort of counselling I have ever experienced. I sobbed and sobbed as I had not done for ages. Amazing: as this was six years down the line. He made me repeat again and again, "Mike I love you, but I release you". This went on until I said, "I cannot do this anymore". We then stopped and Steve brought a little gadget which looked like a remote control and moved it over my head for some time. He then asked me if the pain had gone. I could not say as I was still overwrought about the whole experience.

However, as time has passed, I think I can say with confidence that the excruciating pain that I felt in my solar plexus every time I thought about Mike or that evening, has gone. I can think of him now without tears welling although there are times when this does happen but not nearly as often as it used to. I believe it did work. He wanted me to go for a second session but I just cannot do that again.

We did see a specialist about Brian's problem and he was due for surgery at the end of March. Although we were never pressurised by Dr Steve, he constantly suggested that we think hard about the surgery. We should give the O3 some more time.

About three weeks before the scheduled op, Brian started to show a marked improvement in his bladder control. Not only that, his memory was improving in leaps and bounds; so much so, I can hardly believe it. We decided to cancel the operation much to the specialist's disgust. So far this is another decision that we have not regretted. He is about 98% better and he is coping with life again and I no longer have this awful feeing about his memory. It is now just the normal age related memory loss that we all experience. Thank you Mike and Laureen!

As for me, the fatigue has gone; I have more energy but as yet, no change in the feet. I am frequently told that I look so well. I still live in hope that my feet will improve. Whatever happens, I have nothing to lose and I have seen the most remarkable healing going on at Dr Steve's clinic with other people, that I have now decided that if ever I have a horrid diagnosis of anything, I am sticking with Dr Steve first.

The court case

This has been a very frustrating year. On my birthday in February, I received a phone call from the investigating officer to tell me that he has good news. He said that they had managed to get two members of the gang to sign affidavits and that they would now be indicting the whole gang. This was a Wednesday. He also told me that he would call on Friday to give me more details! I should have known! He omitted to tell me which Friday and silly me, I thought he meant the next Friday. It is now July and I am still to hear from him.

However, I have heard from Karl, from the firm of private detectives, that we have a court date set for the 26th Jan 2015. I can hardly believe it! As yet, I am not aware of any details.

The Mike Thomson Change a Life Trust

This continues to grow. This year the cycle challenge has so far raised R3.5 Million, bringing the total amount donated to anti-crime and youth development projects to date to almost R27 Million.

The achievements of these projects demonstrate the positive impact the Change a Life has on the communities it supports. A few of the recent highlights include:

In January 2014 the Vanessa Lynch and the DNA project celebrated the passing of the DNA Act for which it has been lobbying in parliament for the past six years. This will in time have a profound impact on the South African criminal justice system.

Sbonelo (Eric) Zondi, one of the first beneficiaries of the Martin Dreyer Change a Life Academy, won the prestigious 2014 Dusi Canoe Marathon with his partner Andy Birkitt.

In November 2013, Siphamandla Baku, a project beneficiary in the impoverished Nelson Mandela Township in the Eastern Cape, run by Jan Blom, represented South Africa in the world Age Groups (Junior World Gymnastics Championships) in Bulgaria.

At the November report back last year, a new beneficiary was introduced. It is a very much needed rape crisis centre in Khayelitsha in Cape Town. It is to be run by an inspiring young woman who had been raped herself.

The Karate Dojo has had their first group of Brown belts coming through at the last grading. They are hoping that four students will receive their Black belts by the end of the year. They are:

1. Isaac Mdletshe

2. Moses Sibanda

3.   Siayabonga Nkabinde

4.   Sobhuza "Honest" Ncube

Well done to you all!

This year's cycle challenge is another mystery tour on the Rovos Rail and I think it will be in the Western Cape. It is already fully subscribed.

To summarise, the Mike Thomson Change a Life Trust has made its mark and has to date had some remarkable achievements. There have been many lives changed and many goals reached.

In years to come when the Thomson family and those who knew Mike are no longer around to ensure that "Change a Life" retains its link to Mike Thomson, I hope that there will still be someone who will continue to carry the flag for Mike! My reason for this request is simply this; when someone has had his or her life changed through one of the beneficiaries being the catalyst, that person should always be made aware of or reminded of why it came about that they were given such an opportunity.

Michael Roy Thomson lost his life too soon.

About The Author

Diana Spence was born in Greytown, KwaZulu-Natal on 12th Feb 1943. She was the youngest of three children. She grew up in Johannesburg in Waverley and went to St Mary's school for her primary school years until 1955 and then to boarding school at Epworth in Pietermaritzburg until 1960 when she matriculated.

Diana qualified as a nursery school teacher in 1963 and her first job was to help open the then new Roosevelt Extension Nursery School.

She married Brian Thomson, her high school boyfriend, in September 1964 after they had both qualified. They had four children: Allan, Mike, Debby and Carol.

When Allan and Michael were babies, she garnered support to build a non profit nursery school in Blairgowrie where they had their first home. It took seven years to raise enough money to build a lovely nursery school and staff it with qualified teachers. Thabile nursery school still exists to this day and is considered one of the best in Johannesburg.

Diana then had a part time job for about eight years as an inspectress for the Early Childhood education society.

When her youngest child left school, in order to escape the

empty nest syndrome, she turned her lifelong passion and hobby of landscaping into a business, running a very successful little company for about 16 years.

Diana and her husband bought a share in a game reserve in the Umbabat bordering the Kruger Park in about 1980. It was during the years they spent there every possible moment that they all developed the love of the bushveld and she in particular her passion for indigenous plants. She called her company inDIgenous gardens.

When her son Mike was murdered, her life was shattered. She had always enjoyed writing letters and when she realised that Mike was trying to contact her and she was getting messages from him, she started to record everything as she did not want to forget anything. One day, the thought occurred to her that the occurrences were so unusual and she was helped so much by the contact that she decided to write a book to help others who might be going through the same sort of grief and trauma that she was.

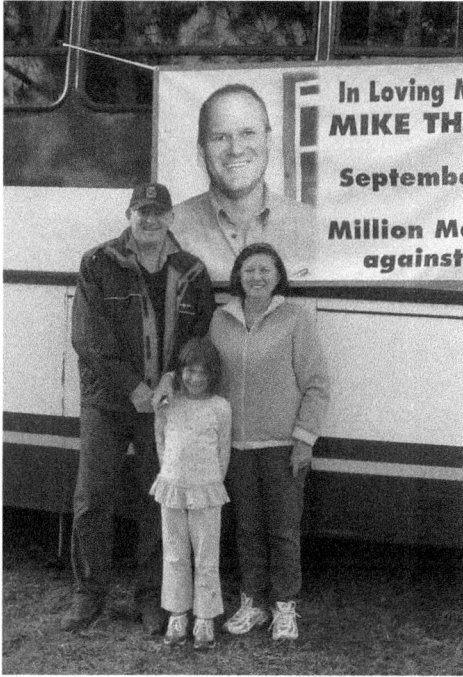

Annie-Rose and friends in front of the "Mike Thomson Bus"

One of the marchers with a noose aound his neck, calling for the return of the death penalty.

Vanessa Lynch - Founder of the DNA Project.

Carolyn Hancock - Board member and co-activist of the DNA Project.

Carole Pedotti Ngono - the initiator and manager behind the "I Choose to Change a Life" initiative.

Martin Dreyer and some of his early beneficiaries of the Martin Dreyer Change a Life Academy.

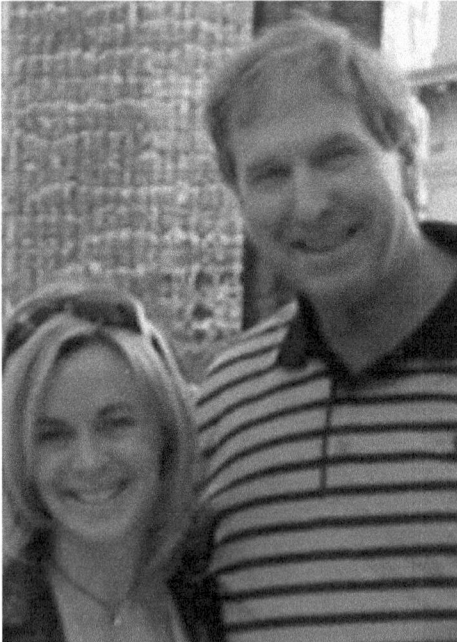
Vanessa Lynch and Derek Watts during the filming of Carte Blanche featuring the development of the DNA Project.

A refreshment stop on one of the cycle challenges.

Scenes from the Kushido Change a Life Karate-Do, run by Mikes brother Allan and is a very special project for the Thomson Family as it honours Mike in every possible way.

The Thomson Family (except Debby and the children) at the launch of the Mike Thomson Change a Life.

Cyclists participating in the annual Mike Thomson Change a Life Cycle Challenge.

An aerial view of the Cycle Challenge Pellaton moving through open African landscape.

Some of the cycle challenge participants in front of a majestic Baobab tree.

Martin, Stan, Ursula nd Jonothan watch on in pride...

Brian, Ursula and Di at the Cycle launch 2014 at Saxon Hotel.

Cyclists on route to the lake in Malawi.

DNA bill passed in parliament early 2014.

The students of Nemato in their humble surroundings.

Stan & Ursula.

Vanessa, Brian and Di at the report back of 2011.

Some of the Martin Dreyer Change a Life Beneficiaries about to take part in a Mountain Biking Challenge.

www.ingramcontent.com/pod-product-compliance
Lightning Source LLC
Chambersburg PA
CBHW070018100426
42740CB00013B/2538